Praise for *The Price of Motherhood*

"A bracing call to arms . . . Crittenden rows against the ideological current and has the temerity to suggest a mind-blowingly sensible alteration of America's present parenting arrangements, and indeed our very way of life."

—BEN DICKINSON, *Elle*

"A landmark book."

—*San Francisco Chronicle*

"Motherhood may be sacred to Americans, but actual mothering is consistently devalued and disrespected. This profoundly important book challenges us to examine how much we really care about children—or about the world of caring in general."

—BARBARA EHRENREICH, author of *Nickel and Dimed*

"Those who nurture young children are essentially punished for performing the very task that everyone agrees is essential . . . Crittenden proposes a unique solution to the motherhood penalty: Consider the work done by mothers a vital national service akin to that performed by soldiers."

—*Glamour*

"Welcome to America, the land where having a child is the worst economic decision a woman can make . . . an important and well-argued study of the huge disparity between the value that mothers produce and the price they are forced to pay."

—CATHERINE ARNST, *Business Week*

"How do we bring up children without putting women down? In this important, well-written book, Ann Crittenden offers serious answers to this preeminent feminist—and human—question. A must read."

—ARLIE RUSSELL HOCHSCHILD, author of *The Time Bind* and *The Second Shift*

"Provocative . . . Not everyone will agree with the remedies Crittenden proposes. But after reading this impassioned work, it's hard not to concur that there is a problem."

—PAM LAMBERT, *People*

"A lively and compelling account of the ways maternal altruism subsidizes our entire economy but imposes high costs on mothers themselves. Ann Crittenden deftly combines facts, figures, interviews, and personal stories to document the unfair—and inefficient—distribution of the costs of rearing children. She has written a great and important book."

—NANCY FOLBRE, author of *The Invisible Heart*

Also by Ann Crittenden

Sanctuary: A Story of American Conscience and Law in Collision

Killing the Sacred Cows: Bold Ideas for a New Economy

The Price of Motherhood

THE PRICE OF MOTHERHOOD

WHY THE MOST IMPORTANT JOB IN THE WORLD IS STILL THE LEAST VALUED

Ann Crittenden

An Owl Book

HENRY HOLT AND COMPANY | NEW YORK

Henry Holt and Company, LLC
Publishers since 1866
115 West 18th Street
New York, New York 10011

Henry Holt® is a registered trademark
of Henry Holt and Company, LLC.

Distributed in Canada by H. B. Fenn and Company Ltd.

Library of Congress Cataloging-in-Publication Data

Crittenden, Ann.
The price of motherhood : why the most important job in the world is still the least valued / Ann Crittenden.
p. cm.
Includes bibliographical references and index.
ISBN 0-8050-6619-5 (pbk.)
1. Motherhood—United States. 2. Motherhood—Economic aspects—United States. 3. Mothers—United States—Economic conditions. 4. Mothers—United States—Social conditions. I. Title.
HQ759.C924 2001
306.874'3—dc21 00-053722

Henry Holt books are available for special promotions and premiums. For details contact: Director, Special Markets.

First published in hardcover in 2001 by Metropolitan Books
First Owl Books Edition 2002
Printed in the United States of America

10 9 8 7 6 5 4 3 2

To the memory of my mother,

Mary Nell O'Banion

Contents

Introduction 1
1 · Where We Are Now 13
2 · A Conspiracy of Silence 28
3 · How Mothers' Work Was "Disappeared": The Invention of the Unproductive Housewife 45
4 · The Truly Invisible Hand 65
5 · The Mommy Tax 87
6 · The Dark Little Secret of Family Life 110
7 · What Is a Wife Worth? 131
8 · Who Really Owns the Family Wage? 149
9 · Who Pays for the Kids? 162
10 · The Welfare State Versus a Caring State 186
11 · The Toughest Job You'll Ever Love 202
12 · An Accident Waiting to Happen 218
13 · "It Was Her Choice" 233
Conclusion: How to Bring Children Up Without Putting Women Down 256
Notes 275
Acknowledgments 305
Index 309

The Price of Motherhood

Introduction

> The good mother, the wise mother . . . is more important to the community than even the ablest man; her career is more worthy of honor and is more useful to the community than the career of any man, no matter how successful.
>
> —Theodore Roosevelt

When my son was small, we loved to read *The Giving Tree,* a book about a tree that gave a little boy apples to eat, branches to climb, and shade to sleep under. This made them both happy. As the boy grew into a man, the tree gave him her apples to sell for money, then her branches to build a house, and finally her trunk to make a boat. When the boy became a tired old man, the tree, by now nothing but a stump, offered him all she had left to sit on and rest. I would read the last line, "And the tree was happy," with tears flowing down my cheeks every time.

The very definition of a mother is selfless service to another.[1] We don't owe Mother for her gifts; *she owes us.* And in return for her bounty, Mother receives no lack of veneration. According to an ancient Jewish proverb, "God could not be everywhere, and therefore He made mothers." The Arabs also have a saying: "The mother is a school; if she is well reared, you are sure to build a nation."

In the United States, motherhood is as American as apple pie. No institution is more sacrosanct; no figure is praised more fulsomely. Maternal selflessness has endowed mothers with a unique moral authority, which in the past has been used to promote temperance, maternal and child health, kindergartens, a more lenient juvenile justice system, and most recently, to combat drunk driving and lax gun controls.

If anything, awareness of the importance of mothers' work is increasing. In 1996 Microsoft founder Bill Gates and executive vice president Steve Ballmer gave Harvard University a $29-million state-of-the-art facility for computer science and electrical engineering. The new building was named Maxwell Dworkin, in honor of their mothers' maiden names. This may have been the first such recognition given to mothers' role in the creation of vast fortunes and an entire new industry.

When I was on a radio talk show in 1998, several listeners called in to say that child-rearing is the most important job in the world. A few weeks later, at a party, Lawrence H. Summers, a distinguished economist who subsequently became the secretary of the treasury, used exactly the same phrase. "Raising children," Summers told me in all seriousness, "is the most important job in the world." As Summers well knows, in the modern economy, two-thirds of all wealth is created by human skills, creativity, and enterprise—what is known as "human capital." And that means parents who are conscientiously and effectively rearing children are literally, in the words of economist Shirley Burggraf, "the major wealth producers in our economy."[2]

But this very material contribution is still considered immaterial. All of the lip service to motherhood still floats in the air, as insubstantial as clouds of angel dust. On the ground, where mothers live, the lack of respect and tangible recognition is still part of every mother's experience. Most people, like infants in a crib, take female caregiving utterly for granted.

The job of making a home for a child and developing his or her capabilities is often equated with "doing nothing." Thus the disdainful question frequently asked about mothers at home: "What do they *do* all day?" I'll never forget a dinner at the end of a day in which I had gotten my son dressed and fed and off to nursery school, dealt with a plumber about a leaky shower, paid the bills, finished an op-ed piece, picked up and escorted my son to a reading group at the library, run several miscellaneous errands, and put in an hour on a future book project. Over drinks that evening, a childless female friend commented that "of all the couples we know, you're the only wife who doesn't work."

Maxine Ross, a stay-at-home mother in Fairfax, Virginia, admitted to me that before she had her child, she too felt nothing but scorn for mothers at home: "We used to live in a four-family co-op, and two of the other women stayed at home with their children. One of them got a cleaning lady and I thought, 'Do you *believe* that? She has so much time, and she doesn't even clean her own house! What does she do all day, watch soap operas?'"

Even our children have absorbed the cultural message that mothers have no stature. A friend of mine gave up a job she loved as the head of a publishing house in order to raise her daughter. One day, when she corrected the girl, the child snapped, "Why should I listen to you? You're just a housewife!"

In my childless youth I shared these attitudes. In the early 1970s I wrote an article for the very first issue of *MS* magazine on the economic value of a housewife. I added up all the domestic chores, attached dollar values to each, and concluded that the job was seriously underpaid and ought to be included in the Gross National Product. I thought I was being sympathetic, but I realize now that my deeper attitude was one of compassionate contempt, or perhaps contemptuous compassion. Deep down, I had no doubt that I was superior, in my midtown office overlooking Madison Avenue, to those unpaid housewives pushing brooms. "Why aren't they making something of themselves?" I wondered. "What's wrong with them? They're letting our side down."

I imagined that domestic drudgery was going to be swept into the dustbin of history as men and women linked arms and marched off to run the world in a new egalitarian alliance. It never occurred to me that women might be at home because there were children there; that housewives might become extinct, but mothers and fathers never would.

A MOTHER'S WORK is not just invisible; it can become a handicap. Raising children may be the most important job in the world, but you can't put it on a résumé.

A woman from Long Island, New York, with a master's degree in special education was advised repeatedly that when she went job hunting she should not mention her thirteen years of caring for a disabled, chronically ill child. All those years of courageous tenacity and resilience would be held against her or, at best, considered irrelevant. She was warned that she had better pad her résumé with descriptions of volunteer work and occasional freelance writing.

The idea that time spent with one's child is time wasted is embedded in traditional economic thinking. People who are not formally employed may create human capital, but they themselves are said to suffer a deterioration of the stuff, as if they were so many pieces of equipment left out to rust. The extraordinary talents required to do the long-term work of building human character and instilling in young children the ability and desire to learn have no place in the economists' calculations. Economic theory has nothing to say about the acquisition of skills by those who work with children; presumably there are none.

Here is how economists have summed up the adverse effects of child-rearing on a person's qualifications: "As a woman does not work [*sic*] during certain periods, less working experience is accumulated. [Moreover] during periods of non-participation, the human capital stock suffers from additional depreciation due to a lack of maintenance. This effect is known as atrophy."[3] In fact, the only things that atrophy when a woman has children are her income and her leisure.

The devaluation of mothers' work permeates virtually every major institution. Not only is caregiving not rewarded, it is penalized. These stories illustrate the point:

• Joanna Upton, a single mother working as a store manager in Massachusetts, sued the company for wrongful dismissal after it fired her for refusing to work overtime—until nine or ten at night and all day Saturday. Upton had been hired to work 8:15 A.M. until 5:30 P.M.; she could not adequately care for or barely even see her son if she had to work overtime. Yet she lost her suit. The Massachusetts Supreme Judicial Court ruled that under state contract law, an at-will employee may be fired "for any reason or for no reason at all" unless the firing violates a "clearly established" public policy. Massachusetts had no public policy dealing with a parent's responsibility to care for his or her child.[4]

• A woman in Texas gave up a fifteen-year career in banking to raise two children. Her husband worked extremely long hours and spent much of his time on the road. She realized that only if she left her own demanding job would the child have the parental time and attention he needed. For almost two decades she worked part-time as a consultant from her home, and for several years she had little or no income. Recently the Social Security Administration sent her an estimate of her retirement income—a statement that was full of zeroes for the years spent caregiving. Social Security confirmed that her decision to be the responsible, primary parent had reduced the government pension by hundreds of dollars a month in retirement income.

• A mother in Maryland had a son who had been a problem child ever since kindergarten. At junior high, the boy was suspended several times; he was finally caught with a gun in his backpack and expelled. The boy's father sued for custody, and the mother countered with a request for more child support, to help pay the $10,000 tuition for a special private school. She also quit her full-time job to have more time for her family. At his new school, the boy showed dramatic improvement both in his academic work and in his behavior. When the case came to court, the father was denied custody, but the judge refused to require him to pay half the costs of the boy's rehabilitation, including therapy and tutoring, despite evidence that the father could afford to do so. A mother who did not work full-time was, in the judge's view, a luxury that "our world does not permit." So the mother was in effect penalized for having tried to be a more attentive mother, and the boy was forced to leave the only school in which he had enjoyed any success.[5]

As these examples reveal the United States is a society at war with itself. The policies of American business, government, and the law do not reflect Americans' stated values. Across the board, individuals who assume the role of nurturer are punished and discouraged from performing the very tasks that everyone agrees are essential. We talk endlessly about the importance of family, yet the work it takes to make a family is utterly disregarded. This contradiction can be found in every corner of our society.

First, inflexible workplaces guarantee that many women will have to cut back on, if not quit, their employment once they have children. The result is a loss of income that produces a bigger wage gap between mothers and childless women than the wage gap between young men and women. This forgone income, the equivalent of a huge "mommy tax," is typically more than $1 million for a college-educated American woman.

Second, marriage is still not an equal financial partnership. Mothers in forty-seven of the fifty states—California, Louisiana, and New Mexico are the exceptions—do not have an unequivocal legal right to half of the family's assets. Nor does a mother's unpaid work entitle her to any ownership of the primary breadwinner's income—either during marriage or after a divorce. Family income belongs solely to "he who earns it," in the phrase coined by legal scholar Joan Williams. A married mother is a "dependent," and a divorced mother is "given" what a judge decides she and the children "need" of the father's future income. As a result, the spouse who principally cares for the children—and the children—are almost invariably worse off financially after divorce than the spouse who devotes all his energies to a career.

Third, government social policies don't even define unpaid care of family dependents as work. A family's primary caregiver is not considered a full productive citizen, eligible in her own right for the major social insurance programs. Nannies earn Social Security credits; mothers at home do not. Unless she is otherwise "employed," the primary parent is not entitled to unemployment insurance or workman's compensation. The only safety net for a caregiver who loses her source of support is welfare, and even that is no longer assured.

For all these reasons, motherhood is the single biggest risk factor for poverty in old age. American mothers have smaller pensions than either men or childless women, and American women over sixty-five are more than twice as likely to be poor as men of the same age.

The devaluation of a mother's work extends to those who do similar work for pay. Even college-educated teachers of infants are often characterized as "baby-sitters," and wages for child care are so low that the field is hemorrhaging its best-trained people. Increasingly, day care is being provided by an inexperienced workforce—what one expert calls "Kentucky Fried Day Care"—while highly trained Mary Poppins–style nannies are officially classified as "unskilled labor," and as such largely barred from entry into the United States.

The cumulative effect of these policies is a heavy financial penalty on anyone who chooses to spend any serious amount of time with children. This is the hard truth that lies beneath all of the flowery tributes to Mom. American mothers may have their day, but for the rest of the year their values, their preferences, and their devotion to their children are shortchanged. As the twenty-first century begins, women may be approaching equality, but mothers are still far behind. Changing the status of mothers, by gaining real recognition for their work, is the great unfinished business of the women's movement.

But revaluing motherhood will not be easy. Even feminists are often reluctant to admit that many women's lives revolve around their children. They measure progress by the distance women have traveled from *Kinder* and *Küche,* and worry that if child-rearing is made a more tempting choice, many women—those natural nurturers—will drift back into domestic subservience. They fear that if women are seen to be mothers first, the very real gains that women have made in the workplace could be jeopardized.

Thus the standard feminist response to the fact that child-rearing marginalizes women is not to raise its status but to urge men to do more of it. Though this has been the cry for more than thirty years, almost 100 percent of the primary caregivers of young children are still women. This suggests that feminism needs a fresh strategy.

Conservatives, for their part, are not willing to put their money where their mouths are. Their eyes grow moist over family values, but they are loath to put any tangible value on the work that a family entails. They cling to the conviction that the only "good" mother is the self-sacrificing, saintly figure who performs the moral, caring work of society at the expense of her own equality and aspirations.

Social conservatives often expect daughters but not sons to renounce ambition and serve their families without compensation. They preach early marriage and childbearing, without warning young women that this increases their chances of divorce and lowers their lifetime income. They embrace an economy that relies on free or badly paid female labor, and then wonder why women express frustration with their lot. As Burggraf has so perceptively noted, "Getting 'women's work' done when women are no longer volunteering their unpaid or underpaid labor is what much of the public discussion of family values is really about."[6]

It is true, of course, that caring for one's child is not a job that anyone does for the sake of remuneration. As *The Giving Tree* implies, raising a child is much more like a gift; a gift motivated by maternal love, the most unselfish emotion in the human repertoire. How can one be paid for a labor of love? The very idea seems emotionally askew, foreign to the essence of care. But just because caring work is not self-seeking doesn't mean a person should be penalized for doing it. Just because giving to one's child is altruistic doesn't mean that it isn't also a difficult, time-consuming obligation that is expected of one sex and not the other. The gift of care can be both selfless and exploited.[7] As Balzac so memorably put it, "Maternal love makes of every woman a slave."

Every now and then, someone calculates what a family would have to pay for a mother's services. In one such exercise, a mother's worth was estimated at $508,700 per year in wages alone, not counting retirement, health, and other benefits. This astronomical sum was arrived at by adding up the median annual salaries of the seventeen occupations a mother is expected to perform, from child-rearing, cooking, and cleaning to managing household finances and resolving family emotional problems.[8] A more realistic assessment would probably value a mother's work at the level of a middle manager, plus the additional occasional services of a psychologist, a financial planner, a chauffeur, and so on. This package could easily add up to $100,000 a year—or $100,000 a year more than a mother is paid.

"No one's crazy enough to work for free but moms," says Ric Edelman, whose firm, Edelman Financial Services, made the $500,000 calculation. "And no one has enough money to hire a good mom. . . . From that perspective our mothers are indeed priceless."

Unpaid female caregiving is not only the life blood of families, it is the very heart of the economy. A spate of new studies reveals that the amount of work involved in unpaid child care is far greater than economists ever imagined. Indeed, it rivals in size the largest industries of the visible economy. By some estimates, even in the most industrialized countries the total hours spent on unpaid household work—much of it associated with child-rearing—amount to at least half of the hours of paid work in the market.[9] Up to 80 percent of this unpaid labor is contributed by women.

This huge gift of unreimbursed time and labor explains, in a nutshell, why adult women are so much poorer than men—even though they work longer hours than men in almost every country in the world.[10]

One popular economics textbook devotes four pages to problems of poverty without once mentioning the fact that the majority of poor people are women and children. The author never considers that this poverty might be related to the fact that half the human race isn't paid for most of the work it does.

In economics, a "free rider" is someone who benefits from a good without contributing to its provision: in other words, someone who gets something for nothing. By that definition, both the family and the global economy are classic examples of free riding. Both are dependent on female caregivers who offer their labor in return for little or no compensation.

IT MAY WELL be that mothers and others who care for children and sick and elderly family members will go on giving, whatever the costs or consequences for themselves. Maternal love, after all, is one of the world's renewable resources. But even if this is so, there is still a powerful argument for putting an end to free riding on women's labor. It's called *fairness*.

An analogy to soldiers might be helpful here. Soldiers, like mothers, render an indispensable national service to their country. The ultimate rationale for offering honors and material rewards to military veterans is to avoid free riding on their services. The public feels it owes its warriors some quid pro quo. The G.I. Bill, for example, was not originally a recruitment tool, as military benefits later became, but repayment of a debt that a grateful nation owed to its fighting men. No one, after World War II, dreamed of being a free rider on the sacrifices of Normandy Beach and Guadalcanal.

By the same token, it isn't fair to demand that the nurturing of human capabilities, the national service primarily rendered by women, be valued any less. It isn't fair that mothers' life-sustaining work forces women to be society's involuntary philanthropists. It isn't fair to expect mothers to make sacrifices that no one else is asked to make, or have virtues that no one else possesses, such as a dignified subordination of their personal agenda and a reliance on altruism for life's meaning. Virtues and sacrifices, when expected of one group of people and not of everyone, become the mark of an underclass.[11]

Establishing a fair deal for mothers would go beyond "wages for housewives," an idea that surfaced in the 1970s; or even mothers' benefits similar to veterans' benefits. What is needed is across-the-board recognition—in the workplace, in the family, in the law, and in social policy—that someone has to do the necessary work of raising children and sustaining families, and that the reward for such vital work should not be professional marginalization, a loss of status, and an increased risk of poverty.

Such recognition would end the glaring contradiction between what we tell young women—go out, get an education, become independent—and what happens to those aspirations once they have a child. It would demolish the anachronism that bedevils most mothers' lives: that although they work as hard as or harder than anyone else in the economy, they are still economic *dependents,* like children or incapacitated adults.

The standard rationale for the status quo is that women choose to have children, and in so doing, choose to accept the trade-offs that have always ensued. As an African safari guide once said of a troop of monkeys, "The mothers with the little babies have a hard time keeping up." But human beings, unlike apes, have the ability to ensure that those who carry the babies—and therefore our future—aren't forever trailing behind.

THIS BOOK IS based on more than five years of research in economics, sociology, history, child development, family law, public policy, demography, anthropology, and evolutionary psychology, as well as hundreds of interviews with mothers and fathers in the United States and Europe.

But this is also a work of the heart, growing out of my own experience as a professional woman and a mother. As a beneficiary of the women's movement, for years I lived the unencumbered life of a journalist; one of the boys in a gender-neutral environment that represented enormous progress for women. For a time I was married, and my husband and I ate out almost every night, had a maid to clean our apartment, and packed our bags on short notice. We weren't even home enough to keep a cat. We eventually separated, and it was more like two roommates going their separate ways than a divorce.

But almost immediately after my marriage dissolved, I was stricken with baby-hunger: a passionate, almost physical longing for a child. I was determined not to become the woman on the T-shirt who looks at her watch and exclaims, "Oh, I forgot to have a baby!" Fortunately, I didn't; within three years I had remarried and become a mother.

I fell hopelessly in love with this tiny new creature, with an intensity that many mothers describe as "besotted." I had taken a lot of trips in my life, but this was the most exotic. The world of motherhood was as strange and unfamiliar to me as a hidden Himalayan kingdom. The first surprise came when I realized how hard and yet how incredibly gratifying motherhood was. I quickly discovered that my husband and I would need all our inner resources if we were to meet the needs of the insatiable and helpless little person we had brought into the world. As Ralph Waldo Emerson put it, "In dealing with my child, my Latin and Greek, my accomplishments and my money stead me nothing; but as much soul as I have avails."

Being a good-enough mother, I found, took more patience and inner strength—not to mention intelligence, skill, wisdom, and love—than my previous life had ever demanded. Nurturing and guiding an ever-changing child was not like housework, a checklist of domestic chores, but highly skilled labor, informed by the same spirit that inspires the best teachers, ministers, counselors, and therapists.

The second surprise came when I realized how little my former world seemed to understand, or care, about the complex reality I was discovering. The dominant culture of which I had been a part considered child-rearing unskilled labor, if it considered child-rearing at all. And no one was stating the obvious: if human abilities are the ultimate fount of economic progress, as many economists now agree, and if those abilities are nurtured (or stunted) in the early years, then mothers and other caregivers of the young are the most important producers in the economy. They do have, literally, the most important job in the world.

I'll never forget the moment I realized that almost no one else agreed. It was at a Washington, D.C., cocktail party, when someone asked, "What do you do?" I replied that I was a new mother, and they promptly vanished. I was the same person this stranger might have found worthwhile had I said I was a foreign correspondent for *Newsweek,* a financial reporter for the *New York Times,* or a Pulitzer prize nominee, all of which had been true. But as a mother, I had shed status like the skin off a snake.

I gradually realized that mothers—and everyone else who spends much time with children—were still in the same boat that women had been in only a few years earlier. After fighting hard to win respect in the workplace, women had yet to win respect for their work at home.

But the moment of truth came a few years after I had resigned from the *New York Times,* in order to have more time for my infant son. I ran into someone who asked, "Didn't you used to be Ann Crittenden?"

That's when I knew I had to write this book.

CHAPTER 1

Where We Are Now

"It is mothers who are picking up the slack, doing . . . what has to be done, whether it makes sense or not, because no one else is available, able, or willing to do the job."

—Suzanne Bianchi, sociologist

One of the misleading impressions left in the wake of the women's movement is that it swept away women's traditional lives, like a sandstorm burying the artifacts of an ancient civilization. The media constantly remind us that women have become doctors, lawyers, merchants, chiefs, implying that no one is left to tend to the children.

The truth, as always, is far more complicated. Mothers have not abandoned home and hearth to go to "work." Mothers are working harder than ever, but their principal place of business is still the home. For all of the ink spilled about the high-tech economy, the majority of American mothers are still primarily engaged in the oldest economy in the world: the household.

Most people seriously underestimate how much of their lives contemporary American women spend on their children. There is even evidence that today's mothers are taking the tasks of reproduction more seriously than any previous generation. Recent research indicates, for example, that American mothers—whether they work outside the home or not—may be spending more time with their children than they did in the past.[1] And married fathers are also putting in more time with the kids, although mothers as a group continue to devote far more hours to children than fathers do.[2]

These new data put the lie to conservative fears that once liberated, women would liberate themselves from the responsibilities of child-rearing. They also raise questions about feminist hopes that men would become coparents, sharing equally in the massive labor required to produce a well-prepared child. Neither the fears nor the hopes have come to pass. For whatever reasons—biology, social conditioning, institutional inertia, choice, or no other choice—children's lives are still overwhelmingly shaped by women, and children are still the focus of most women's lives.

Educator Johnnetta Cole once commented that for every child, someone has to be the mommy; the one who is responsible; the one who can be counted on day in and day out, on good days and bad. Whether she has a Ph.D. or an M.D., a B.A. or a G.E.D.; whether she is a conservative traditionalist or a Yuppie professional, for the most part, the mother is still the mommy.

Falling in Love

I first met Eleanor when she was an undergraduate at Yale in the mid-1970s. A tall, red-haired Irish-American girl from the working-class suburb of Winthrop, Massachusetts, she became one of the first women to graduate from that august institution. Blessed with boundless energy and enthusiasm, she proceeded to take on the world, confident that she would make her mark on it. She worked for various advocacy groups, served as a top aide to the lieutenant governor of Massachusetts, and even made a long-shot, unsuccessful run for Congress.

One late spring day a few years ago, we were having lunch in Boston's North End when Eleanor brought up the crucial life decision facing her. She had been trying for seven years to get pregnant, with no success. Now at age thirty-seven she and her husband, Jack, were weighing two alternatives: either to adopt or to put their dreams of having a child aside for good.

A few months later, Eleanor called to say that she and Jack were leaning toward adoption. They had been introduced to a three-and-a-half-year-old child who was in a foster home after being removed from abusive parents. Jack and Eleanor had started seeing Veronica on weekends, and although they knew that she was troubled, they felt there was a good chance that they could bring some stability and happiness into her life.

I visited Eleanor and Jack a couple of times after Veronica began living with them. One night when I arrived for dinner, the house was filled with balloons, left over from Veronica's fourth birthday party. The little brown-eyed sprite was running around in her nightgown, obviously excited, and eager to show me her new toys. She finally went to bed without too much trouble, and Eleanor and Jack discussed her progress. They were still letting Veronica spend some of her time with her last foster mother, to ease the adjustment into their home, and although she had "bad days," they believed that the adoption would work. As hard as it was with her sometimes, they had decided that it was worth it.

Several months later, I received a call from Eleanor. She was having doubts. That was putting it mildly—she was in agony. Veronica would be fine for a few weeks and then would go to pieces, a hellion by day, screaming at night. Eleanor had calculated that she was putting in fifty-eight hours during an average week just on child care. Her husband and a baby-sitter were together spending an additional twenty hours a week on Veronica. Eleanor was not going to bed until one or two in the morning and getting up again at five or six.

"It is such an enriching experience—that dimension is wonderful. . . . But it's also emotionally exhausting. It's killing me. I don't know what to do."

Veronica had just been legally freed for adoption. Her mother was a drug addict, her father an alcoholic. It was hard to imagine two people more unfit for parenting. Eleanor knew what it would do to Veronica if she didn't go through with an adoption, but what would an adoption do to her?

She had just finished a year with Boston Edison, leading a team of about twenty people in designing an award-winning energy conservation program. For the first time in her life she was earning a six-figure salary, and her boss had approached her about the possibility of the two of them starting their own energy-efficiency consulting firm.

She was also working on a book and was president of Women of Vision, a network of prominent women interested in promoting institutional change on behalf of women. She thought that she might be able to do *one* of these projects and be a mother to Veronica, but that two, not to mention all three, would be impossible. She was willing to accept the trade-offs, but they were excruciating.

"I love my work, and I've always derived a large part of my identity through my work," she told me. "I'm truly tortured. Men get a standing ovation if they miss a meeting because of parenting; women miss whole careers.

"Sometimes I think only a few people should choose motherhood as a vocation. But then I think, no—that's not fair either. Why do we have to choose like this?" Hers really was a choice; she was free to decide not to go through with the adoption. She was facing an exaggerated version of the American mother's dilemma.

Her friends had offered conflicting advice. One woman who had adopted a little girl had described it as "thirty-five years of misery." Another friend had urged her not to do anything that might make her less effective in her work. "Most women can be mothers," she had told her, "but only you can do what you can do for the world."

Eleanor finally made her decision after a particularly difficult night. Here is how she described the events in a letter to Veronica's foster mother: "I heard a piercing scream from Veronica's room, and I jumped up and flew to her bedside. She was standing on her bed, crying. I took her in my arms and brought her back to bed with me, holding her on top of me, stroking her back, saying, 'It's OK, Veronica. You're safe with us. We'll take care of you.' After a while, she calmed down, and I brought her back to her room. Two hours later she knocked on my door, came over to my bed, threw her arms around me, and said, 'Will you be my mommy?' It was Mother's Day morning."

Eleanor later told me that she believes there are two main avenues to love. One is falling in love, a spontaneous, heartfelt response to a few enchanting people you may meet in life. The other avenue is choosing love, a rational commitment to another person to share your life with them, to care for and support them through good times and bad. Unlike falling in love, choosing love is a conscious decision with momentous, permanent consequences. Eleanor and Jack had already fallen in love with Veronica. And on Mother's Day, they also chose to love her, for life.

Jack has continued in his job with the city of Boston. But Eleanor has opted to work on a variety of independent projects that give her flexibility. She now spends more time on Veronica than on any other part of her busy life.

THIS IS WHERE we are. Most women, like Eleanor, are still embracing motherhood, with all of its glorious, messy entanglements, assuming the awesome responsibility of being a primary parent. This is why homemaking, the fundamental task associated with raising the young, is still the largest single occupation in the United States. As a group, working-age homemakers outnumber secretaries, stenographers, and typists; food-preparation and service workers; schoolteachers; construction workers; mechanics and repairers; farmers, foresters, and fishermen; mathematical and computer scientists; and all of the writers, artists, entertainers, and athletes combined—not to mention lawyers, doctors, and other professionals. Even among women in their thirties, by far the most common occupation is full-time housekeeping and caregiving.[3]

Among married mothers with children under age eighteen, 28.4 percent of all those in the prime working years of twenty-five to fifty-four are not in the labor force, meaning that the only employment of these 6.9 million women is their home and children.[4]

The persistence of traditional family patterns cuts across economic, class, and racial lines. Uneducated married mothers are the least likely to be employed, having the least to gain from a job. They calculate, quite correctly, that as long as there is one breadwinner in the family, their presence at home can create more value, and be more satisfying, than much of the (under)paid work they could find. But the United States also has one of the lowest labor force participation rates for college-educated women in the developed world; only in Turkey, Ireland, Switzerland, and the Netherlands does a smaller proportion of female college graduates work for pay.[5]

The college-educated stay-at-home mother is a fixture in American business and professional circles. With sixty-plus-hour work weeks the norm at the higher levels of the economy, a full-time "wife" is often the only thing that makes family life possible. A survey of chief financial officers in American corporations found that 80 percent were men with stay-at-home wives. Another survey of managerial employees revealed that 64 percent of the male executives with children under age thirteen had nonworking spouses.[6] "The presence of a wife at home to care for family and personal matters is almost as much a requirement for success in business today as it was a generation ago," consultant Charles Rodgers told me, in an interview in his office in Cambridge, Massachusetts.[7]

A second large group of wives and mothers—approximately 20 percent of married mothers with children under age eighteen—is officially classified as "working," but these women are employed part-time while their principal job is at home.[8] The government classifies a person as "working"—that is, in the labor force—if he or she is employed for as little as one hour a week, is merely looking for paid work, or works unpaid for at least five hours a week in a family business. Thus a "working mother" can be the wife who lends a hand one afternoon a week in her husband's office; the mother who works a few evenings a week as a waitress after being home all day; or the consultant or editor who works out of a home-based office.[9] Even new mothers who are on maternity leave are "working mothers" because they remain employed.

Cheryl Evans, a Baltimore mother of four, was a licensed day-care provider in her own home while her children were little, making her officially a working mother. And Deborah Fallows, a writer in Washington, D.C., who described herself as a "stay-at-home mom" for years, was a "working mother" because she earned a few hundred dollars a year from freelance writing. But in every real sense both of these women were mothers at home. Counting them as "working mothers" contributes to the false impression that most mothers are not available to their children during the day. On the contrary, a substantial majority of working mothers appear to be reducing their work hours during the child-rearing years. In 1996, for example, married working mothers on average put 1,197 hours into their paying jobs, a mere half of the 2,132 hours averaged by married fathers.[10]

Still, many mothers don't want or can't afford to put their jobs and careers on the back burner. Almost 18 million, roughly half of all women with children under eighteen, do work full-time; that is, at least thirty-five hours a week. And the tendency of mothers to work full-time is the long-term trend. Between 1994 and 1999 alone, nearly 1 million women a year moved from part-time to full-time employment, including a record number of mothers of even very young children.[11]

This historic movement of mothers into the workplace has aroused legitimate concern, particularly over the fate of infants who are placed in surrogate impersonal group care for long hours early in life. Yet there is no clear and consistent evidence that the change in family life has been harmful to children. Some of the most alarming assertions that working mothers are shortchanging their kids are based on "evidence" that upon close inspection melts away. One allegation—that American parents spend 40 percent less time with their children than they did in 1965—is simply false. After being repeated by countless officials and media pundits, and cited in congressional hearings, think tank reports, and books, the alarmist "40 percent decline" finally appeared in a correction, where it belonged.[12]

Another worrisome statistic appeared in a report issued in 1999 by the president's Council of Economic Advisers. This document contained a widely publicized warning that parents had 14 percent less time available for their children in 1999 than in 1969.[13] But that does not mean fathers and mothers actually do spend less time with their kids. They could be sacrificing other activities. Fathers may be spending less time bowling, going fishing, or having a drink after work with their colleagues, and mothers may be devoting fewer hours to shopping or playing bridge. In fact, this is exactly what is happening.

A closer look can assure us that the family is not undergoing a meltdown, that the essential function of the family—the care and upbringing of children—is not in crisis because mothers have gone to work. On the contrary, all the signs indicate that women today are taking on motherhood with a greater-than-ever awareness of its importance.

From Quantity to Quality

Back in the 1970s, Arleen Leibowitz, an economist at RAND, was one of the first researchers to discover that, all else being equal, as women become better educated, they tend to devote *more* time and attention to their children. Apparently, as women's horizons expand, and their opportunities multiply, their hopes and aspirations for their offspring increase as well. They delay child-bearing, have fewer children, and invest more time and resources in each one. All over the world, across continents and cultures, as women advance they stop "having babies" and start "raising children," a process economist Ted Schultz described as a shift from "quantity to quality" in human reproduction.

Leibowitz speculated that as the average American woman gained better schooling and spent more of her life in the paid labor force, she would also probably spend more time with her children, not less.[14] This prediction proved uncannily accurate. Sociologists, economists, demographers, and historians have all reported a profound shift from quantity to quality in child-rearing, not just in the United States but almost everywhere on the globe. Researchers have confirmed, for example, that the number of hours of primary care (that is, feeding, bathing, etc.) per child by white married mothers in the United States almost doubled between the 1920s and the 1980s, a period in which the improvements in women's education and opportunities were nothing short of revolutionary.[15] Mothers in 1985 also spent more *overall* time on child care than did mothers in the 1920s. When domestic economists W. Keith Bryant of Cornell University and Cathleen Zick of the University of Utah looked at the time diaries of American farm wives in the 1920s, they noticed that the women were so busy with a myriad of chores that they had little time for any one member of their large broods.

Sociologists have also discovered that mothers today spend as much if not more time with their children as mothers did in the 1960s, despite the massive movement of mothers into the workplace during the intervening years.[16] Sharon Hays, a sociologist at the University of Virginia, found for example, that despite their busy schedules, the professional women she interviewed used more intensive time-consuming child-rearing techniques than less educated women. They not only talked and read more to their children; they also favored giving their children choices. They engaged in negotiation rather than demanding strict obedience to firm rules, and put a high premium on developing independence and critical thinking, all of which take more time than simply laying down the law.[17] But Hays also observed that mothers at every socioeconomic level now take it as a given that child-rearing is a very serious business, requiring a huge expenditure of time and effort. "I've had grandmothers tell me their daughters work far harder and spend more time with their children than they did," says Hays.

Sandra Espinoza, of Washington, D.C., a married mother of two, is a good example of this maternal determination. For six years, she worked as a full-time housekeeper for a family near her son's primary school, and for five more years she worked two jobs, as a housekeeper and a teacher of English as a second language. Every morning she had to get up at 6:30 A.M., fix breakfast for the family, and pack a lunch for her husband, a mechanic. She took a long bus ride across the city to her teaching job, which began at 8:00 A.M. and ended at 2:30 P.M. Then another bus to her second employer's home, where dirty dishes, unmade beds, piles of laundry, and all the rest awaited her. Four hours later, at 7:00 P.M. she left for home, arriving back where she had started, just in time to fix dinner, help with homework, and on and on and on.

Through all these years, Mrs. Espinoza's overriding focus was her children. She and her husband never had dinners out alone, or vacations, or time enough to exercise. Their lives revolved around their church and their kids.

At his mother's urging, Rafael, who was a friend of my son's, went to summer school for extra tutoring. Thanks to her efforts, he won scarce summer scholarships to city-run sports camps and attended a weeklong merchant marine program she discovered. She never missed a back-to-school night or a teacher conference, especially during the precarious early teen years. When her daughter, Rebecca, won a college scholarship for Hispanic girls, Sandra took one of her first trips ever out of the city to take her to school in Virginia.

I spoke to Mrs. Espinoza recently, and she told me she had finally decided to cut back to part-time work, quitting the domestic work. "I can't go on; I'm absolutely exhausted," she said. "I'm forty-three, the kids are in good shape, and I need some rest."

Sandra Espinoza's exhausting efforts help explain why the movement of mothers into the labor market appears to have had so little measurable impact on children's well-being, despite vigorous efforts by traditionalists to prove otherwise.[18] Working mothers just don't rest.

The Leisure Gap

Working mothers put in longer hours than almost anyone else in the economy. On average, they are estimated to work more than eighty hours a week.[19] Time-use surveys confirm that as women enter the workplace, they take on the equivalent of two full-time jobs, forcing them to cut back on everything in their lives *but* paid work and children.

The first thing to go is housework. According to John P. Robinson, a sociologist at the University of Maryland, between 1965 and 1985, working mothers reduced the amount of housework they did from twenty-seven hours a week to twenty.[20] In the mid-1960s, for example, the average dinner took two and a half hours to prepare; today, it's ready in fifteen minutes, according to a survey by grocery manufacturers.[21]

But cookie-baking nostalgia aside, the shift to fast food has not destroyed the family or displaced that ritual marker of togetherness, the family dinner. In a 1998 survey two-thirds of all American families claimed that they managed to eat dinner together at least five nights a week, and an additional 23 percent said they ate together three or four times a week.[22] So what if it is over pizza or at McDonald's?

The other incredibly shrinking thing in working mothers' lives is leisure. Women are protecting their children from a parental "time famine" by subjecting themselves to a "time crunch." Their grueling schedules explain why so many eventually decide to give up their paychecks, if they can afford to. It may be the only way they can get a good night's sleep.[23]

In intensive interviews with thirty-seven mothers who were working full-time in a California hospital, sociologist Anita Garey found that some were getting only three and a half to four and a half hours of sleep. "I'd say most were getting five or six hours a night," Garey told me in a telephone interview. "Sleep—not their children—is what they are giving up directly, along with couple's time. . . . The toll is tremendous."[24]

The root problem here is not the working mother, but the triumph of "turbo-capitalism," which has brought with it a steadily lengthening workday for white-collar employees and managers.[25] By the year 2000,

Americans had the heaviest workload in the industrialized world, including Japan. There is no question that this speedup is putting unbearable pressure on conscientious parents, reflected in poll after poll, with both men and women calling for a shorter work week.[26]

The pressures are obviously greatest on single mothers. Almost 27 percent of American children are in families headed by a lone parent, usually a mother. A University of Michigan survey found that preteen children living with single mothers spent twelve to fourteen fewer hours a week with parents than children living with married parents.[27] When a 1995 *Washington Post* poll asked 702 randomly selected teenagers, "Do your parents spend too much time or too little time with you?" only 26 percent of those with married parents said too little time. Even more—30 percent—said their parents spent too much time with them. But half of the kids whose parents were divorced said they had too little time with their parents, and only 18 percent felt they spent too much time.[28]

Children report that the parent who is in truly short supply is the father, whether their parents are married or single, whether their mothers work or not. According to demographer Cheryl Russell, most children "say they spend enough time with their mothers. Most say their mothers 'almost never' miss events and activities important to them. In contrast, most children say their fathers 'frequently' or 'sometimes' miss important events. Many children say they would like to spend more time with their fathers."[29] For teenagers, according to a study by the National Center on Addiction and Substance Abuse, "a bad relationship with fathers is so much more common than with mothers. . . . It's much rarer for moms to be absent or distant."[30]

Where Are the Fathers?

The mirror image of the myth that "mothers have flown the coop" is the myth that fathers are becoming equal parents. Many feminists want to believe this, because they want to think that traditional gender roles are being eliminated. Corporations want to believe it, because they want to assume that all their employees can be worked as if work were all there is to life. And men themselves are not averse to taking credit for turning over a new leaf. Thus the politically correct term for child-rearing is "parenting"—neatly disguising the fact that the mothers are doing most of the work. And a father's every paternal gesture is interpreted as a sign of the long-awaited new man. But wishing won't make it so, and for the most part, it isn't.

Almost everyone agrees that men are doing more housework and child care than their own fathers did, particularly in households where the wife earns a hefty part of the family income. There is also good evidence that married fathers are spending almost as much time with their children on weekends as mothers do, taking them to sporting events and other outside activities.[31]

But the fact remains, as one recent study put it, "despite an overall increase in the relative involvement of fathers, household activities, caring for infants, studying and reading (with children) remain domains in which fathers have a very low relative contribution."[32] In the relatively rare households where the mother is the bigger breadwinner, mothers still spend more than thirteen hours a week more than fathers on child care and household chores. This doesn't jibe with any theory about rational economic behavior. "The puzzling thing for an economist," says Richard Freeman, a Harvard economist, "is if her hourly earnings are higher than his, she should be the one who works more hours outside the home, and he should do more of the work in the home. And that isn't happening."[33]

Even when a wife earns more than half of the family income, the husband will typically contribute no more than 30 percent of the domestic services and child care. And that estimate comes from surveys based on men's own statements about their family contributions, surveys that experts agree are biased on the upside. Even if a married man becomes unemployed, his proportion of housework and child care almost never exceeds 30 percent. By contrast, when a married woman becomes unemployed, the percentage of domestic work she does averages 75 percent. "Our data shows that there is not a true gift exchange in marriage," economist George Akerlof told me. "Although there is a lot of variation, between most spouses there is not complete reciprocity."[34]

The care of babies and toddlers is still clearly a female monopoly. In families with preschool children, mothers appear to be putting in roughly three to four *times* as many hours as fathers. One study of thirty-s... families of young children, representing various classes, races, and work patterns, found that the man rarely had primary responsibility for any *single* child-rearing duty. In *no* household did a father take responsibility for *all* child-rearing tasks.[35]

Before the arrival of the first child, couples tend to share the housework fairly equally. But something about a baby encourages the resurgence of traditional gender roles. One woman who worked in advertising before she became a stay-at-home mother of two described the dynamic. "My husband used to shop, put something in the oven. . . . When you're both out there all day, you're in it together. Once the children arrived, however, things changed. He works all week, and on the weekends he wants to relax. I'll have a list of five or six things I want him to do, but he wants to relax, watch sports on TV. . . . The baby will throw food on the floor, and even when he's sitting right there, I'll have to pick it up, put it away, take her away, put her to bed."

She remembers the moment when they started to play the "where" game:

She: "Would you set the table?"

He: "Where are the napkins?"

She: "We've lived in the same house for twelve years and they're where they've always been."

Whether they work full-time, part-time, or not at all outside the home, mothers are much more willing to do what has to be done for children. Maryland psychotherapist Leah Steinberg told me, "In all my years of practice I've never had a man come into my office and say 'I need to cut back; I need to work part-time.' Women say this all the time." It is most often Mom who drops everything and runs if a child has an accident. Working mothers are more likely than working fathers to take time off to care for a sick child, resulting in far higher absentee rates. During an average week in 1989, full-time working mothers who were married and had a child under age six had more than double the average rate of absenteeism. Married fathers with preschoolers were well below the average.[36]

Mothers, working or not, go to more teacher conferences, attend more school meetings, and volunteer at school events more often than fathers. They even make up one-third of Little League softball coaches.[37] At a luncheon at my son's school for active parent volunteers, I counted three men in a roomful of roughly fifty women. At another parent meeting, it was a dozen mothers and three fathers—a typical ratio.

Mothers run the errands. Nationwide, working mothers of young children run more than twice as many errands on their way home from work as fathers do. A survey in Washington, D.C., found that women stopped at schools and day-care centers twice as often as men on the commute from work and were more likely to detour for errands. Men were twice as likely to go to a bar or restaurant.[38]

Despite the media's fondness for Mr. Mom, he remains an aberration. Of the 20.5 million American children under the age of five, only about 320,000 have fathers as their primary guardian—a minuscule 1.5 percent.[39] Recently, more *single* men have been living with children, often teenage sons. But single fathers are more likely than single mothers to have someone else in the household who helps with or actually provides the child care. "Most are men living with women, such as their own mothers," says sociologist Andrew Cherlin, "and they're doing the real care for the children."

In 1994, 73 percent of men and women polled said taking care of the kids was the woman's primary responsibility, along with the cooking (80 percent), the grocery shopping (79 percent), the laundry (80 percent), the housecleaning (76 percent), and the dishes (73 percent). Of all the household chores, men took primary responsibility for only one: deciding how the money would be spent (55 percent).[40]

YEARS AGO, GLORIA STEINEM approvingly observed that "we've become the men we wanted to marry." She meant that women no longer have to look to a man to fulfill their dreams of accomplishment or economic security; they can achieve these things themselves. This is true, but only if a woman decides not to have children. With the arrival of a child, a mother's definition of accomplishment becomes more complex, her work load goes up, and her income and independence go down. For all the changes of the last decades, one thing has stayed the same: it is still women who adjust their lives to accommodate the needs of children; who do what is necessary to make a home; who forgo status, income, advancement, and independence. Nowhere is this more dramatically illustrated than in the experience of the nation's most educated women—the ones who had the best shot at having it all.

CHAPTER 2

A Conspiracy of Silence

> We have done better at playing according to the men's rules than changing them to our own.
>
> —Susan Estrich, the first female editor of the *Harvard Law Review*

One of the worst-kept secrets of the past two decades is the quiet exodus of highly trained women from corporations and the leading professional firms. Faced with institutions that have no tolerance for anyone with family responsibilities, many mothers have taken the only available option—just say no.

Not that mothers are dropping out of the labor force. On the contrary, as we have seen, more women with children are employed full-time than ever before. But they are not necessarily working at the careers for which they have been trained, or at the most challenging levels of those careers, or at the salaries that their training would normally command.

I know of what I speak. After my son was born, I was faced with having to resume an all-consuming work schedule at the *New York Times*. I loved my job, but I felt I couldn't do it anymore. There was no question that I would have preferred to stay at the newspaper, had it offered a part-time alternative, but in 1983 it didn't. And I hadn't waited as long as I did to have a baby in order to turn him over to someone else for most of his waking hours.

In the course of my interviews, I met dozens of working mothers who had had to make similar decisions, from the psychiatrist who gave up the time-consuming training that would have enabled her to rise in her profession, to the academic biologist who took herself off a tenure track in order to work a twenty-hour week, to the physician who relinquished the ob- part of her ob-gyn practice, to former managers, executives, and economists who became freelance consultants at home. None of us were prepared to do what most men do willingly—reduce our parental role to that of a fond breadwinner.

Be a Man

The unwritten requirement for success in corporate America is to be a corporate man, says one disgruntled female executive who tried but failed. Young women today are urged to finish school, find a job, acquire skills, develop seniority, get tenure, make partner, work endless hours, and put children off until the very last minute. When and if they do give birth, they are expected to treat the event like an appendectomy, take a brief time-out for recuperation, and then resume the truly important business of business.

Buried in the fine print of the 1995 report of the federal Glass Ceiling Commission was the gritty truth: most women don't want to follow this model. In comments included in the report, which revealed that white men occupy 95 out of 100 senior management positions, male executives complained over and over again that the problem with women was that they just weren't men. Women weren't "tough enough," they groused; women didn't play enough golf, or like to go fishing, or use baseball metaphors. One woman testified that when she won company awards and contests, "they'd give me money clips and tie tacks."

"What's important is comfort, chemistry, relationships, and collaborations," said one white male executive. "When we find minorities and women who think like we do, we snatch them up."[1] The trouble is, mothers are the least likely women to think like "we" do, when "we" are men who see their children a few minutes a day and on weekends.

This is not the way anyone thought it would be, back in the 1970s and early 1980s, when an army of briefcase-toting twenty-something women poured out of universities into the offices of corporate America. But when these women began to want babies of their own, they discovered that their equality at work was only as deep as their commitment to the unencumbered life. Those who had children soon found out that trying to compete in a race designed for the unattached was like running in a marathon with a ten-pound weight strapped to each leg. By the end of the 1980s, mothers and women who planned to be mothers were quietly exiting the institutions they had so recently entered.

One of the first people to mention the attrition publicly was Geraldine Laybourne, a prominent television executive. In a 1989 speech to women in cable television, Laybourne, then the head of Nickelodeon, asserted that "women are becoming frustrated and leaving corporate America in droves. There are fewer senior-level women in management today than in 1982. . . . The glass ceiling isn't the only reason women are leaving," she continued. "They are also leaving for child-rearing concerns. In America we tend to take a short-term view of this issue, and because of the need to show results every day, we lose the employee."

Laybourne had broken a feminist and corporate taboo against talking about maternal defections. After all, weren't women the same as men? As smart, as ambitious, as hardworking? As suited to high office? Few were bold enough to suggest that a woman might want a slightly different career path, at least while her children were young.

But Laybourne's candor didn't land her in the hot water that scalded another truth teller, the late Felice N. Schwartz. Schwartz was the founder and president of Catalyst, a not-for-profit organization that advocates the advancement of women in business. She had spent almost thirty years fighting to open up opportunities for women in corporate America, and she was troubled by the obstacles to their rise to top-level positions. She understood the problems firsthand, because she had experienced them herself.

Schwartz had had the first of her three children at age twenty-three and had worked part-time at home for eight years while they were young. She saw such a "time-out" as a reasonable option for many mothers, if companies would accept it without stigmatizing those who chose that route. In a controversial article published in the *Harvard Business Review,* she argued that women are different from men—they have babies—and because of biology, tradition, and socialization, many might want to reduce their work pace for a time to raise their children. This made women more expensive to hire than men, Schwartz wrote, because some will need flexibility and a temporarily slower career path. But providing these things is in employers' interest, she maintained, because the cost of losing talented women is greater than the cost of employing them.[2]

Schwartz's reasoning was marred by an excessively rosy view of business attitudes. The corporate establishment had shown no interest whatsoever in changing its modus operandi to accommodate family life and had only begun to admit women in the executive ranks on condition that they conform to established male norms. Yet she professed shock when female graduates of the Wharton School of Business told her they took their wedding rings off before going to job interviews. They knew that any hint that a baby was a possibility would hurt their chances. (Wharton men, in contrast, *borrowed* wedding rings, so they would look more responsible.) She was horrified to learn that a recruiter from a "prominent financial services company" was asking women in job interviews whether they would have an abortion if they got pregnant.[3]

Nonetheless, Schwartz clung to her convictions that corporations could be made to see the light. In the mid-1990s, she predicted in a speech that companies would soon be offering generous family benefits in order to keep valued female employees. One of my friends, an attorney and mother of three who was in the audience, was skeptical. "Law firms want single people they can work to death," she told me bluntly.

In her article Schwartz never once used the term "mommy track." Nor did she mean to imply that women who choose a slower career path should be permanently sidelined. She certainly never dreamed, she assured me in 1994, that her article might hand male executives an excuse to "give up on women." But she did make the mistake of talking about "career-primary" women, who could be treated like men, and "career-and-family" women, who might need more time to reach positions of responsibility. She assumed that only women might want a "non-career-dominant" period in their lives, and that only mothers are more costly to hire, overlooking the factors, including excessive competitiveness, that make some men expensive propositions as well.

For her sins, Schwartz was pilloried by the very people who shared her concerns. Feminists, work/family experts, congressional liberals all piled on, claiming that she was trying to shunt female employees off on a slow road to nowhere. Despite a lifetime of advocacy for women, she was painted as an enemy of female progress. Stunned and hurt, she convened a meeting with women's magazine editors from *Savvy, Working Mother, Working Woman, Executive Female,* and *New York Woman* to discuss how they could get beyond the controversy and move the debate forward. "The message they gave me was strong," she later wrote. "It may be true what you're saying, but we just cannot discuss these things at this point."

Schwartz concluded that there was a "conspiracy of silence" about what was happening to mothers in the workplace.[4] Women's advocates weren't confident enough yet to challenge the corporate culture head-on. Corporate leaders, for their part, didn't want to acknowledge that their rigid ways were driving women away. Schwartz had been groping for a way to persuade the "male structures and conventions of business" to accommodate women's preferences. But no one else was ready to admit that women were different at all.

The incompatibility of conventional career patterns with motherhood was documented by economist Claudia Goldin. Goldin, who turned fifty in 1996, was curious about how the lives of women of her generation had turned out. Her college-educated contemporaries had had a clearly stated goal: to "have it all," both a career and a family. How successful, she wondered, had they been in their quest?

Not very, as she discovered in her survey.[5] Fewer than 20 percent of college-educated baby-boomer women had managed to achieve both motherhood and a career by their late thirties or forties. Though their generation was probably the first to contain even a small group of women "who managed to reach mid-life with both career and family," that group was small indeed: no more than 13 to 17 percent of all the women who graduated from college between 1966 and 1979.[6] No wonder "having it all" had acquired such a hollow ring by the mid-1990s.

The trade-offs between career and family have been stark. A female baby boomer's success in the employment arena was directly correlated with whether or not she had children. The women without children have been *twice* as successful in achieving a career as the women with children. Fully *half* of the women who had attained a career by midlife were childless.[7]

Claudia Goldin knows something about this trade-off herself. The first female professor to receive tenure in economics at Harvard, she is unmarried and has never had a child. Privately, according to Harvard colleagues, she believes that a serious, high-level career and primary responsibility for children cannot be combined. Plenty of people agree with her. A 1995 survey of employees at Eli Lilly, one of the most family-friendly companies in the country, found that only about one-third of them believed that it was possible to advance their careers and devote enough time to their families.[8]

Goldin put the college-educated boomers' lives in historical perspective by comparing them with several previous generations of American women. The first group of American women to receive a higher education—those graduating around 1910—virtually had to renounce motherhood and family life if they wanted a career. More than half of the female college graduates of that generation never had children. Theirs was a clear-cut either-or choice: *career or family*. If they chose a career, it almost always involved teaching, one of the few fields open to women.

The next generation, those graduating around 1933, typically worked at a fairly menial job for a few years and then dropped out of the labor force, in a *job then family* pattern. After them came the graduates of the 1950s, who had substantially higher marriage and fertility rates than their predecessors, and who went to work after their children were older. Their pattern was *family then job,* for almost all the doors to the professions were still closed to them with the exception of teaching.

These were the women who launched the modern women's movement. Dissatisfied with their constraints, they began the drive to open up life choices and serious professions for women. Their immediate successors, the college-educated baby boomers, were the first to try to put it all together: to have it all.

As is now becoming clear, they were not able to pull it off. By all indications they have followed a pattern of *career then family,* pursuing their professional dreams and postponing children until they run up against the biological clock, and then, as they approach middle age, putting those children first. This is the pattern my friend Eleanor is following, and it rings true to me, because it was my own pattern as well. The fact is that no generation of American women has yet been able to achieve what most college-educated women have said they wanted for more than 100 years: a meaningful career *and* a chance to raise children of their own.

Goldin's findings are reflected in the experience of 902 women who graduated from Harvard's professional schools between 1971 and 1981. Judy Walker, a personnel officer at Harvard, and her coauthor, Deborah Swiss, had set out to produce a compilation of stories on how this elite group of highly trained women had managed to succeed. In the early stages of the project, Walker and Swiss assumed that their survey of a large population of women with top-flight professional credentials would reveal many examples of support in the workplace for women confronting the career/family dilemma.[9]

One may marvel at the authors' naïveté, but they were simply reflecting a common assumption that the 1980s and 1990s were a saga of success for talented, energetic women. In fact, Walker and Swiss found "a different, nearly opposite picture": fully 25 percent of the female Harvard M.B.A.s of the 1970s, some of the most expensively trained and highly motivated people in the country, had left the workplace *entirely* by the early 1990s. Many said they had been forced out of the best jobs once they became mothers.

The women felt "blindsided"; they hadn't expected it to be so difficult to combine motherhood with a career. Their expectations and self-esteem were high, based on their superb education and proven competence. They had simply not anticipated two things: the degree to which they would fall in love with their new baby, and the high professional price they would be forced to pay for that love.

Many mothers reported that they were completely unready for the almost immediate necessity of abandoning their babies while the mother-infant romance was still at its height. Eighty-two percent of the mothers had taken a maternity leave of four months or *less,* whereupon they were expected to return to "normal."[10]

Most of the women couldn't accept a model of parenthood that saw a baby as a temporary blip on a career screen. Even though the great majority believed that reducing their hours of work would be detrimental to their career, fully 70 percent cut back anyway after the birth of their first child. The feelings this aroused were complex. The fifty-two women interviewed in depth expressed a tangled mixture of satisfaction, frustration, anger, and a wistful sense of loss over what they viewed as a totally unnecessary conflict between caring for their child and pursuing professional goals they had spent their lives, and a great deal of money, preparing for.

One banker, depressed and angry about how her image in the office had changed after a *three*-month leave—hardly a retreat into domesticity—said that such a break was "not what people expect from a dedicated, high-performing employee. They want your soul." Another woman felt "almost desperate" about having to make a choice between doing work she had fought long and hard for and being an intimate part of her child's life.

A physician and mother at a major Boston hospital, who was still required to attend meetings scheduled after a twelve-hour day, commented that "any deviation from accepted practice stands out, requires explanation, causes resentment, and interferes with the male environment's tunnel vision." A Boston doctor who took a three-month, mostly unpaid maternity leave overheard the following comment by a male colleague: "She's sure milking the system for all it's worth." This man, like the other male physicians who solemnly agreed with him, had encouraged his own wife to stay home with their young children.

The double standard was evident in the advice these women volunteered for younger women. Things would have been easier, they said, if they "had only one child," or "had no kids," or had "been born a man."[11]

Workplace Realities

In sum, women may have come a long way, but mothers have a lot farther to go. This is particularly true in business. A recent Catalyst survey of male and female M.B.A.s revealed that among those who have risen to within three levels of the CEO position, fewer than half (49 percent) of the women have children, compared with 84 percent of the men.[12] Moreover, in profession after profession, the accepted structures and conventions repel dedicated parents like a body rejects a foreign object.

Accounting

By 1990 the defection of female professionals had prompted a number of major corporations to conduct in-house surveys on why the women were leaving. One of the most concerned firms was Deloitte and Touche, which like all the big accounting firms was experiencing a female brain drain. Roughly 50 percent of Deloitte and Touche's new hires were women, but, as a female partner at Price Waterhouse observed in 1992, "women are not staying in the pipeline. Look at the percentage of women hired ten years ago and how many are still here; the percentages have not held." Between 1982 and 1992 the percentage of female partners in the largest CPA firms had barely risen, from 1 percent to a grand total of 5 percent.

Deloitte and Touche calculated that it cost between 95 percent and 150 percent of an annual salary to replace every female professional who left. In an effort to cut these losses, the accounting firm decided to get to the bottom of women's disaffection. An in-house survey found, among other things, that when a person asked for a flexible schedule in order to accommodate child-rearing, she was given the message that she had just committed career hara-kiri.[13] In a separate random survey of 1,450 female C.P.A.s, many of the women revealed that while they wanted children, they were afraid that motherhood would damage their chances for promotion.

Deloitte subsequently began promoting some women on flexible schedules to partner and discovered that almost all of those who were offered flexibility stayed with the company. By 1997 the percentage of partners who were women had risen to almost 10 percent, the highest among the big firms. Women's magazines hailed this as a significant victory for working mothers.[14]

Law

"Act like a man and time your pregnancies appropriately," advised a 206-page guidebook put out by the Harvard Women's Law Association in 1995. *Presumed Equal: What America's Top Women Lawyers Really Think About Their Firms* explained the facts of life in the leading law firms:

- Two men in one firm were so afraid to leave work that they didn't join their wives in the delivery room when their children were born.
- A female associate at Baker & Botts said she and her husband had decided not to have children, because she couldn't pursue a partnership otherwise.
- An associate at Paul, Weiss, Rifkind, Wharton & Garrison reported that "the only conditions under which a woman could succeed is if she remained unmarried and certainly childless."[15]

While being recruited by a prominent firm, a Harvard Law School graduate had the following experience: She had been wooed through three rounds of interviews, had met almost all the partners, and was sitting down to a final lunch when she laid her cards on the table. "I work really hard, and I know I can do a good job," she told her suitors. "But I need to get home at the end of the day because I have a one-year-old."

End of courtship. She never heard from the firm again.[16]

Women are not dropping out of the law. A national study has found only a 1 to 2 percent difference in the number of men and women leaving the practice of law. According to the *ABA Journal,* 95 percent of women lawyers who have a child return to work within a year. What women are dropping out of are the large firms. Typically, female graduates flock into the big firms, work morning, noon, and night for a few years, and then depart, leaving the fat pickings of partnership to the men. According to the *National Law Journal,* in 1995 only 13 percent of the partners in the 1,160 largest law firms, and only about 7 percent of the equity partners, who share in a firm's profits, were women. A survey of the 1972 to 1975 graduates of the University of Michigan Law School found that fifteen years after graduation the men were more than twice as likely as the women to be practicing at a large firm. The women were in public interest law, small firms, and working for government.

This is the typical pattern. Women are more apt to go into the relatively low paying, less pressured areas of government and legal services, and, increasingly, corporate in-house counsel. The reason is children. Recently I met a woman in her late twenties who had quit a prominent law firm to go to work for the Securities and Exchange Commission because, she explained, at the government agency she would have to work "only" eight or nine hours a day instead of ten or twelve or more.

A friend of mine—who asked that her identity be disguised—actually managed to succeed in a prominent Midwestern firm while raising two children. After earning her law degree in 1974, she became a tax attorney and practiced for more than twenty years, much of it with the same firm. She deliberately waited until she made partner before having her first child, then took a three-month maternity leave and became the first partner to be granted a part-time (80 percent) schedule. She went on to have another child, and while the two were small, she reduced her schedule to 60 percent.

For years she was the *only* partner in the firm on a part-time schedule, and the partners referred to the arrangement as the "Joan Stern" policy. The policy was not automatically available to every new parent but had to be negotiated anew by anyone who wanted to work part-time. Many other women—and men—in the firm wanted a reduced workweek, Stern says, but never dared to ask for one for fear of what it would do to their future.

In 1996 Stern's children were ages eight and ten. She went home three days a week at 3:30 P.M., in time to meet her son as he got off the school bus. In the afternoon she was available for her kids if they needed her, and in the evening, after everyone was fed and read to and down for the night, Stern was usually back to work. She often worked until 10:30 or 11:00 P.M. and then was up again at 4:45 A.M. "I'm free between 11:00 at night and 4:30 in the morning if you want to reach me," she joked at the time.

Joan's husband, a university professor, also worked on a part-time schedule for a year, but, she says, "spending more time at home ate into his research, which was why he had become an academic in the first place." So she is the more flexible parent. "I made these choices," she says. "I'm comfortable with them." But when a local newspaper wanted to feature her in a story on how some firms allowed partners to have family time, she refused. "It might cause my clients to wonder and might hinder me in getting new clients," she explained.

A few years later Stern finally left her firm and she is now working as an independent tax consultant. She says she feels nothing but relief to be out from under the pressure that permeates the practice of law today.

So what's wrong with this picture? One could make a case that women can succeed, and find much more balance in their lives, in smaller law firms, in academia, and in advocacy work, carving out new legal territory rather than following in the footsteps of men into the big firms. But not only are the largest firms the most lucrative in the profession, they are the traditional breeding grounds for high government officials, judges, and other positions of authority. A selection process that winnows women out of this stream has the effect of keeping a disproportionate number of qualified women out of top government jobs, off the bench, and out of the loop for corporate directorships and other leadership positions. The large firms' inhospitality to parents perpetuates women's marginality.

If anything, things appear to be getting worse. A report by an American Bar Association panel in 1995 confirmed that the partnership rate for women fell even farther behind the rate for men during the 1990s, as many firms retrenched and the demand for ever more billable hours intensified. (By one estimate, lawyers in 2000 were billing 500 to 600 more hours a year than just a few years earlier.)

Science

In science the "woman situation" has been compared to a leaky pipe: a roiling Amazon of smart graduate students at one end reduced to a trickle at the other. "Science is really hard work," says Dr. Bruce Alberts, president of the National Academy of Sciences and a molecular biologist at the University of California in San Francisco. He adds, "It really helps to have a wife."[17] Most women don't.

In 1995, at Dr. Albert's university, fully half the graduate students in biology were women. But where will those students end up? One study found that one-fifth of the women who were employed in science and engineering at the beginning of the 1980s had dropped out of those fields by 1989, compared with one-tenth of the men. As the study pointed out, this waste of a huge investment in advanced training not only harms individuals but is a drain on the entire economy.[18]

Only a handful of female graduate students make it to tenured positions in academic science departments. In 1995, women still accounted for less than 10 percent of full professorships in science and engineering, only slight progress from roughly 3 percent of tenured professors in 1973. A review at MIT found that as of 1994, there were 252 men and 22 women in the six departments of science combined. Of the 17 tenured women scientists at the university, only 7 had children.

Stephanie Diment, a pathologist, claims that she never met a woman who left science to take four or five years out for child-rearing who subsequently returned to a tenure track. Most of her female colleagues who became mothers, she adds, averaged four weeks or less of maternity leave.

Diment herself spent six years on a ten-year tenure track at New York University, before leaving in December 1994 to take a job as an editor at a scientific publisher. There, her 8:30 A.M. to 4:30 P.M. day was four hours shorter than her typical day in the lab, leaving her with some time for her four-year-old daughter. The intense pressures in science and the ferocious competition for grant money penalize men as well as women with families, Diment points out. "The younger guys are facing the same situation. One young scientist I know at NYU, whose wife works full-time, was told by his department chairman that he would have to see less of his children if he wanted to make it."

Yet the conspiracy of silence in the labs and the universities is as great as it is in the corporate world. Diment, like numerous others I interviewed, says that no one dares to talk about the problems for fear of being labeled a complainer or being seen as less than fully dedicated to their work. In 1994, she reports, "a questionnaire went around [NYU] asking about family issues, and a couple of women I know, who had strong opinions on the subject, wouldn't fill it out. There was no way they could be convinced that the answers would be anonymous. So you don't even get information on the extent of the problem."[19]

Engineering and Technology

Several years ago, the magazine *Woman Engineer* profiled a general manager in the civil service division at Westinghouse, holding her up as "a good example for young women engineers." Her typical workday began at 8:30 A.M. and ended at 8:30 P.M., followed by dinner with a customer or a business-related function until about 11:00 P.M., plus a few more hours of work on Saturday and Sunday.

"All the long hours are worth it," she enthused. "And I balance my work with an equally active personal life. I work hard, but I also—to use a corny phrase—play hard."

Maybe so, but she hasn't yet tried the hardest thing of all: balancing her work and her play with a family.

Women make up only about 9 percent of American engineers and 27 percent of the nation's programmers and computer scientists, according to Commerce Department figures. The reasons are many and complex, but they do not include the inability of women to master technology or engineering. Women, after all, were instrumental in the development of the earliest computers, and invented Common Business-Oriented Language, or COBOL, not to mention Kevlar (the bulletproof material used in vests), the dishwasher, Scotchgard, windshield wipers, and the automatic drip coffeemaker. But women were not instrumental in inventing the 24/7 culture surrounding high-tech companies. It is unimaginable that any person primarily responsible for a young child could have a demanding position with a new technology company—much less start one—without delegating virtually all of the care to someone else.

This is surely why the lunchroom at Microsoft in Seattle is full of young men and only a sprinkling of women. Why less than 5 percent of venture capital money loaned to high-tech start-ups goes to female-headed companies. Why only 3 percent of Internet companies have a woman on their board. And why 94 percent of the richest technology professionals—those who earn $300,000 a year or have a net worth of at least $3 million—are men.[20]

Government Service

In 1992 a government panel looked into the puzzling fact that only about one in ten of the top executive positions in the federal government were held by women. Sure enough, the panel discovered that overall, "women with children have received fewer promotions than women without children and than men," even after controlling for length of service, education, and other factors.[21]

The panel also found that women with children were sometimes seen as being less committed to their jobs. This was strange, since only

2 percent of women with children at home worked less than forty hours a week, and more than half (55 percent) were working *more* than a forty-hour week. The female senior executives also received performance appraisals as good as *or better* than the men's and expressed just as much commitment to career advancement.[22]

But that apparently was not enough. "She's clearly made a priority decision," said one male executive of a subordinate who had requested maternity leave. "There's nothing irrational about [her] decision, but it's much less likely she'll get a managerial shot."

Another offered this explanation for why mothers were not promoted: "As a successful senior executive you come in at 7:00 A.M. and you stay longer and work harder than anybody else and you really don't start your rumination about really important things until 10:00 or so at night." A number of women were passed over, the top guns admitted, because they had children who were still home in those evening hours.[23]

Medicine

More than 40 percent of the new entrants to medical schools are now women. One out of every five doctors is a woman. As American medicine moves toward group practice and more emphasis on preventive care, part of the revolution is the demise of the male monopoly within the profession.

But a 1992 study by the National Institutes of Health concluded that the problem of reconciling family and career is "the most difficult to address" of all the obstacles facing aspiring female doctors. The report revealed that the medical profession has made only minimal adjustments to the timetables and rhythms of people trying to raise children.

The N.I.H. report found that:

- nearly half of all U.S. medical programs still had no written maternity leave policy;
- only 37.5 percent of medical schools had formal maternity leaves;
- only 18 percent of medical schools provided child care, and half of all teaching hospitals had no child-care facilities;
- only 14 percent of residency programs offered part-time or shared residency positions.

The report concluded that a new definition of a "successful career" was required, so that women—the report ignored men—who take time for family responsibilities are not viewed as less committed physicians or penalized in their advancement.[24]

If young women doctors are willing to behave exactly like traditional men, they do just fine. The wage gap in medicine has virtually disappeared among physicians under age forty-five—*provided* that they work the same hours, pick the same specialties, and work in the same practice arrangements.[25]

But of course, they don't. Women doctors work on average fifty-one hours a week versus sixty-two hours for the men—an obvious artifact of their greater family responsibilities. Women are also more apt to be in less lucrative specialties, like pediatrics and family medicine, and to be in staff positions in hospitals or health maintenance organizations, which offer more regular hours.[26]

Not only do these early decisions lower women's income, they effectively block the great majority of female doctors from rising to the top in later life or doing the research they once set out to do, including research on women's health. The best appointments in medical schools go to those who can put in sixty- to seventy-hour weeks in their thirties and forties, something most women with children can't or won't do. Of the 126 medical schools in the United States, only four had female deans in 1994. Fewer than 5 percent of department heads were women. And fewer than 10 percent of full professors were female—the same percentage as in 1980.[27]

Buried in these numbers are a lot of abandoned dreams.

Unions

Ironically, unions, the very organizations that are supposed to defend workers' interests, have just as few women leaders as other American institutions and professions. And for the same reason. A survey of 298 local unions in the United States concluded that "family responsibilities are a major barrier to women becoming local union officers."[28]

The typical top union official is a forty-six-year-old married white male with a high school education, according to this survey. Less than 10 percent of top local officers are women, who are *less likely to be married than their male counterparts*. This means that mothers are not at the bargaining table, not likely to handle grievances, and have little responsibility for enforcing contracts. Consequently, the arrangements mothers need, if they are to earn a reasonable income, much less maintain a career—paid maternity leaves, flexible hours, part-time work with prorated benefits, and help with child care—are unlikely to become priorities of organized labor. Or a reality.

WHEN MOTHERS' MARGINALIZATION in the workplace is acknowledged, it is usually shrugged off as something women "choose" or as part of life's inevitable compromises.[29] But we should pay attention to the overwhelming and systemic evidence that mothers can never achieve economic equality in the labor market as things now stand. Put another way, whoever cares for the kids will always get the short end under current arrangements. "We've gone down the path of 'equal' treatment and it's gotten us so far. But not far enough," says economist Jane Waldfogel.

Workplace marginalization has cumulative negative effects on a primary caregiver's income, her status in marriage, her children's security, and even the economy as a whole. It is time someone looked at these costs, and we will.

But it is also time to pay serious attention to the work mothers *are* doing, in lieu of what they aren't; to take account of all the hours of unpaid labor a mother does, and all the value she creates while raising children and making a home. It is curious, to say the least, that when a woman accepts what everyone agrees is the most important job in the world, her economic contribution literally disappears off the charts. Her unpaid work is the dark matter in the universe of labor.

How did this come to be? How did one of the most productive activities on earth—arguably the *most* fruitful activity—come to be denied the status of "real work"? Here's the story.

CHAPTER 3

How Mothers' Work Was "Disappeared": *The Invention of the Unproductive Housewife*

> I go to professional gatherings as my husband's wife and when I say I'm at home with two children, people never talk to me about anything serious. . . . They say, "Oh, it's so important what you're doing." I have actually said in reply, "You don't really believe that. Everything in this culture tells me that what I was doing before was more important. The rest of it is vacuous, empty words."
>
> —A former vice president of a Washington-based trade association

Any woman who has devoted herself to raising children has experienced the hollow praise that only thinly conceals smug dismissal. In a culture that measures worth and achievement almost solely in terms of money, the intensive work of rearing responsible adults counts for little. One of the most intriguing questions in economic history is how this came to be; how mothers came to be excluded from the ranks of productive citizens. How did the demanding job of rearing a modern child come to be trivialized as baby-sitting? When did caring for children become a "labor of love," smothered under a blanket of sentimentality that hides its economic importance?

In recent years a new generation of female scholars—historians, law professors, economists, and sociologists—have begun to piece this story together. Their research, to put it bluntly, explains how mothers were robbed; how the hardest-working people on earth came to be defined as "dependents" who "don't work" and who have to be "supported" by a spouse who is officially the only "working" member of the household.

The early feminists, most of whom were wives and mothers, did not accept the denial of a mother's worth without a fight. Before the Civil War, feminists claimed that a married woman's unpaid labors entitled her to nothing less than an equal share of family wealth and income. But this demand proved far too radical, and the women's movement increasingly concentrated on the more attainable goal of female suffrage. Not until the 1970s were the assets accumulated in a marriage deemed to belong to both spouses. And as for so-called "family" income, to this day it remains the exclusive property of the spouse who earns it.

IN THE PRECAPITALIST era a "good wife" was considered a major *economic* asset. "Four things necessary in a house are a chimney, a cat, a hen, and a good wife," declared John Florio in the early seventeenth century, equating a spouse with other useful animals and appliances. A wife's skills at "housewifery" were considered as important to a family's standard of living as a husband's skills of yeomanry. The sturdy "goodwife"—that bustling candle maker, pie baker, and chicken plucker now celebrated in reconstructed colonial villages all over New England—supported her husband with her labor, and no man of substance could be without one.

Yet the fruits of female labor legally belonged to men. Until the middle of the nineteenth century, married women had no right to property of their own. The common law gave a woman's husband an absolute right to her "services," including any outside income she might earn. Unless her family was wealthy enough to provide property for her in trust, a woman entered marriage as a dependent, and a dependent she remained. Wives had no legal say in family financial decisions, and widows were treated as an "encumbrance" on a man's estate, which was passed on to his heirs. As the first feminists often pointed out, it was hard to distinguish this servile state from that of a slave.

When most families lived at a bare subsistence level, these glaring inequities were somewhat irrelevant. Husband and wife shared bed and board with no great economic disparities between the two. But in the nineteenth century, as the cash economy spread, men gradually began to work for wages or were able to accumulate money through commercial transactions, while women for the most part remained in the barter economy of the family. "Work" or "labor" became synonymous with cash income and with "men's" work. The stage was set for the assumption—still with us—that men "supported" their wives at home, as if unpaid work were not productive and not part of the "real" economy.[1]

One of the first appearances of the monetary definition of "productive" is in Alexander Hamilton's 1791 *Report on Manufactures,* an argument for national investment in manufacturing industries. Only goods that could be sold to create revenue were included in Hamilton's definition of "the total produce" of society. He attributed a "superiority of . . . productiveness" to labor whose product was geared for exchange outside the household. Thus he argued that women and children "are rendered more useful" by going to work in manufacturing establishments and earning cash than by remaining at home.[2] In *A Vindication of the Rights of Woman,* written at about the same time, Mary Wollstonecraft pointed out that under the new political and economic system that was emerging, "Either women can become [like] men, and so full citizens; or they continue at women's work, which is of no value for citizenship."[3]

As women's family labor lost status as "work," it was increasingly sentimentalized as a "labor of love." Feminist economist Nancy Folbre put it neatly: "The moral elevation of the home was accompanied by the economic devaluation of the work performed there."[4] In the late eighteenth and early nineteenth centuries the frugal, hardworking colonial wife was slowly replaced in popular mythology by the "angel of the hearth," a moral exemplar who tended to the spiritual, emotional, and physical needs of her brood, leaving the material aspects of life to her husband.

For men was reserved the world of money, commerce, and industry. For middle- and upper-middle-class white women, the ideal was to become the embodiment "of pure disinterested love, such as is seldom found in the busy walks of a selfish and calculating world," as one New Hampshire gentleman wrote in 1827.[5] Under this doctrine of "separate spheres," the "true woman" was the upholder of private morality and the caring sentiments. She would never stoop to ask for any monetary compensation for her labors. She was put on a high pedestal but asked to carry a very heavy load.*

It has been suggested that this ideology served to keep educated, relatively privileged women from taking the republican ideals of liberty and equality to heart. After the French and the American Revolutions, many educated women had presumed to dream that they too might be liberated from arbitrary authority. Wollstonecraft's *A Vindication of the Rights of Woman* expressed these hopes in impassioned polemic, devoured by female readers on both sides of the Atlantic. Wollstonecraft posed the perfectly logical question: How could societies founded on the principles of universal human rights deny those rights to women?

The ingenuous solution to this challenge to patriarchal dominance was to cede to women the exalted task of nurturing the new free men. Rather than seeking their own personal gratification, women were urged to find fulfillment in the all-important task of creating the citizens of the new republic.

The emerging ideology of "separate spheres" thus served a dual purpose: it discouraged women from demanding greater participation in public and economic life, and it gave mothers license—and the moral authority—to rear their children as they saw fit. It ratified the withdrawal of fathers from the home and the expansion of mothers' responsibilities within it. Women's new assignment brought with it a significant strengthening of their domestic position. Prior to this time, the family had been a "patriarchal sovereignty," in the words of one satisfied early-eighteenth-century paterfamilias. Fathers had sole legal custody and could apprentice or marry off their children without a mother's consent. A woman's duty to her offspring took a distant second to her obligations to her husband, the rooster who ruled in every roost. All of this gradually changed, until by the mid–nineteenth century American women in many states had won the right to share joint custody of their children. Writer Lydia Sigourney could assure her female readers that their dominion

*This ideology is still alive and well in the twenty-first century. Mothers at home are "the moral backbone of the country," wrote social conservative David Gelernter in a 1998 fund-raising letter for the Family Research Council, a lobbying group for the traditional father-headed family.

over their young ones, which had hitherto known "bounds and obstructions," was now "entire and perfect."[6]

On the other hand, the new emphasis on conscientious motherhood did succeed in keeping American women out of the mainstream, as numerous foreign travelers observed. A visitor to the United States during the 1830s, Francis Grund, attributed the general ill health of married women "to the great assiduity with which American ladies discharge their duties as mothers. No sooner are they married than they begin to lead a life of comparative seclusion; and once mothers, they are actually buried to the world."[7]

Alexis de Tocqueville was also struck by the "extreme dependence" of American women and the degree to which they were "confined within the narrow circle of domestic life." "American women never manage the outward concerns of the family or conduct a business or take a part in political life. . . . Nor have the Americans ever supposed that one consequence of democratic principles is the subversion of marital power," he wrote. "They hold . . . that the natural head of the conjugal association is man." American women, he concluded, paid for their lofty moral and intellectual stature with "social inferiority" and arduous toil.[8]

But the increasing weight given to the job of caring for children was far more than just a strategy to distract women from participating in public life. It was also necessary to the development of a vibrant capitalist economy. By the late eighteenth century in France, England, and the United States, the countries with the most dynamic economies of the day, the rising bourgeoisie understood that their children would have to become educated, motivated little achievers if they were going to improve or even maintain their station in life.[9]

This required a new approach to child-rearing. In a static, agrarian economy people cannot, and need not, make huge investments of time or emotion in their children. Early in life, with little or no schooling, children are able to become valuable economic assets, who work in the fields and the kitchen, tend the babies, care for the animals, and help in the family enterprise. An Indian baby in Guatemala can be safely tucked in a hammock all day with no harm done to his future as a subsistence farmer. A peasant child in Europe could be harshly treated and kept in line with no risk to his future as an underling. Even an aristocratic child could be treated with indifference and still safely count on inheriting his class privileges.

But these practices provide poor preparation for success in a fluid and meritocratic society. It takes years of hard, patient work to mold infants into individuals who have the imagination to find a place for themselves in a competitive, mobile world, the self-confidence to strive, and the self-discipline to plan for an uncertain future. "Breaking the will" or even benign neglect are not the best ways to ensure that a child will have what it takes to be a real go-getter.[10]

Upper- and middle-class fathers, increasingly drawn away from the home by commerce and industry, were not in a position to undertake this new parental challenge. Thus mothers were exhorted to step into the father's traditional place as the family's principal teacher, disciplinarian, and moral arbiter. As Benjamin Rush of Philadelphia, one of the signers of the Declaration of Independence, put it: since men would not have the time to govern their offspring as they had in the past, mothers would have to assume the task. If they were to meet the challenge, Rush predicted, they would need education and training, because raising children was becoming an increasingly complex job.

The mounting demands of child-rearing thus provided the rationale for the education of women. The education of girls for the crucial assignment of producing workers with "a capitalistic spirit" as well as "Christian virtue" became a distinctive feature of early-nineteenth-century America. Numerous special schools for girls were established, with the express purpose of preparing women for enlightened motherhood. Between 1790 and 1850, female literacy in the United States rose at an unprecedented rate, unmatched anywhere in the world. By the middle of the nineteenth century, the literacy rate for white American women was roughly equal to that for white men. By 1860, only 5 percent of white women in New England and 20 percent of white women in the South could not read.[11]

Literate mothers devoured magazines offering "how-to" advice on child health and discipline and reminding them that they were shaping "the character of the whole of society." Again and again, the message of the educational reformers of the Enlightenment was repeated: Successful child-rearing requires a kinder, gentler, more patient hand, and an enormous amount of care and vigilance. Cold, rigid authoritarianism could not do the job of instilling in children the desirable qualities of self-reliance, honesty, industry, and thrift.[12] Thus women were recruited to the crucial task of producing the kind of human capital that the modern industrial economy needed.[13]

This story has been left out of economic history. As the story of the family is conventionally told, virtually all serious economic activity had left the household by the mid–nineteenth century, as manufacturing migrated from farms into factories. The household evolved from a workplace, where most necessities were produced, into a place of leisure, consumption, and emotional replenishment; a "haven in a heartless world." Ostensibly, industrialization put families, and the women in them, "out of business."

In fact, the family remained an intrinsic part of the economy. There was simply a transformation of the type of goods and services produced in the home. The new domestic product was the intensively raised child. According to anthropologist Wanda Minge-Klevana: "During the transition from preindustrial society to industrial society, the family underwent a qualitative change as a labor unit—from one that produced food to one whose primary function was to socialize and educate laborers for an industrial labor market."[14] By producing new worker-citizens, families became, in the words of Shirley Burggraf, "the primary engine of economic growth."[15]

Child-rearing, of course, was still only a small part of the work of the nineteenth-century household. As the economy became more commercial, women by default had to perform what had been men's and even children's domestic work—for children too were leaving the home, to go to school.* The family's unpaid labor force was shrinking down to the adult women, who had to handle chores with animals, gardens, and repairs on top of the traditional work of cooking, cleaning, and child care.[16] The angel of the hearth was increasingly on her own, up to her elbows in coal dust and soapsuds.

---

*Nineteenth-century governments as well as families contributed to the production of human capital by banning child labor and establishing public primary schools that all children were required to attend. But the principal producers of and "investors" in the new worker-citizens were their own families.

Commentaries of the period refer to wives' overwork and lack of leisure in language reminiscent of contemporary complaints about the "second shift." In a letter to the editor of a New England newspaper in 1846, "Cleo Dora" suggested that husbands needed to be reminded of the meaning of the word "helpmeet." It meant to *help,* she wrote, not to perform *all* of the family labor, and certainly not to be kept hard at work long after her husband had come home to relax. "I pray you . . . now and then exhort husbands to do their parts," she concluded.[17] The sheer demands of everyday household management are reflected in the advice manuals for middle-class women of the antebellum period. In her enormously popular 1841 *Treatise on Domestic Economy,* for example, Catherine Beecher argued that the economy of housework required the "wisdom, firmness, tact, discrimination, prudence, and versatility" of a politician and the "system and order" of a business. In Beecher's opinion, domestic accounting procedures actually surpassed the often "desultory" practices of business.[18]

Jeanne Boydston, the leading historian of the nineteenth-century domestic economy, argues that both husbands and employers enjoyed a free ride on wives' unpaid labor. Boydston has calculated that the cash value of the work done by working-class and middle-class wives was far greater than the cost of their maintenance. Their activities enabled employers to pay extremely low wages, a factor that "was critical to the development of industrialization in the antebellum Northeast." Wives were a bargain, which explains why young men, if they wanted to get ahead, were advised to marry.[19]

Thus, behind the myth of the "true woman," whose calling was emotional and moral, lurked the reality of the overworked mother, whose output was economically productive. And behind the myth of the male breadwinner and the self-made man lurked the free labor provided by a wife.[20]

For decades neither sex challenged the gendered split between "work" and "home." Women imagined that their moral and domestic authority compensated for their lack of economic and political power. And men imagined women as givers of love and arbiters of virtue too pure for the marketplace—conveniently overlooking the fact that as long as women had no right to property or access to cash income, their domestic "gifts" were given in return for food, shelter, and protection.[21]

The reigning family myth—that men "supported" women as well as children—prevented the great majority of women from seeing themselves as valuable economic players and equal marriage partners. They couldn't feel cheated of the fruits of their labor if they didn't believe that what they were doing *was* labor. Even as accomplished and astute a woman as Harriet Beecher Stowe couldn't see through the ideological veil. In 1850 she wrote to her sister-in-law, relating her recent activities: the household had moved to Maine the spring before; she had made two sofas, a chair, diverse bedspreads, pillowcases, pillows, bolsters, and mattresses; painted rooms; revarnished furniture; given birth to her eighth child; run a huge household; and somehow also managed to make her way through the novels of Sir Walter Scott—all within a year.

"And yet," she confided, "I am constantly pursued and haunted by the idea that I don't do anything."[22]

The Joint Property Claim

These were the circumstances in which the early women's rights movement emerged in the eastern United States in the 1840s. And not surprisingly, most of its leaders were educated middle-class married mothers who had begun to question the idea that their work was "unproductive" and hence unworthy of material recognition.

Elizabeth Cady Stanton, the best-known advocate of women's rights in the nineteenth century, had seven children. Her feminism developed in her early thirties, after she moved with her husband and several young children to a new town, Seneca Falls, New York, where she knew no one. Her husband traveled most of the time, leaving her feeling isolated and overworked.[23]

Although Stanton had household help, as her prominence grew she was continually struggling to find time for her lectures and political activities. In a note to Susan B. Anthony in 1853, she asks her friend to find a lawyer who can look up some points of law for her. "You see," she explains, "while I am about the house, surrounded by my children, washing dishes, baking, sewing, etc., I can think up many points, but I cannot search books. . . . I seldom have one hour undisturbed in which to sit down and write. Men who can, when they wish to write a document, shut themselves up for days with their thoughts and their books, know little of what difficulties a woman must surmount to get off a tolerable production."[24]

In 1857, while Stanton was nursing her sixth child, the unmarried Anthony complained that "those of you who have talent to do honor to poor—oh! how poor—womanhood have all given yourselves over to baby-making; and left poor brainless me to do battle alone."[25]

But Susan B. Anthony was the exception. Most early feminists did it all.

Antoinette Brown Blackwell, the first female minister in the United States, had seven children, as did Martha Coffin Wright, an adviser to Anthony and Stanton who later became an officer of the National Woman Suffrage Association. Lucy Stone, a teacher who kept her own name after marrying Antoinette Blackwell's brother-in-law, raised one child, made her own yeast, bread, and soap, cured meat, kept chickens and cows, and grew vegetables. Lydia Maria Child supported herself and her husband by writing, and noted in her diary that in one year she prepared 722 meals and made thirty-six pieces of clothing and seventeen items of household furnishing. Ida B. Wells, who as a courageous young journalist documented southern lynchings, later raised six children while organizing African-American women in Chicago to demand the vote.

These feminist foremothers knew firsthand about a wife's contributions to the household economy. They could speak from experience to women like the anonymous author of "The Revolt of Mother," a short story based on the writer's memories of farm life in pre–Civil War Massachusetts. The storyteller described a farm wife, Mrs. Penn, who toiled for years in silent resignation—raising the children, preparing the food, washing and ironing the clothes, cleaning the house—while all of the family's earnings were poured into the husband's farm business. When Mr. Penn decided yet again to make a big expenditure on what interested *him* (a new barn) instead of what *she* wanted (a spruced-up house), an avalanche of accumulated anger and resentment came pouring down on him: "You see this room, here, father, you look at it well. You see there ain't no carpet on the floor an' you see the paper is all dirty, an' droppin' off the walls. . . . You see this room, father, it's all the one I've had to work in an' eat in and sit in sence we was married."

This fictitious wife found a solution: she moved the family into the new barn.[26]

The early leadership of the woman's rights movement had close ties to the antislavery movement and saw obvious parallels between the institution of slavery and the institution of marriage. But rather than attack marriage itself, as some nineteenth-century utopian socialists and communitarians had done, the antebellum feminists came up with a strategy that took the doctrine of separate spheres literally. If women's work in the home is so exalted, they asked, why isn't it valued equally with men's work? By virtue of their labor, they argued, wives earned joint rights to all the property accumulated during a marriage.

This joint property claim was on the agenda of the First National Woman's Rights Convention, held in 1850 at Worcester, Massachusetts. The convention's resolutions opened with a demand for women's suffrage and closed with a vow to remember the million and a half women trapped in slavery in the South. In between, the delegates resolved to revise the marital property laws "so that all rights may be equal between (married parties);—that the wife may have, during life, an equal control over the property gained by their mutual toil and sacrifices, be heir to her husband precisely to the extent that he is heir to her, and entitled, at her death, to dispose by will of the same share of the joint property as he is."[27]

In the following year's convention at Worcester, the joint property claim was spelled out in greater detail. It was resolved: "That since the economy of the household is generally as much the source of family wealth as the labor and enterprise of man, therefore the wife should, during life, have the same control over the joint earnings as her husband."[28]

In 1854, Stanton, then age thirty-eight, gave her first major public address, before the New York state senate. In a black silk dress with a white lace collar secured with a diamond pin, she made a bold bid for full legal citizenship for women, and for female equality in marriage. She demanded for married women the right to earn money and inherit property, a share of marital property, shared custody of children, and the right to divorce.

This was an uncompromisingly radical agenda. The attempt to win legal and economic equality for women *in the family* was far more sweeping than the demand for the vote, and far more threatening to men's economic dominance. Indeed, more than a century later, the vote has long been won, but mothers are still waiting for full economic equality in the family.

Stanton's demands, and subsequent campaigning, did achieve results. The New York state legislature had in 1848 passed the Married Women's Property Act, allowing married women to hold property in their own names, and insulating their separate estates from a husband's debts. In 1857 and again in 1860, the act was amended to give married women, for the first time, the right to collect their own earnings, to share joint custody of their children, and to inherit equally with their children when widowed. This was the most liberal marital property reform that had ever been adopted in the United States.

In the 1860s and 1870s, similar laws were enacted in other states, granting wives rights to the land and property they brought into a marriage and the right to their own earnings. But these Married Women's Property Acts, or "earnings statutes," passed by all-male legislatures, did not affect the economic status of the great majority of women, who had little if any property or outside earnings of their own.

In 1860, when New York state finally granted a wife the right to her own earnings, only 15 percent of all free women in the United States had any earnings from paid labor, and most of these women were single or widowed. As late as 1890, the national census counted only 3.3 percent of all white married women as working for wages (compared with roughly 40 percent of all African-American women).[29]

Many feminists immediately recognized that the 1860 New York statute would still leave husbands in full control of all property created during a marriage. It was a help to poor women who had to work for a living, one feminist wrote. "But what shall the great mass of women, the wives of the middling classes . . . do? What right have they in the property obtained after marriage?" The answer was poignantly conveyed in this 1876 letter from an anonymous farm woman to the editor of a suffrage magazine:

> Married in pioneer times a poor man, and by our joint efforts have made us a home worth several thousand dollars; have

> borne nine children, and took the whole care of them. Five are men grown, four of them voters. The first twenty years I did all my house-work, sewing, washing and mending, except a few weeks at the advent of the babies. For the last sixteen years have had help part of the time; but have had from two to four grandchildren to care for the last three years, one of them a baby. And now I want to go to the Centennial and cannot command a sixpence for all my labor. Husband owns and controls everything and says we have nothing to spend for such foolishness. Have no more power than a child. Now if my labor has been of any value in dollars and cents I want those dollars and cents to do as I please with. I feel like advising every woman not to do another day's labor unless she can be the owner of the value of it.
>
> All the property that I possess in my own right is this pen and holder; a present from my brother in California. PEN HOLDER

The nation's courts were deaf to such cries. Wives' labor within the home was presumed to be rendered *voluntarily* on behalf of the family, and not in expectation of financial reward. The Iowa Supreme Court, for example, found that the state's earnings statute, passed in 1873, "did not intend . . . to release and discharge the wife from her common law and scriptural obligation and duty to be a 'help-meet' to her husband. If such a construction were to be placed upon the statute, then the wife would have a right of action against the husband for any domestic service. . . . For her assistance in the care, nurture, and training of his children, she could bring an action for compensation. She would be under no obligation to superintend or look after any of the affairs of the household unless her husband paid her wages for so doing. Certainly, such consequences were not intended by the legislature."[30]

Certainly not!

AFTER THE CIVIL WAR, in the face of this kind of unyielding opposition, the women's rights movement in the United States gradually turned away from the issue of economic equality between husbands and wives. The leadership increasingly focused on legal equality, including the right to hold office, to be tried by peers, to equal treatment under the criminal code, and, most notably, the right to vote. By the 1880s the claim that wives had a right to joint marital property had been dropped from the suffragists' legislative agenda.

Instead of demanding that equal *value* be placed on women's work of child care and homemaking, many women's rights advocates began to challenge the traditional gender division of labor itself. American feminists began to describe work within the family as labor that women had to *escape,* if they were ever to achieve equality and freedom. They began to imagine two-career marriages and schemes for cooperative housekeeping that would free women to earn an income and relieve them from the drudgery of housework. In other words, they began to sound like contemporary feminists in their assumption that women could only avoid subservience and economic dependency by becoming wage earners.

This shift reflected the dramatic changes in the U.S. economy taking place after the Civil War. By 1870, for the first time in American history, more men were employed, earning wages, than were producing their own livelihood themselves. In the new money economy, wives increasingly depended on their husbands for income to run the household. The principal economic unit was no longer considered the household, but the individual, whose wages were legally his alone.

Fifty years earlier, when the federal census first began to measure economic activity it had tallied the number of families, not individuals, engaged in agriculture, commerce, and manufacturing. It was assumed that all members of a household contributed to the family enterprise, whether it was a farm, a handicraft, or a business. As working for wages became more common, however, the federal census began to inquire into the occupations of *individuals*. The 1850 census wanted to know the "profession, occupation, or trade" of each male person over fifteen years of age. In 1860 this question was extended to women, the great majority of whom described their occupation as "housekeeper."[31]

In 1870 Francis Walker, a prestigious economist who later served as president of the Massachusetts Institute of Technology, took command of the U.S. census. A Civil War veteran who liked to be addressed as

"General," Walker did not believe that women's household work was of particular economic value. "We may assume that speaking broadly, [a wife] does not produce as much as she consumes," he confidently wrote.[32] Under Walker's aegis, the census explicitly stipulated that those who described themselves as "housekeepers" had to be people receiving wages for the service. "Women keeping house for their own families, or for themselves, without any other gainful employment, will be entered as 'keeping house,'" he decreed. Thus the work of family maintenance—all of the gardening and canning and cooking and cleaning, the animal raising, the sewing and mending, the care of the sick and the elderly—not to mention the task of rearing the next generation of productive workers, was stricken from the list of productive employments.

Precise on this point, Walker was surprisingly cavalier about the systemic undercounting of the cash earnings that women did have. His census takers, by his own admission, overlooked most women's income, earned by taking in boarders and lodgers, for example, or contracting industrial piecework from manufacturing firms. As a result, virtually *all* of women's toil from dawn to dusk was dismissed as irrelevant to the real productive activity of the bustling, growing nation.

This massive slight did not go unnoticed. Speaking at a woman's congress in 1874, Mary Livermore argued that "women had a monetary value as wives and mothers, and they ought to insist upon a recognition of that value. Eight millions of American women were wives and housekeepers, but according to the census they were 'doing nothing.'" In 1878 a protest was issued by the Association for the Advancement of Women, a group of the most highly educated women of the time, including Maria Mitchell, a Harvard astronomer, Julia Ward Howe, a prominent feminist activist, and Melusina Fay Pierce, an advocate for the collectivization of housework.

In a letter to Congress these notables complained that "more than twelve millions of American women [were] overlooked as laborers or producers or left out . . . and not even incidentally named as in any wise affecting the causes of increase or decrease of population or wealth." They suggested that a more accurate accounting could be obtained if the Census Bureau employed "intelligent women to collect vital statistics concerning women and children."[33]

The suggestion was ignored. By 1900, wives and daughters without paying jobs were officially classified as "dependents." As the new century began, the married woman had become "just a housewife." In 1900, in an essay published in *Cosmopolitan* magazine, one Flora Thompson penned these words: "Women have forced economic recognition of their labor in men's spheres, but especial woman's work remains the economic cipher. Domestic labor is accorded no rational recognition in the mind of political economy or in the heart of labor reform."[34]

One hundred years later, this is still true.

Interestingly, the state of Massachusetts, the home of so many educated and distinguished women, held out against the trend longer than most. In the Massachusetts census of 1875, unpaid housewives were included in an occupational category along with housekeepers, servants, nurses, and washerwomen. Married women were not automatically assumed to be either productive or unproductive. Some were described as "having nothing to do but superintend the households," and others, in the census's own words, were "simply ornamental." (By some unknown method of accounting, these were estimated to be fewer than 2 percent of all wives.) Gradually, however, the Massachusetts census bowed to the inevitable. By 1905, housework was listed in the "not gainful" class, along with students, retirees, those unemployed for twelve months, and dependents.[35]

The British census evolved in a similar fashion. Before 1851, British census takers, like those in the United States, had inquired after the occupations of families rather than individuals. When individual occupations were first listed, "wives, mothers and mistresses" were placed in a category by themselves, distinct from the class of "dependents," which included children, the sick and infirm, gypsies and vagrants, and certain "ladies and gentlemen of independent means."[36]

The censuses of Britain and of England and Wales from 1851 to 1871 were under the direction of the renowned medical statistician William Farr, who viewed a nation's population as its "living capital." In one section of his 1851 report, Farr defined the head of the family as "the husband-and-wife." Farr also had a strong appreciation of the value of the work of child-rearing. "The most important production of a country is its population," he wrote in 1851. In 1861 he elaborated: "These women [wives and widows] are sometimes returned as of no occupation. But the occupation of wife and mother and housewife is the most important in the country, as will be immediately apparent if it be assumed for a moment to be suppressed."[37]

By 1871, however, the head of household had been redefined as "the householder, master, husband, or father." In 1881, all women engaged in unpaid domestic duties were explicitly placed in the "Unoccupied Class." In 1891, a year in which as many women were engaged as wives and mothers as men were engaged in all the other occupations, the British census dropped the category of wives and mothers altogether. The bureaucrats apparently felt a little guilty about erasing mothers from the rolls of the fruitful: "The most important, however, of all female occupations . . . is altogether omitted from the reckoning, namely the rearing of children and the management of domestic life."

The great English neoclassical economist Alfred Marshall had no qualms about this bold stroke. Testifying before a parliamentary committee in 1898, Marshall held up a recent German census as an example of superior methodology. It described married women as "dependents."

In Australia as well the work of women was "disappeared." By 1890 the population had been divided into two categories: breadwinners and dependents. Women doing domestic work were "dependents," along with children and "all persons depending upon private charity, or whose support is a burthen on the public revenue."[38]

Thus all over the Anglo-Saxon world by the beginning of the twentieth century, the notion that women at home were "dependents" had acquired the status of a scientific fact. The idea that money income was the only measure of human productivity had triumphed. With official blessing, husbands could consider wives not as economic assets but as liabilities.

The theft was breathtaking.

So complete was this victory that it was accepted by some of the most prominent turn-of-the-century feminists. In 1909 two women's organizations sponsored a debate between Charlotte Perkins Gilman, the celebrated author, and Anna Howard Shaw, the president of the National American Woman Suffrage Association. The topic was the economic value of a wife's household labor.

Gilman took the position that the vast majority of American women, the "immense middle class," were unproductive parasites. Even though a wife might work ten to fourteen hours a day for the family, raising the children, maintaining the home, and extending the purchasing power of her husband's wages by her thrift, Gilman maintained that "her labor is not productive industry." An "unpaid wife," Gilman declared, was "a domestic servant in the extremely wasteful and expensive class of one servant to one man."

Gilman's position was elaborated in her widely acclaimed book, *Women and Economics* (which was said to be "the Bible of the student body at Vassar"). In it she ridiculed the notion that "the wife [is] an equal factor with the husband in producing wealth" and insisted that women are supported by their husbands. She repudiated the struggles of earlier feminists by denying that work for the family could have any claim to equal status or reward. "There is no equality in class between those who do their share in the world's work in the largest, newest, highest ways and those who do theirs in the smallest, oldest, lowest ways," she wrote of the traditional division of labor in marriage. For Gilman, only the collectivization of domestic labor and the "break up [of] that relic of the patriarchal age—the family as an economic unit" could emancipate women. She wanted to abolish the private home and have people live in apartment houses, with professionally staffed facilities for meals, cleaning, laundry, and child care.

It is not hard to detect in this program a profound distaste for family life. For Charlotte Gilman, maternity had none of the solace that might have mitigated its oppressions. She lumped the care of children with all of the other menial labor women were assigned, as if child care were equivalent to dishwashing, and as if women could flee their children as easily as they could run away from dirty laundry. She literally threw the baby out with the bathwater.

Gilman's thinking was strangely congruent with that of male-dominated legislatures and courts, which also denigrated the economic importance of women's "labor of love." She was in effect abandoning a position—that wives had an equal right to marital property—that had threatened the very foundations of male economic power.

In the historic 1909 debate, Anna Shaw challenged Gilman's assumption that mothers were analogous to servants. She made a fundamental distinction between the work of a mother and that of a domestic servant.

The former, she explained, creates a *home* for her children; the other merely maintains it. Shaw claimed that wives "put something economically valuable into [the husband's income] which has increased, if not its incoming power, at least its outgoing power." For that, she concluded, wives and mothers should be compensated with earnings proportionate to the position that their family held in society.[39]

A reporter covering the debate for the *New York Evening Call* reported that the female audience had no problem deciding which side of the argument they were on. At the close of the debate, when the audience was asked whether a wife was supported by her husband, "[a] few scattered ayes were heard, but when the judge asked for the 'noes' the answers were so vigorous and numerous that it was easily apparent that the vast majority of the audience had no doubts."

Shaw won the debate but lost the battle.

As that evening in New York illustrated, at the turn of the twentieth century, the women's movement contained two contradictory strands: one that denigrated women's role within the family, and one that demanded recognition and remuneration for it. The first argued that only one road could lead to female emancipation, and it pointed straight out of the house toward the world of paid work. The second sought equality for women within the family as well and challenged the idea that a wife and mother was inevitably an economic "dependent" of her husband.

For the rest of the twentieth century, the women's movement followed the first path, and it led to innumerable great victories. But in choosing that path, many women's advocates accepted the continued devaluation of motherhood, thereby guaranteeing that feminism would not resonate with millions of wives and mothers.

Married women in the United States were to remain legally and economically subservient to their husbands for several more generations. Until 1970, husbands still had sole power to manage all property acquired during the marriage. A wife had no clear legal remedies to prevent her husband's mismanagement of marital property, and no clear right even to know the extent or location of the communal assets. A married woman with no separate property of her own could not even obtain credit without her husband's consent.

In the 1970s, the joint property claim finally became the law of the land. Assets accumulated during a marriage, except for those that are inherited, are deemed to belong to both spouses. But to this day, in only three states—California, Louisiana, and New Mexico—are wives unequivocably entitled to half of marital assets. (In six other states there is a judicial presumption that marital assets are owned fifty-fifty.)[40] Moreover, in many courts of law it is still considered *unnatural* for a wife and mother to claim a material reward for her labors on behalf of the family. If a wife is promised benefit from her husband in exchange for the performance of household labor, and he reneges on his part of the bargain, no court will assist her in enforcing the agreement. The courts have declared that her labor was "presumed gratuitous" or "rendered freely," with no expectation of any quid pro quo.

As recently as 1993, for example, a California court refused to enforce an agreement made between a married couple after the husband suffered a stroke. Although he had been advised by his doctors to enter a nursing home, his wife had consented to nurse him at home in return for inheriting certain properties. She provided the care, but he died without keeping his promise. The judge declared that he would abide by "the long-standing rule that a spouse is not entitled to compensation for support." "Even if few things are left that cannot command a price, marital support remains one of them," this judge opined, in a ruling that brought the full weight of history down on the hoodwinked wife.[41]

Free riding in the family endures.

CHAPTER 4

The Truly Invisible Hand

> How did we ever come to believe that it was more important for somebody to have a meaningless job than to raise their children well? This doesn't make sense even in simple accounting terms.
>
> —Robert Theobald, in *Reworking Success*

The invention of the "unproductive housewife" still has tremendously negative consequences for women, and for our understanding of the true origins of our prosperity. If the creation of human capital that takes place in the home is not accorded any monetary value, then it is unlikely that it will be supported, or encouraged, or rewarded as it should be. And for that, everyone, not just caregivers and children, is the loser.

The assumption that the unpaid labor of child-rearing has nothing to do with the real economy was cast in stone as early as the 1920s. By that time the official decision had been made to include in measures of the United States' output only transactions in which money changed hands. When the first prototype of what later became the Gross National Product was developed in the early 1930s, its calculations were limited to the total monetary value of goods and services that were sold. Services provided under any other terms did not, by definition, add to the national wealth and were therefore excluded from the GNP. Thus almost all of the activities of married women were omitted from the scorecard of capitalism.

Simon Kuznets, the statistician who developed the GNP (and won a Nobel prize for his efforts), clearly saw the limitations of his handiwork. In his very first report to Congress in 1934, Kuznets warned that "the welfare of a nation" can "scarcely be inferred" from the measurement system that was emerging.[1] The system could only measure *tangible* things, like tons of steel or bushels of grain, the number of fish caught or trees cut. *Intangibles,* such as improvements in a surgical technique, the value of clean water, or the care provided by a family member, could not be quantified. Social science had not progressed enough to be able to measure some of the most important things in life.

But the concept of the GNP was seductively simple, and by 1950 all of the world had adopted the same guidelines, later enshrined in the United Nations System of National Accounts. Sir Richard Stone, the man who was instrumental in developing the international system, was also subsequently awarded a Nobel prize, the only Nobel, ironically, that has never gone to a woman. The GNP (officially renamed the Gross Domestic Product in 1991) became the world's economic measuring stick. Today countries are competitively ranked according to their growth in GDP; that is, by their volume of *monetary* transactions.

Thus the great part of women's work does not figure. Nothing counts unless it is bought and sold. This produces absurd perversities: a nurse feeding formula to a baby counts as a productive activity, but a mother's breast-feeding doesn't; care for an aging relative in a nursing home counts, while at-home care by an unpaid family member doesn't; paying bills and taxes and planning family investments counts when done by an accountant, but not when done by a spouse; charitable contributions of money are tax-deductible, but volunteer donations of time are not;[2] teaching twenty children in a classroom counts, while home schooling one's own children doesn't.

I once heard Marilyn Waring, New Zealand activist and the world's foremost advocate of putting unpaid work in the GDP, give a speech in which she asked the audience what kind of system would count a soldier sitting eight hours a day in a missile silo as usefully employed, but consider a mother taking care of two preschoolers "unoccupied." The answer was obvious: a system that devalues women.

WOMEN HAVE ALWAYS had a hard time being "counted." The verb "to count" has several meanings: "to matter," "to make a difference," "to enumerate." Women have long been regarded as deficient in all of these ways, including the idea that they are not very good at math. But in the days when men were still the undisputed heads of the household, there was great respect for the activity that takes place in the home—and a recognition that it did, in fact, generate wealth. The very word "economics" derives from the Greek root *oikonomia,* the management of the household. Aristotle had the highest regard for oikonomia and made an important distinction between it and *chrematistics*. Oikonomia referred to the management of a household so as to increase its use value to all of its members over the long run. Chrematistics was the manipulation of property and wealth so as to maximize short-term exchange values.[3] The man who planted olive trees and built olive presses was practicing oikonomia; the man who leased all the olive groves in the winter and charged monopoly rates for renting them out at harvest time was practicing chrematistics. One activity enhanced future productivity to the ultimate benefit of the community, while the other sought short-term gain for the individual. The man who practiced oikonomia was highly respected, whereas the chrematistic speculator was held in low esteem.[4]

These attitudes have been turned upside down. Much of what passes for economic activity in capitalism, from the seventeenth-century speculation in tulip bulbs to twenty-first-century stock market churning, is chrematistics. And what was once condemned as the vice of shortsighted self-aggrandizement has been transformed into a virtue.

Chrematistics found its rationale in classical economic theory, which casts "economic man" as the chief actor in the drama of wealth creation. Economic man is both the one who plants the olive trees *and* the one who rents them out, but in this new theory the moral differences between the two become irrelevant. The individual's pursuit of personal gain theoretically adds to the sum total of riches. No matter how self-interested he may be, economic man's strivings to garner wealth for himself will be guided as if by an invisible hand to produce more resources than could ever be generated by the well-meaning plans of government or the community.

This is what is called the "magic of the marketplace." The beauty of the free market, according to Charles L. Schultze, economic adviser to President Lyndon B. Johnson, is that it reduces "the need for compassion, patriotism, brotherly love, and cultural solidarity as motivating forces behind social improvement. . . . Harnessing the 'base' motive of material self-interest to promote the common good is perhaps the most important social invention mankind has achieved."[5]

But this satisfying scenario, assuring us that we can all be as selfish as we like and still be doing good, is only half of the story—the second half. In the beginning, we are all helpless babies, and another economic actor, "conscientious mother," holds center stage. Without conscientious mother, there would be no economic man.

Here is another way the story of wealth creation might begin: Conscientious mothers, motivated by feelings of compassion and love, nurture, protect, and train children for adulthood. Fathers, other female caregivers, and relatives may play a part in this process, but mothers have the primary role. Their altruism, and willingness to do all that they can for their offspring, left unfettered, will be guided as if by an invisible hand to produce healthy children who will become the productive, enterprising economic men and women of the future.

Conscientious mothers, in other words, are the contemporary practitioners of oikonomia: the building and preservation of long-term communal value that used to be the essence of economics.

WHEN I FIRST met Virginia Williams in November of 1998, she was decked out in a colorful print dress, purple sweater, and a black stole covered with glittering musical notes. Her ample bosom was draped with necklaces, crosses, and a Star of David, tokens of her Catholic faith and a reminder of a great-grandfather who was Jewish. As I soon discovered, Virginia, a seventy-two-year-old African-American, was a one-woman rainbow coalition, if not a one-woman band. (Her business card identified her as "evangelist, singer, community activist.")

She and her late husband, Lewis, a fellow postal service worker, had raised eight children, including Anthony, who at that time was the Democratic candidate for mayor of Washington, D.C. Tony had been adopted at age three. As Virginia tells the story, a white postal office coworker kept bringing in pictures of his little foster son. "I looked at those pictures and I said, 'That's not a white child!' We later found out the boy's mother was white, an unmarried seventeen-year-old, and the father was black. Her family wouldn't let the girl keep the baby, and she had put him into foster care.

"I believe the foster father loved that child dearly. But I think his wife may have neglected him," she continued. "I worried about that, and about a black child growing up in a poor white neighborhood. I sent his picture around to all of my black friends who didn't have children, but not one would adopt him; they all had one reason or another. His head was a little bit disfigured from lying in the crib . . . and although he was three years old, he hadn't said a word yet. The foster parents had him tested, and the father told me they were going to send him to a home for retarded children.

"I knew that child wasn't retarded. I told my husband that I felt like God wanted us to have this child. Tony was exactly two years younger than my oldest, Lewis, and two years older than my second child, Virginia. I firmly believed that God had left that space for Tony.

"My husband thought I was crazy. We already had two young kids, and I was pregnant again. Our priest said I shouldn't do it; that it wouldn't be fair to our other children, who had very high IQs, to bring a retarded child into the house. But my husband said if you can get the money to adopt him, you can."

Virginia sang professional light opera whenever she could, and she raised money for the adoption by recording for the sound track of the film *Carmen Jones*. Only a couple of weeks after Tony came to live with the family, she had an inkling of what he had been through.

"I was changing the bed with the kids and the phone rang," she said. "I told them all to wait a minute in the hall, and I went to talk, and when I finally got back, about an hour later, the other two were long gone, but Tony was still standing there, alone, in the hall. That's when I knew that someone had abused that child. I got down on my knees and held him and cried. I never would let them test him after that."

The Williamses brought their children up as Catholics, and all attended parochial school. There never was any doubt that they would all go to college—"it was always *when* you finish college, never *if*," she said—and they all did. Lewis is a graduate of MIT and a professor of economics at the University of California at Redlands. Tony, the "retarded" child, attended both Harvard and Yale and went on to acquire a reputation as a brilliant manager in several city governments, including Washington, D.C., where as chief financial officer he steered the city away from fiscal collapse.

Virginia, who throughout our interview answered her endlessly ringing telephone with a chirpy "Tony Williams's mother," readily admitted that her influence alone did not turn a mistreated orphan into one of the country's most prominent African-Americans. "I had plenty of help," she confided. Her own mother pitched in, as did her sister Myrtle, who had no children.

She was also blessed with a job that allowed her to take time off whenever she had to, even to travel on short singing engagements. And above all, she had a husband who worked nights and stayed home during the day, allowing him to be deeply involved with his family.

"When I married Lewis, in 1947, he said he wanted three things in life: to have six kids, to be married fifty years, and to live to be eighty. He got all three," she told me. Her husband, who died in 1998, was a strong moral influence. She described an incident that occurred when Tony was in the eighth grade. The boy had come home bruised and scratched, and told his parents that he had been hit by a car that had suddenly come barreling out of an alley. They subsequently learned from one of Tony's teachers that he was the one who had come barreling out of the alley, right into the path of the car.

Her husband sat Tony down and said, "I want you to tell the truth about how the accident happened." When the boy admitted that he had caused the accident, his parents asked why he had lied. "Kids told me we could get a lot of insurance money if it was the driver's fault," he explained, "and I know we can always use more money."

Lewis said nothing, but as Virginia tells it, the next day the insurance agent arrived, papers were signed, and the insurer turned over a check of several thousand dollars to her husband. He dramatically tore it up. "When we start needing money that bad, I'll let you know," he told his son. "You'll never lie to get anything and think that I'll appreciate it."

"That showed character," Virginia declared emphatically.

On the day of our conversation, the voters in the nation's capital, tired of a mayor who took drugs and let every basic city service deteriorate, essentially decided an election on the issue of character. Two-thirds of the voters cast their ballot for Tony Williams for mayor of Washington, D.C. It was quite a victory for a onetime retarded child, who had been headed for institutionalization as a ward of the state before Virginia Williams saw his picture.

This is not the kind of story you will read in an economics textbook. And Virginia Williams is not the kind of person who is celebrated as a source of national wealth. But her story suggests that something fundamental has been left out of conventional economics. She reminds us that altruism is a driving force in human betterment, and that "irrational" mother love, backed by steadfast fathers and supportive kin, makes the material world go round.

Human Capital

The quality of early care is one of the most important determinants of human intellectual and emotional capabilities. This is as clear as a summer sky over Texas. A large and growing body of research in child development has shown that care and guidance of the young child lays the essential groundwork for the formation of human knowledge, skills, creativity, and entrepreneurship.

Economists are also beginning to realize that human capital—or human capabilities—is an even more important component of a nation's riches than natural capital (land, minerals, water) or physical capital (bricks and mortar, machines, roads). In 1995, when the World Bank started to include estimates of human capital in measuring countries' wealth, the bank's first rough estimates turned up the surprising finding that 59 percent of the wealth in developed countries is embodied in human and social capital (that is, educational levels, skills, a culture of entrepreneurship). The remainder consists of natural resources (25 percent) and manufactured capital (16 percent). Since most natural resources are a given—you can't create more oil or arable land—this means that *in the wealthiest countries, human capital accounts for three-quarters of the producible forms of wealth.*[6]

Being There

It is admittedly hard to measure an activity as subtle as sensitive child care. Mothers themselves often refer to the essence of child-rearing as simply "being there," putting one's time at the disposal of another and signaling that the other's needs come ahead of one's own. "Like the sentry or the night nurse," writes Kari Waerness, a Norwegian sociologist, the caregiver's role "is to be on call."*

The "good-enough" parenting described by English child psychologist D. W. Winnicott is so unobtrusive and self-effacing that husbands may not notice their wives providing it, and mothers may not notice it when day-care workers and nannies are doing the job. The more skillful the caregiver, the more invisible her efforts become. Ideally, the recipients themselves don't even notice that they are being cared for, other than to accept caring as part of the natural order of things. If a well-prepared meal is regularly on the table, it is enjoyed and taken for granted, noticed only in its absence. If a parent reads to a child every night before bedtime, it becomes an accepted ritual, only noticed if Mom or Dad is too busy. Like the work of a fine seamstress, the tiny stitches that build character and confidence are invisible to the eye.

I once witnessed one of those exquisitely subtle caring moments in the home of a family-care provider. She was serving lunch to a

*Kari Waerness, "The Invisible Welfare State: Women's Work at Home," *Acta Sociologica* (Oslo) 21 (1978—supplement): 194, 195, 201.

Human capital is more important today than it has ever been. Skilled human beings are the raw material of the new economy, the key ingredient in the recipe for prosperity in the postindustrial age. Harris Miller, president of the Information Technology Association of America, has said that "running out of IT workers today is like running out of iron ore in the Industrial Revolution." Or as Wall Street economist Roger group of five youngsters, ranging in age from eighteen months to five years. When a four-year-old tipped over a glass of milk, she calmly said, "Uh-oh, that's why we have plastic over the table." She fetched a cloth and wiped up most of the spill, then handed it to the boy to finish the job. Within a minute he was happy again, unaware of all that had gone into the incident: the preparation of a child-friendly, accident-proof environment; the everyone-makes-mistakes acceptance of a small child's natural clumsiness; the avoidance of blame; the efficient, can-do solving of a problem; the child's assumption that he was part of the solution, expected to clean up a mess he had made and presumed to have the competence to do it. In another household, the accident could easily have been a disaster for him.

How do you weigh this invisible touch and put a value on it? Its quiet unobtrusiveness is surely a major reason why unpaid care is accorded so little worth. Still, if being there can be counted in the case of the night nurse and the sentry, it can also be counted in the case of mothers and fathers. I was reminded of this when Baltimore Orioles shortstop Cal Ripken became a baseball immortal in 1995 just for being at the ballpark, day in and day out, attending more consecutive games (2,131) than any other player in history. This feat prompted a note from a friend. "To put Cal Ripken's recent achievement in perspective," she wrote, "we should all be congratulated for the number of days we have worked without a break raising our children. I've been at it 3,316 days with Michael. You've been at it even longer with James. I think we also deserve a standing ovation in Camden Yards. . . . That will be the day."

Kubarych once remarked, "Human capital is everything; look at Singapore"—a small and prosperous city-state whose only resource is its industrious population.[7]

If most of our national prosperity reflects the productivity of our human capital, then the people who provide primary care to children are the single most important source of our most valuable economic assets. Put another way, conscientious mothers are key players in the drama of economic growth, the stars who never receive top billing. This is the back story, still largely untold by the economics profession.

The profession remains stubbornly reluctant to think about the maternal contribution to the economy, prompting Shirley Burggraf to joke that most economists don't know where babies come from. The prevailing assumption is that the formation of productive skills *begins* with formal education, when a child goes off to school.[8] Somehow, in the abstract world of economics, curious babies spontaneously evolve into eager students, ready to read and write.

One of the most popular economics textbooks for college undergraduates, for example, acknowledges that "recent research on economic growth has emphasized that human capital is at least as important as physical in explaining international differences in standards of living." But then the author, a Harvard professor, defines human capital as "the knowledge and skills that workers acquire through education, from early childhood programs such as Head Start to on-the-job training for adults."[9] Thus, with one stroke, he deletes thirty years of infant research showing that before formal learning can begin, there have to be years of nurturing, confidence building, creative play, and curious exploration, all under the guidance of caring mentors. Utterly undigested is the harsh truth, in the words of one child psychologist, that "beginning education at age five is too late."[10]

Even when psychologists identify some of the mechanisms by which mothers produce human capital, their findings are ignored by economists. In the 1950s, Harvard psychologist David C. McClelland became interested in the cultural and psychological underpinnings of economic growth and decline. In his 1961 book, *The Achieving Society,* McClelland described how child-rearing practices can inculcate the traits that make individuals and societies entrepreneurial.

He cited a group of studies that pinpointed what some mothers did to produce in their sons a drive for achievement, the principal character trait that has fueled the rise of modern capitalism. (Daughters were not included in any of these 1950s studies.) In one particular study of twenty-nine white middle-class families in the American Midwest, researcher Marion Winterbottom identified the child-rearing practices that explained why some boys had a notable drive for achievement by the age of eight, while others showed little or none. The mothers of the "high" achievement-oriented sons expected them to have more independence and mastery of various tasks. The boys were expected to do more for themselves, to make their own friends, to try harder in competitions. The mothers of the other boys reported putting more restrictions on their sons at the same age; that is, on playmates, entertainment, and on such decisions as how to spend their allowance and what books to read.[11]

Subsequent investigations confirmed Winterbottom's conclusions on the essential role of primary caregivers in instilling ambition, but these provocative findings have never been integrated into the study of economic growth.

The one economic theory to treat parents as serious economic producers is the "New Home Economics" developed by Gary S. Becker of the University of Chicago. Recognizing that a steady supply of skilled workers cannot simply be taken for granted, Becker decided to look deeper into the all-important question of how human capital is formed. He concluded what every parent knows: that families do the bulk of the work. He estimated that direct investments by families account for more than three-quarters of all investment in human capital.[12] Parental investments in their offsprings' "skills, health, learning, motivation, 'credentials,' and many other characteristics," he wrote, are even more important than schools or specialized training.*[13]

But this pioneering effort to analyze the family as a serious economic enterprise became the butt of jokes within the profession. For years the New Home Economics was not taken any more seriously than the old home economics had been. (One earlier male writer on the family's economic contribution was condescendingly dismissed as a "potty chair" economist.) Becker was virtually ostracized by other economists, not because his portrayal of family dynamics was unrealistic but because he took activities within the family seriously at all. He finally earned the

---

*Shirley Burggraf has estimated that 95 percent of the costs of raising a child in the United States are borne by parents. This is why she calls the family the "greatest investment institution" in the country.[14]

respect of his peers and was awarded a Nobel prize in 1992. But many of his colleagues continue to brush off the issue of women's unpaid labor like a piece of lint on a fine dark suit.

This attitude is particularly puzzling in light of the sheer magnitude of unpaid work in the home. A spate of new studies reveals that nonmarket labor, including the care and education of young children, is far greater than anyone have ever dreamed. In Australia, for example, where data on nonmarket labor are highly sophisticated, one analyst calculated that at least half of all economic production in 1992 came from work within households.[15] In 1994 the Australian bureau of statistics calculated that the value of unpaid work was equivalent to 48 to 64 percent of the GDP. Other studies have found nonmarket production to be as large as 55 percent of GDP in Germany, 40 percent in Canada, and 46 percent in Finland. These estimates include all nonmarket work, such as auto repair and home remodeling, but much of it is associated with child care; that is, with the formation of human capital.

Making a home for a family is so time-consuming, in fact, that many men who have never done much of it simply cannot believe the numbers. Norwegian economists Charlotte Koren and Iulie Aslaksen report that when estimated GDP figures for household work in Norway were first published, "some men commented that the numbers must be overestimated, for everybody knows that a housewife isn't that busy."[16]

Similarly in the early 1980s, when Nechama Mesliansky was asked to calculate the yearly value of a typical housewife's work for inclusion in a legal text, she came up with a figure of more than $60,000. According to Mesliansky, executive director of the National Center on Women and Family Law, her male boss protested that they couldn't publish such a high figure.[17] They didn't.

Economists, most of whom are men, reinforce this denial of the bustling domestic activity that is often going on under their very noses. One current economics text, for instance, argues that "in the most advanced industrial economies, the nonmarket sector is relatively small, and it can be ignored."[18]

Another popular text devotes all of four sentences to the discussion of the value of household labor: "Many people, particularly leaders of the women's movement, argue that household work should be given a value and included in GNP. This is worth thinking about. Would it be a reasonable thing to do? If so, how would one go about valuing household production?"[19] End of discussion.

Even as recently as 1995, the best-selling textbook by Paul A. Samuelson and William D. Nordhaus made virtually no mention of the enormous amount of unpaid labor going into the upbringing of children. The distinguished authors note that the GDP does not include some key items that contribute to human well-being. As an example, they mention "do-it-yourself" work done at home, such as "cooking meals, growing tomatoes, or educating the children." These "do-it-yourself" activities are listed under a heading of "Leisure Time."[20]

Economists often maintain that the omission of unwaged labor from the GDP contains no gender bias. But women supply at least twice as much of the world's unpaid labor as men. This is the principal distinction between "women's work" and "men's work": men are paid for most of the work they do and women aren't. In industrial countries, according to United Nations statistics, women spend roughly one-third of their total working time on paid work and two-thirds on work that is unpaid and unrecognized. For men, the proportions are reversed.[21]

"Economists have been profoundly uncomfortable—even resistant—to the notion that time devoted to children is economically important," says Nancy Folbre. "What they really resist is the idea that altruism might be one of the engines of economic growth. This would destroy their model that self-interest drives everything."[22]

What men are also resisting is the subversive idea that the imbalance in unpaid labor should be righted, either by men doing more of it, or by women being reimbursed for their work. Sweeping this topic under the rug makes both of those alternatives less likely. As Elizabeth Enders, a New York artist and mother, puts it, "If caring work is unacknowledged and denied, then no one has to be directly responsible for it. . . . Working men don't have to feel guilty about not sharing housework and child care, especially if they don't exist."[23]

Society as a whole can also avoid paying for work if that work doesn't officially exist. Because unpaid child care is not measured and counted as labor, caregivers earn zero Social Security credits for raising children at home. As a result, millions of American women forfeit billions of dollars a year in retirement income. And if a mother faces divorce, she quickly discovers that courts in many states are permitted to ignore the value of her caregiving. If it isn't in the GDP, how can it be considered an economic contribution to the marriage?

A 1995 United Nations report made it starkly clear why "everybody" wants to believe that "housewives aren't that busy." Women receive a disproportionately small share of the world's resources, the report found, considering the massive amount of work they do. The report recommended that "the fruits of society's total labor should be more equitably shared."[24] The principal author of this report, the late Mahbub ul Haq, commented that "there is an unwitting conspiracy on a global scale to undervalue women's work and contributions to society. If women's work were accurately reflected in national statistics, it would shatter the myth that men are the main breadwinners of the world."[25]

This little stick of dynamite, backed by reams of data, passed virtually unnoticed by the major media.

Economic Woman

During the 1990s, a growing number of female economists began to challenge their profession's failure to incorporate women's work. Given the indifference to those who produce our precious human capital, these critics wondered, why would anyone choose to do this work? As Shirley Burggraf points out, the woman who chooses motherhood today has more to lose than any generation of women before her.

In her provocative book *The Feminine Economy and Economic Man,* Burggraf describes how the costs of family obligations have risen dramatically. In the epochal 1970s, women gained the freedom to pick and choose what they wanted in the big bazaar of life: they could enter a profession, earn a decent wage, marry or stay single, have children or not. With this sudden liberty, Burggraf argues, something new under the sun was born: a species she calls *femina economica,* or "economic woman."

Economic woman, like economic man, is a rational, independent, and informed individual whose time is worth money. She surveys her

How to Value Unpaid Labor

It is not actually all that difficult to establish value for unpaid household labor, however subtle that labor might be. The first step is deciding which nonmarket activities in the home are work and which are leisure. The best test is the so-called third-person criterion, developed by economist Margaret Reid in 1934: if a third person could be paid to do the activity, then it is work. Cooking, cleaning, child care, yard work, and repairs all fall into that category. A leisure activity, in contrast, is something you couldn't pay someone to do for you, like watch a movie, eat a meal, or listen to music.

Just because a person may enjoy an activity—playing a game with children, playing professional ball, or playing a part in a movie—doesn't mean that what they are doing is not work. Most people try to find work that is enjoyable and satisfying, and if they succeed, that doesn't mean they aren't working.

Once the time spent on nonmarket work is established, the next step is determining what that time is worth. In the case of unpaid work, this has to be estimated, or "imputed." Imputations are done for all sorts of nonmarket activities included in the GDP, such as the production of food for consumption, and even, in some countries, of criminal transactions, including the drug trade, prostitution, and the black market. This prompted Gloria Steinem to surmise that many countries, including the United States, may know more about illegal drug traffic than they know about legal homemaking.

The monetary value of work in the home can be imputed in several ways. The most common method is to estimate the cost of hiring someone to do all the jobs performed by a wife and mother: the "housekeeper wage" approach. A second method is the "specialist wage" approach, based on the cost of hiring different specialists for the various services, from cleaning to cooking to child care, each valued at the going wage. In practice these two approaches come up with much the same results.

Feminists have objected that both of these methods seriously underestimate the value of women's unpaid labor because they are based on the artificially low wages paid for work traditionally done by women—especially caring labor, which has never been recognized as highly skilled. By one such method, for instance, it would cost only about $16,000 (in 1991 dollars) to buy all the services performed in an American home for one year, comparable to the average salary of a hotel clerk, receptionist, or security guard. The Canadian Human Rights Commission tried to correct for this problem by applying an "equal pay for work of equal value" standard to homemakers' tasks. It found that this raised a homemaker's worth by 200 to 300 percent, to the level of a middle manager or social worker—not counting overtime pay.

A third approach, producing larger valuations, is based on a homemaker's "opportunity costs." Her unpaid work is valued at the amount she could earn outside the home, based on the wages she most recently earned or could expect to earn. Thus the work of a lawyer who stays home with a child would be valued far more than that of a high school graduate, regardless of how well he or she did the job. This "opportunity cost" method is increasingly used by divorce lawyers in calculating a caregiver's contribution to a marriage.

Duncan Ironmonger, an Australian economist, suggests that the value of unpaid household work, including but not limited to caregiving, should be called Gross Household Product (GHP). It could be added to the current GDP, which could be called the Gross Market Product (GMP). Together they would account for the Gross Economic Product (GEP), the total value added by productive human activity.

possibilities and sees that her time is worth $150 an hour or more as a professional, $50 an hour or more in some businesses, $15 an hour or so as a teacher, $5 to $8 an hour as a day-care worker or teacher of young children—and zero as a mother. She sees that a child is often a "career buster," and that modern marriage is no more binding than a lover's promise. Given what she sees, Burggraf wonders whether economic woman, any more than economic man, would answer this ad in the twenty-first century:

> Wanted: Parents willing to bear, rear, and educate children for the next generation of Social Security taxpayers, and to carry on the American culture of learning and progress. Quality children preferred. Large commitment of time required. At least one parent must work a double shift and/or sacrifice tenure and upward mobility in the job market. Salary: $0. Pension benefits: $0. Profits and dividends: $0.[26]

In *Who Pays for the Kids?* and in numerous articles, Nancy Folbre explains how, as the costs of raising children have steadily risen, they have steadily devolved upon women. With the disappearance of the extended patriarchal family, followed by the decline of the two-parent family, women's advances in freedom have been offset by men's decreasing responsibility for children. As she puts it, "Woman have gained new rights and men have resisted new obligations." Mothers and woefully underpaid female caretakers are increasingly the only adults left to meet children's daily needs.[27]

This raises a serious public issue, Folbre argues. In her view, children are "public goods," whose future productivity is essential to everyone's economic well-being. The Social Security system, for example, depends on their future contributions. The public, whose retirement will be underwritten in large part by the taxes paid by other people's children, has a stake in seeing that these children are raised to become productive, upstanding citizens. It is therefore in the public interest for society to assume more of the costs of raising children. When I asked Folbre how she handled the argument that having a child was a purely personal choice and private obligation, rather like the decision to raise a pet, she shot back: "I just remind people that when their Lab grows up it's not going to pay their Social Security."[28]

MARILYN WARING HAD a dream and a plan of action to give unpaid caregiving greater weight and visibility. She suggested that if every woman in every country told the census takers that she was an "unpaid worker," instead of "unemployed" or "not in the labor force," the authorities would be forced to "count" women's work. In 1996 Waring's dream came true in Canada, thanks to a forty-six-year-old homemaker and mother of three in remote Saskatchewan. Carol Lees, a lone housewife, literally compelled the government to rewrite the national census to include most forms of unpaid labor.

Five years earlier, when the national census taker came to her door, Lees had looked down at a question asking "number of hours worked in the past week." She realized that this meant "worked for pay" and that she would have to answer "zero." Her labor, as she said to me later, was "not legitimized as work, for Pete's sake."[29]

On March 8, 1991, International Women's Day, Lees wrote to the minister in charge of the Canadian census to inform him that she was refusing to respond to the census and was starting a national movement to encourage other homemakers to do the same until their labor was counted as productive.

Lees had never taken part in any political movement before. But in her letter she literally dared the government to do its worst, which in this case was a $500 fine or three months in jail. "The government will not show well if it levies a fine on a mother of three with no income because she is refused recognition for her labours in raising her children," she wrote. "Removing the mother from the home to send her to jail will not go down well either," she added. Lees copied the letter and sent it to Gloria Steinem.

The bluff worked. The government did not dare prosecute Lees, and she went on to organize a campaign calling on Canadian women to boycott the 1996 census unless it counted their unpaid labor. In the meantime, the homemaker from Saskatoon unveiled an unexpected talent at publicity. At one point she did a television interview in which she put water, salt, sugar, shortening, and yeast into a clear glass bowl. She explained that she was making bread but was leaving out a basic ingredient—the flour. So what she got wouldn't really be bread. The government does the same thing when it measures what is going on in the economy, she said, because it leaves out roughly half of what should be included—all of the work that Canadians do for free.[30]

Almost no one but the press and Canadian public opinion supported Lees's campaign. In 1993, when an organization called Statistics Canada sponsored the first international conference on how to include unpaid work in the GNP, Lees was discouraged from attending. "I asked them if I could speak to the conference on behalf of unpaid workers, and they sent me a letter saying that this would be a 'highly technical' conference of 'experts,'" she told me in a telephone interview. "I wasn't an 'expert'; I just did the unpaid work they were going to talk about."

REAL Women, an organization of conservative women, wouldn't back Lees, telling her that they didn't like the idea of big government collecting census information in the first place. (Concerned Women for America, the largest conservative women's group in the United States, takes a similar position.) And when Lees asked feminists at the local university to cosponsor a national conference on the topic of unpaid work, they declined, saying that they disagreed with her child-care policy.

"What *is* your child-care policy?" I asked her.

"To value it wherever it occurs, in or out of the home," she said.

Coming from the women Lees thought would be natural allies, these reactions disappointed her, but as she put it, "it convinced me that I was on exactly the right course."

In August 1995, the government relented. While many of Canada's most politically active women were in Beijing for an international women's conference (where women's unpaid labor was a major topic of discussion), the bureaucracy quietly announced that it would include three new questions in the May 1996 census. People would be asked how many hours in the previous week they spent on the following unpaid activities: (1) home maintenance, housework, and yard work; (2) supervision of children, either their own or others'; and (3) care or assistance of the elderly.

Lees had hoped that unpaid volunteer work would be included as well, but this was a good beginning. Marilyn Waring had argued that as long as women's work as producers and reproducers remained invisible, women "would be invisible in the distribution of benefits."[31] When Waring was a member of the New Zealand Parliament, she found that it was impossible to prove that the country needed child-care facilities after women began working outside the home, because unpaid child care at home had never officially existed. (Similarly, when the U.S. welfare laws were changed in 1996, requiring all mothers of toddlers to seek employment, Congress overlooked the fact that someone would have to step in to take care of their children during the day.)

Canada is moving to correct these omissions, thanks to the efforts of Carol Lees's tiny organization, the Canadian Alliance of Home Managers. Lees's campaign brings to mind a comment once made by Margaret Mead: "Never doubt that a small group of thoughtful, committed citizens can change the world; indeed, it is the only thing that ever has."

The United States Drags Its Feet

The United States is a conspicuous laggard in these developments. Grassroots women's organizations, statistical agencies, and scholars have successfully urged governments in Australia and in most western European countries to pay more attention to nonmarket labor. Third World women's groups in particular, anxious to prevent the "disappearance" of women's economic contributions in their own countries, as happened in the West, have made the recognition of unpaid labor a major priority.

After intense lobbying, the United Nations Statistical Commission recommended in the early 1990s that member countries' national statistical offices prepare so-called satellite GDP accounts estimating the value of unremunerated work. In 1993, the United Nations further recommended that countries add to GDP two important unpaid tasks performed by women in the developing world: the gathering of firewood and the carting of water.

By the late 1990s the national statistical offices of Canada, Australia, Austria, Germany, Norway, Italy, France, Israel, and Burkina Faso (which had a female chief statistician) had begun to collect information on the amount of nonmarket work being performed. The European Union plans to conduct its own harmonized survey.[32]

The United States, where GDP accounting began, is the great holdout. The issue has attracted almost no grassroots interest or enthusiasm, and even among women's advocates there is widespread skepticism about whether an "add women and stir" approach to the GDP would make much difference for women.

Nancy Folbre, who has written much of the history of the exclusion of nonmarket work, says she was surprised by the level of feminist opposition to the idea. I ran across this myself during an interview with Barbara Bergmann, an authority on women in the U.S. economy. Bergmann told me that she couldn't understand why an accounting change deserves attention when such basic necessities as subsidized child care are still not available to most American families. According to Folbre, many old-line feminists like Bergmann believe in their heart of hearts that "anything that romanticizes housework and childcare is bad for women."[33] Conservatives, for their part, worry that if the government discovers how much valuable work is really going on at home, it might find some way to tax it as income.

In the absence of strong support, the United States is doing very little in response to the UN recommendation. At first the Clinton administration was sympathetic to a 1993 congressional bill calling for a time-use survey of nonmarket work. But it didn't take long before the secretary of labor realized that he was not the secretary of unpaid labor. In June of 1994 Secretary Robert Reich wrote a letter to the measure's principal sponsor explaining that because economists couldn't agree on methodology, and because the Department of Labor didn't have "the funds or the personnel" to undertake the effort, the administration couldn't support the legislation.

"Moreover," Reich added, in an obvious bow to conservative sensibilities, "even if one concluded that the Government could obtain the data, there is the question of whether it should intrude into individual lives to the extent necessary to determine how Americans spend their personal lives."

A fax network of feminists in Washington, D.C., quickly responded. "If more men in high places had to do their own laundry, iron their shirts, take care of the kids, cook their meals, and clean the johns, don't you think this work would get valued and included in a hurry?"[34]

At last report, the Bureau of Labor Statistics was preparing for the possibility that Congress might mandate surveys of time use.

YEARS AGO NOBEL prize–winning economist Theodore W. Schultz observed that the development of human capabilities does not come free. There are always costs that someone has to pay. According to Schultz, who has been dubbed the "father of human capital theory," the basic questions about human capital are:

- Who will bear the costs?
- Who will reap the benefits?

The answer to the first question is families, and mothers in particular. The answer to the second question is everyone. The entire society benefits from well-reared children, without sharing more than a fraction of the costs of producing them. And that free ride on female labor is enforced by every major institution, starting with the workplace.

CHAPTER 5

The Mommy Tax

> In the U.S. we have no way to address women's economic disadvantages except through the concept of gender. We see the problem as discrimination on the basis of gender. But what's really going on is a disadvantaging of *mothers* in the workforce.
>
> —Susan Pedersen, historian

On April 7, 1999, the Independent Women's Forum, a conservative antifeminist organization, held a news conference at the National Press Club in Washington, D.C. Displayed in the corner of the room was a large green "check," made out to feminists, for ninety-eight cents. The point being made was that American women now make ninety-eight cents to a man's dollar and have therefore achieved complete equality in the workplace.

The sheer nerve of this little exercise in misinformation was astonishing. Upon closer examination, it turned out that the women who earn almost as much as men are a rather narrow group: those who are between the ages of twenty-seven and thirty-three and who have never had children.[1] The Independent Women's Forum was comparing young childless women to men and declaring victory for all women, glossing over the real news: that mothers are the most disadvantaged people in the workplace. One could even say that motherhood is now the single greatest obstacle left in the path to economic equality for women.

For most companies, the ideal worker is "unencumbered," that is, free of all ties other than those to his job. Anyone who can't devote all his or her energies to paid work is barred from the best jobs and has a permanently lower lifetime income. Not coincidentally, almost all the people in that category happen to be mothers.

The reduced earnings of mothers are, in effect, a heavy personal tax levied on people who care for children, or for any other dependent family members. This levy, a "mommy tax," is easily greater than $1 million in the case of a college-educated woman.[2] For working-class women, there is increasing evidence both in the United States and worldwide that mothers' differential responsibility for children, rather than classic sex discrimination, is the most important factor disposing women to poverty.[3]

"This is the issue that women's and children's advocates should be raising," argues Jane Waldfogel, a professor at Columbia University School of Social Work. "Women's equality is not about equal access to education or equal job opportunities anymore—those things are done. The part that's left is the part that has to do with family responsibilities."[4]

The much-publicized earnings gap between men and women narrowed dramatically in the 1980s and early 1990s. All a girl had to do was stay young and unencumbered. The sexual egalitarianism evident in so many television sit-coms, from *Friends* to *Seinfeld* to *Ally McBeal,* is rooted in economic reality. Young women don't need a man to pay their bills or take them out, any more than men need a woman to iron their shirts or cook their dinner. Many childless women under the age of thirty-five firmly believe that all of the feminist battles have been won, and as far as they're concerned, they're largely right.

But once a woman has a baby, the egalitarian office party is over. I ought to know.

Million-dollar Babies

After my son was born in 1982, I decided to leave the *New York Times* in order to have more time to be a mother. I recently calculated what that decision cost me financially.

I had worked full-time for approximately twenty years, eight of those at the *Times*. When I left, I had a yearly salary of roughly $50,000, augmented by speaking fees, freelance income, and journalism awards. Had I not had a child, I probably would have worked at least another fifteen years, maybe taking early retirement to pursue other interests. Under this scenario, I would have earned a pension, which I lost by leaving the paper before I had worked the requisite ten years to become vested. (The law has since changed to allow vesting after five years with one employer.)

My annual income after leaving the paper has averaged roughly $15,000, from part-time freelance writing. Very conservatively, I lost between $600,000 and $700,000, not counting the loss of a pension. Without quite realizing what I was doing, I took what I thought would be a relatively short break, assuming it would be easy to get back into journalism after a few years, or to earn a decent income from books and other projects. I was wrong. As it turned out, I sacrificed more than half of my expected lifetime earnings. And in the boom years of the stock market, that money invested in equities would have multiplied like kudzu. As a conservative estimate, it could have generated $50,000 or $60,000 a year in income for my old age.

At the time, I never sat down and made these economic calculations. I never even thought about money in connection with motherhood, or if I did, I assumed my husband would provide all we needed. And had I been asked to weigh my son's childhood against ten or fifteen more years at the *Times,* I doubt whether the monetary loss would have tipped the scales. But still, this seems a high price to pay for doing the right thing.

The mommy tax I paid is fairly typical for an educated middle-class American woman. Economist Shirley Burggraf has calculated that a husband and wife who earn a combined income of $81,500 per year and who are equally capable will lose $1.35 million if they have a child. Most of that lost income is the wages forgone by the primary parent.[5] In a middle-income family, with one parent earning $30,000 per year as a sales representative and the other averaging $15,000 as a part-time computer consultant, the mommy tax will still be more than $600,000. Again, this seems an unreasonable penalty on the decision to raise a child, a decision that contributes to the general good by adding another productive person to the nation.

In lower-income families, the mommy tax can push a couple over the brink. Martha F. Richie, a former director of the U.S. Census Bureau,

Where Is the Mommy Tax the Lowest?

An appreciation of a mother's needs can be added to the list of things, like food and fashion, that the French simply do best. Certainly everyone who has ever studied family policy comes away from France with the same blissful expression that one would wear after a great meal.

The country spends more than twice the percentage of its GDP on social welfare as the United States: 29 percent versus 14 percent. And much of that money goes to mothers and children.[6] *Every* French mother, rich or poor, married or single, receives not only free health care but a cash allowance for each child. The allowance can be spent in any way she wants, including hiring help at home. If she hires a licensed nanny, the government will even cover the costs of her contributions to the nanny's pension program.

Single mothers are also entitled to a package of benefits, including housing subsidies, worth about $6,000 a year. These special benefits are sharply reduced when a child reaches the age of three.[7] But time limits do not have the same harsh effects that they would have in the United States, because of the universal medical care, and because public nursery school is available for every three-year-old. By that age virtually every French child is enrolled in one of the world's best preschool systems, free of charge. These programs, combined with a year-long paid maternity leave, make it easy for French mothers to take care of their infants *and* to be employed.[8]

The mommy tax on French women is consequently one of the lowest in the world. The earnings differential between working mothers and childless working women in France is about 8 to 10 percent, compared with at least 20 percent in the United States and 50 percent in Great Britain and Germany.[9] Put another way, babies are much cheaper in France. They are also better off. The combination of relatively high maternal income and a strong safety net keeps the child poverty rate in France down to 6 percent, compared with 17 percent in the United States—despite similar rates of out-of-wedlock births.

told me, "There is anecdotal evidence—no real research—that for a lower-earning married couple the decision to have a child, or a second child, throws them into poverty."[10]

Those who care for elderly relatives also discover that their altruism will be heavily penalized. A small survey of individuals who provided informal, unpaid care for family members found that it cost them an average of $659,139 in lost wages, Social Security, and pension benefits over their lifetimes. The subjects reported having to pass up promotions and training opportunities, use up their sick days and vacations, reduce their workload to part-time, and in many cases even quit their paid jobs altogether. This exorbitant "caring tax" is being paid by an increasing number of people, three-quarters of them women. A 1997 study discovered that one in four families had at least one adult who had provided care for an elderly relative or friend.[11]

The mommy tax is obviously highest for well-educated, high-income individuals and lowest for poorly educated people who have less potential income to lose. All else being equal, the younger the mother, and the more children she has, the higher her tax will be, which explains why women are having fewer children, later in life, almost everywhere.

The tax is highest in the Anglo-Saxon countries, where mothers personally bear almost all the costs of caring, and lowest in France and Scandinavia, where paid maternity leaves and public preschools make it easier for mothers to provide care without sacrificing their income.

Most women never think about the mommy tax until they have an encounter with rude reality. Virginia Daley was an interior designer for Aetna Life & Casualty in Hartford, Connecticut. After almost ten years with the company, and consistently good performance reviews, raises, and promotions, Daley was fired in 1993 from her $46,640-a-year job. The dismissal occurred after she had had a baby and then tried to arrange a more flexible work week, in accordance with the company's stated policies.

Not only were her requests for flexibility denied, her workload was actually increased in the wake of a massive corporate downsizing. Already frustrated, Daley was furious to learn in late 1992 that Aetna's chairman Ronald Compton had been awarded a "Good Guy" award from the National Women's Political Caucus for his support of model family-leave programs. (Aetna also consistently made *Working Mother* magazine's annual list of best companies for employed mothers, and in 1992 was touted as one of the *four* "most family-friendly companies" in America by the Families and Work Institute.)

Daley dashed off a memo to Compton, charging that "when it comes to offering flexible family arrangements, Aetna's performance is far from award-winning." The memo concluded that "realistic options for Aetna employees to meet their family obligations without sacrificing their careers are not generally available today. To continue to represent to Aetna employees and the national media that these options are available is unconscionable."

Three months later Daley was terminated, on the grounds of poor performance.

She sued, and the case went to trial in 1997. Aetna maintained that Daley had lost her position because she wasn't able to handle the additional responsibilities that she was assigned after the downsizing (and the baby). The jury essentially agreed with Aetna. It also agreed with the company that Daley was not speaking out on a matter of public concern when she complained that numerous employees were being denied family-friendly schedules. Her memo to Compton was therefore not "protected speech," i.e., an important statement that entitles an employee to protection from retaliation. Daley lost the case, as well as a subsequent appeal.

(Information obtained from a court-ordered survey of all salaried employees below the level of corporate officer confirmed that *slightly less than half* of the Aetna employees who asked to work at home part of the week had had their request granted, in the period between January 1, 1991, and March 1, 1993. Most requests for job sharing and for compressed work weeks were also denied. On the other hand, the great majority of people who wanted to work part-time, usually a thirty-hour week, were granted such a schedule.)

According to Daley's lawyer, Philip L. Steele, the jury foreman told him after the trial that although the panel was very sympathetic to Daley, its members felt she had probably "overextended" herself. "They believed it was just too hard for a woman to raise little kids and do a good job," Steele told me. "The thinking was, how can a woman do all that, not how could a company do that?"

The decision cost Daley dearly. She calculates that over the next five years following her departure from Aetna, her income as a part-time consultant was from $90,000 to $154,000 lower than if she had stayed at the company. And that doesn't include the loss of Aetna's annual contribution to her 401K retirement plan. "I figure that if I'd stayed at Aetna another ten years," Daley told me, "their contribution to my 401K alone would have been more than $25,000. That could easily become more than six figures by the time I am retirement age. . . . People need to know that once you have a child you'll definitely be poorer."[12]

Sixty Cents to a Man's Dollar

In the Bible, in Leviticus, God instructs Moses to tell the Israelites that women, for purposes of tithing, are worth thirty shekels while men are worth fifty—a ratio of 60 percent.[13] For fifty years, from about 1930 to 1980, the value of employed women eerily reflected that biblical ratio: The earnings of full-time working women were only 60 percent of men's earnings. In the 1980s, that ratio began to change. By 1993, women working full-time were earning an average of seventy-seven cents for every dollar men earned. (In 1997, the gap widened again, as the median weekly earnings of full-time working women fell to 75 percent of men's earnings.)

But lo and behold, when we look closer, we find the same old sixty cents to a man's dollar. The usual way to measure the gender wage gap is by comparing the hourly earnings of men and women who work full-time year-round. But this compares only the women who work like men with men—a method that neatly excludes most women. As we have seen, only about half of the mothers of children under eighteen have full-time, year-round paying jobs.[14]

To find the real difference between men's and women's earnings, one would have to compare the earnings of all male and female workers, both full- and part-time. And guess what one discovers? The average earnings of *all* female workers in 1999 were 59 percent of men's earnings.[15] Women who work for pay are still stuck at the age-old biblical value put on their labor.

My research turned up other intriguing reflections of the 60 percent ratio: A survey of 1982 graduates of the Stanford Business School found that ten years after graduation, the median income of the full- and part-time employed female M.B.A.s amounted to $81,300, against the men's median income of $139,100. Again, the women's share is 58 percent. Another study, of 1974 graduates of the University of Michigan Law School, revealed that in the late 1980s the women's average earnings were 61 percent of the men's—despite the fact that 96 percent of the women were working, and that the men and women were virtually identical in terms of training. The authors of this study concluded that the women's family responsibilities were "certainly the most important single cause of sex differences in earnings."[16]

Conservatives frequently tout women's economic gains in order to charge that women's advocates who haven't folded their tents and gone home must be making up things to complain about. In a polemic titled *Who Stole Feminism?* Christina Hoff Sommers lambasts feminist activists for wearing a button stating that women earn fifty-nine cents to a man's dollar, which, she claims, is "highly misleading and now egregiously out of date."[17] Sommers is right if we skim over what she calls such "prosaic matters" as the fact that people who have primary responsibility for a child have different work patterns from people without caring responsibilities. But if we are interested in the real differences in the earnings of employed men and women, those buttons still tell the real story.

The Cost of Being a Mother

A small group of mostly female academic economists has added another twist to the story. Their research reveals that working mothers not only earn less than men, but also less per hour than childless women, even after such differences as education and experience are factored out. The pay gap between mothers and nonmothers under age thirty-five is now larger than the wage gap between young men and women.

The first comprehensive estimates of the cost of motherhood in terms of lost income were made in England by Heather Joshi of the City University in London and Hugh Davies of Birkbeck College of the University of

London. The two economists estimated that a typical middle-class British mother of two forfeits almost *half* of her potential lifetime earnings.[18]

In the United States, similar work has been done by Jane Waldfogel at Columbia University. Waldfogel set out to assess the opportunity cost of motherhood by asking exactly how much of the dramatic wage gains made by women in the 1980s went to women without family responsibilities. How many of the female winners in the 1980s were people like Donna Shalala, Janet Reno, Elizabeth Dole, and Carole Bellamy, the director of UNICEF: childless women whose work patterns were indistinguishable from those of traditional males.

Back in the late 1970s, Waldfogel found, the difference between men's and women's pay was about the same for all women. Nonmothers earned only slightly higher wages. But over the next decade things changed.[19] By 1991, thirty-year-old American women without children were making 90 percent of men's wages, while comparable women with children were making only 70 percent. Even when Waldfogel factored out all the women's differences, the disparity in their incomes remained—something she dubbed the "family wage gap."[20]

WHY DO WORKING mothers earn so much less than childless women? Academic researchers have worried over this question like a dog over a bone but haven't turned up a single, definitive answer.[21]

Waldfogel argues that the failure of employers to provide paid maternity leaves is one factor that leads to the family wage gap in the United States. This country is one of only six nations in the world that does not require a paid leave. (The others are Australia, New Zealand, Lesotho, Swaziland, and Papua New Guinea.)[22] With no right to a paid leave, many American mothers who want to stay at home with a new baby simply quit their jobs, and this interruption in employment costs them dearly in terms of lost income. Research in Europe reveals that when paid maternity leaves were mandated, the percentage of women remaining employed rose, and women's wages were higher, unless the leaves lasted more than a few months.[23]

In the United States as well, women who are able to take formal paid maternity leave do not suffer the same setback in their wages as comparably placed women who do not have a right to such leaves. This is a significant benefit to mothers in the five states, including California, New York, and New Jersey, that mandate temporary disability insurance coverage for pregnancy and childbirth.[24]

Paid leaves are so valuable because they don't seem to incur the same penalties that employers impose on even the briefest of unpaid career interruptions. A good example is the experience of the 1974 female graduates of the University of Michigan Law School. During their first fifteen years after law school, these women spent an average of only 3.3 months out of the workplace, compared with virtually no time out for their male classmates. More than one-quarter of the women had worked part-time, for an average of 10.1 months over the fifteen years, compared with virtually no part-time work among the men. While working full-time, the women put in only 10 percent fewer hours than full-time men, again not a dramatic difference.

But the penalties for these slight distinctions between the men's and women's work patterns were strikingly harsh. Fifteen years after graduation, the women's average earnings were not 10 percent lower, or even 20 percent lower, than the men's, but almost 40 percent lower. Fewer than one-fifth of the women in law firms who had worked part-time for more than six months had made partner in their firms, while more than four-fifths of the mothers with little or no part-time work had made partner.[25]

Another survey of almost 200 female M.B.A.s found that those who had taken an average of only 8.8 months out of the job market were less likely to reach upper-middle management and earned 17 percent less than comparable women who had never had a gap in their employment.[26]

Working-class women are also heavily penalized for job interruptions, although these are the very women who allegedly "choose" less demanding occupations that enable them to move in and out of the job market without undue wage penalties. The authors of one study concluded that the negative repercussions of taking a little time out of the labor force were still discernible after twenty years.[27] In blue-collar work, seniority decides who is eligible for better jobs, and who is "bumped" in the event of layoffs. Under current policies, many women lose their seniority forever if they interrupt their employment, as most mothers do. Training programs, required for advancement, often take place after work, excluding the many mothers who can't find child care.[28]

Mandatory overtime is another handicap placed on blue-collar mothers. Some 45 percent of American workers reported in a recent survey that they had to work overtime with little or no notice.[29] In 1994 factory workers put in the highest levels of overtime ever reported by the Bureau of Labor Statistics in its thirty-eight years of tracking the data. Where does that leave a woman who has to be home in time for dinner with the kids? Out of a promotion and maybe out of a job. Increasingly in today's driven workplace, whether she is blue- or white-collar, a woman who goes home when she is supposed to go home is going to endanger her economic well-being.

The fact that many mothers work part-time also explains some of the difference between mothers' and comparable womens' hourly pay. (About 65 percent of part-time workers are women, most of whom are mothers.)[30] Employers are not required to offer part-time employees equal pay and benefits for equal work. As a result, nonstandard workers earn on average about 40 percent less an hour than full-time workers, and about half of that wage gap persists even for similar workers in similar jobs.

Many bosses privately believe that mothers who work part-time have a "recreational" attitude toward work, as one Maryland businessman assured me. Presumably, this belief makes it easier to justify their exploitation. But the working conditions they face don't sound very much like recreation. A recent survey by Catalyst, a research organization focused on women in business, found that more than half of the people who had switched to part-time jobs and lower pay reported that their workload stayed the same. Ten percent reported an increase in workload after their income had been reduced. Most of these people were mothers.[31]

Another factor in the family wage gap is the disproportionate number of mothers who operate their own small businesses, a route often taken by women who need flexibility during the child-rearing years. Female-owned small businesses have increased twofold over small businesses owned by men in recent years.[32] In 1999, women owned 38 percent of all U.S. businesses, compared with only 5 percent in 1972, a remarkable increase that is frequently cited as evidence of women's economic success. One new mother noted that conversations at play groups "center as much on software and modems as they do on teething and ear infections."[33]

Less frequently mentioned is the fact that many of these women-owned businesses are little more than Mom-minus-Pop operations: one woman trying to earn some money on the side, or keep her career alive, during the years when her children have priority. Forty-five percent of women-owned businesses are home-based. And the more than one-third of businesses owned by women in 1996 generated only 16 percent of the sales of all U.S. businesses in that year.[34]

In 1997, although women were starting new businesses at twice the rate of men, they received only 2 percent of institutional venture capital, a principal source of financing for businesses with serious prospects for growth. Almost one-quarter of female business owners financed their operations the same way that they did their shopping: with their credit cards.[35]

Some researchers have suggested that mothers earn less than childless women because they are less productive. This may be true for some mothers who work at home and are subject to frequent interruptions, or for those who are exhausted from having to do most of the domestic chores, or distracted by creaky child-care arrangements. But the claim that mothers have lower productivity than other workers is controversial and unproven. It is easier to demonstrate that working mothers face the same old problem that has bedeviled women in the workplace for decades.

It's Discrimination, Stupid

It is revealing that those occupations requiring nurturing skills, such as child care, social work, and nursing, are the most systematically underpaid, relative to their educational and skill demands.[36] These are also, of course, the occupations with the highest percentage of females. But men who are primary caregivers also pay a heavy price: a "daddy tax," if you will. This suggests that at least part of the huge tax on mothers' earnings is due to work rules and practices and habits of mind that discriminate against anyone, of either sex, who cannot perform like an "unencumbered" worker. In other words, discrimination against all good parents, male or female.

Surveys have found that wives may adore husbands who share the parenting experience, but employers distinctly do not. A majority of managers believe that part-time schedules and even brief parental leaves are inappropriate for men.[37] When Houston Oiler David Williams missed one Sunday game to be with his wife after the birth of their first child, he was docked $111,111.

A survey of 348 male managers at twenty Fortune 500 companies found that fathers from dual-career families put in an average of *two* fewer hours per week—or about 4 percent less—than men whose wives were at home. That was the only difference between the two groups of men. But the fathers with working wives, who presumably had a few more domestic responsibilities, earned almost 20 percent less. There it is again: a 20 percent family wage gap.[38]

"Face time still matters as much or more than productivity in many companies," Charles Rodgers, a management consultant in Boston, said. Rodgers told me about a man in a high-tech company who regularly came to work two hours early so that he could occasionally leave early for Little League games with his son. He was given a poor performance rating.[39]

Such discrimination is hard to quantify, but it is potentially a powerful political issue. When the Clinton administration announced that it was banning employment discrimination against *parents* working in the federal government, there were so many calls to a White House staffer assigned to the case that her machine stopped taking messages.

Only eight states currently have laws prohibiting discrimination against parents in the workplace. Examples include taking a primary parent off a career track out of an assumption that the individual couldn't do the work; hiring someone without children over a more qualified person with children; forcing a primary parent to work overtime, or else; and refusing to hire a single parent, though the employer hires single, childless people. In the course of my reporting, I encountered numerous mothers who felt that their employer's refusal to arrange a shorter workweek, particularly after the birth of a second baby, amounted to career-destroying discrimination.

The Second Baby

Cindy DiBiasi, a former reporter for WUSA-TV, a Gannett-owned station in Washington, D.C., is one of the countless mothers who found that the birth of a second baby, and the impossibility of arranging a short workweek to accommodate it, destroyed her career.

DiBiasi is a slim, attractive, dark-haired woman with a brisk air of self-assurance instantly recognizable as the glossy competence displayed every night on the evening news. In 1989, she became the medical reporter for WUSA, a job that she had long coveted. Two days before she was scheduled to begin her new position, DiBiasi discovered that she was pregnant. She hadn't yet signed a contract, and she didn't tell her bosses for seven weeks. But she was able to put her pregnancy to use, producing a series on having a baby, even arranging for a camera crew to be at the hospital when her daughter was born in August of 1990. She remembers being on camera even after her water broke. "They didn't have to worry about me being committed," she commented wryly.

After a ten-week maternity leave, DiBiasi was back on the job from 10:00 A.M. until 6:00 P.M., producing a five-minute live segment for the 4:00 P.M. news show and a taped piece for the 6:00 P.M. news. All went well until just before her child's first birthday, when DiBiasi had to take three days off to visit her sick father in Illinois. A week later, her child's nanny was unable to come to work for two days in a row. DiBiasi was about one hour late on the first day and two hours late on the next. (Her husband took off work on both days to be at home.)

She was subsequently called into her boss's office and told that she would lose vacation time for the days she took to go to Illinois. "I was amazed," she told me. "I asked if it had anything to do with my being late those two days and explained what had happened. I asked if there was a problem with my work. He said no, but he was getting red in the face. . . . A long time ago a female reporter told me that whenever my child got sick, I should always say it was *me* who was sick. I remember thinking, that's bullshit. How could they want me to be dishonest? But now I wasn't so sure.

"I didn't like the feeling I was getting, so I asked for a meeting with the two top executives. They told me that there was a perception that I was not working 'full days.' I reminded them that I was on the air twice a day, every day, and that nights at home I was reading medical journals to keep up in my field. 'How does the desk know that?' they asked.

"Then they mentioned, almost casually, that they might want to take the medical unit in a different direction, but 'that has nothing to do with you or your work,' they assured me.

"At one point one of them said something like 'the problem is that you think you're the only one who has a family.'. . . Now the guy who said this had a son in college, and the other two men with children had stay-at-home wives. I pointed out that I had a *one-year-old*. And that if I had problems dealing with it I'd tell them. They just looked at me, with this blank, flat look."

During the next six months, DiBiasi was asked to do a live segment on the 5:00 P.M. news, along with her pieces for 4:00 P.M. and 6:00 P.M. She agreed, thinking, "As long as I'm not away from my kid any more time, I'll kill myself for them—that'll solve this. . . . Then I found out that I was pregnant again. I realized that I couldn't keep up the pace, so I asked if I could switch to a three-day week, with a prorated salary cut. The news director said he would think about it.

"I worked all the way up to my delivery, which was in June of 1992. I had eight weeks of maternity leave. Two days before I was to go back, I had a call from the assistant news director. 'We really need help on general assignment,' he said. So after I get back, for the next two months I'm doing fires, accidents, you name it, and I'm not getting home at six-thirty anymore. One day they asked me to do a live shot in Annapolis at the end of the day, and I said I couldn't—it meant I wouldn't get home until nine P.M. My boss said, 'Can't your nanny just stay?'

"I said, 'Number one, no, she can't stay, and number two, if she *could* stay, I don't want to get home that late. If I do that, I won't see my kids at all.'

"He just looked at me. Then he said, 'So, you'll see them tomorrow.'"

DiBiasi's new position was a demotion, but she continued a while longer, getting home late regularly. Finally, she told the desk that there was no way to be a general assignment reporter if one had to be at home at 6:30 P.M. She was told she had to continue on general assignment.[40]

The managers at WUSA had put DiBiasi in a job they knew she couldn't do. She hired a lawyer and began the process of suing the station. The important thing, her lawyer told her, was to stay on the job, no matter how bad it got. Otherwise, management could argue that she had left voluntarily. However, the demands of staying on the job, and preparing a case, proved overwhelming.

"I was supposed to be secretly tape-recording all our meetings," DiBiasi said, "and then come home and transcribe the tapes at night. I had the job, I had to deal with the attorney, my husband was traveling a lot, and I had two little babies. . . . I finally had to quit when it all became just too much of an emotional drain. I would have had to sell short everything in my life I cared about; there would have been no more essence to me."

DiBiasi also decided not to sue: "I knew that if I pursued this, they would say I wasn't a good reporter. And there is a contradiction in these kinds of suits, because in order to get punitive damages, you have to show *damage;* you have to show that you're a wilting flower who has been hurt by all this. If you're strong, and are determined not to be a victim, they can argue, so what's the problem?"

So, after fifteen years in television reporting, DiBiasi lost a job she loved, a six-figure income, her health insurance, and her economic independence. Slowly, she was also losing public recognition, a newsperson's working capital. All because she had had the temerity to try to work for fewer days a week while her two children were young. For all of her talent, energy, and drive, DiBiasi, like millions of other mothers, was suddenly only a husband away from financial disaster.[41]

As Cindy DiBiasi's story illustrates, the most popular form of family planning in the United States and other wealthy countries—two children, spaced not too far apart—is incompatible with most women's careers. Even if a new mother and her employer can cope with one child, the second baby is often the final straw. The most sympathetic employers can prove surprisingly resistant to the second baby. A well-known feminist economist told me that she had gone to great lengths to bend the rules at her university to accommodate one of her graduate students who had become pregnant. The woman was given a year's extension on her schedule and time out to be with her new infant. Then, just before she was due to come back, she became pregnant again.

My friend, who believed she had been as progressive as was humanly possible, felt betrayed. She thinks the woman was foolish not to realize that the system can only accommodate so much deviation. "You have to play by the rules to some extent, especially when other people have stuck their neck out for you," she said. This professor, by the way, has no children herself, but she does have tenure.

How to Lower the Mommy Tax

Until now, narrowing the gender wage gap in the United States has depended almost entirely on what might be called the "be a man" strategy. Women are told to finish school, find a job, acquire skills, develop seniority, get tenure, make partner, and put children off until the very last minute. The longer a woman postpones family responsibilities, and the longer her "preparental" phase lasts, the higher her lifetime earnings will be.

Ambitious women of the baby-boom generation and younger have by and large tried to be a man in this way. A good example is Susan Pedersen, a historian who achieved tenure at Harvard in the mid-1990s. By that time, she was married and in her late thirties, but she had postponed having children until her academic career was secure. Motherhood was something she wanted very much, she commented during an interview, but it posed a serious threat to her professional dreams and had to be delayed.[42]

As Pedersen's success demonstrates, this strategy does work—for the very small number who are able to pull it off. And women who have their children later in life do have higher lifetime earnings and a wider range of opportunities than younger mothers. The advice dished out by writers like Danielle Crittenden—no relation—an antifeminist ideologue who has urged women to marry and have their babies young, ignores this, along with some other hard truths. Crittenden never tells her readers that young parents tend to separate and divorce much more frequently than older couples, leaving young mothers and children vulnerable to poverty. Large numbers of the women who end up on welfare are there because they have done exactly what she recommends: married and had children young and then been left to support them alone.[43]

But trying to be a man has its own risks. Many baby-boomer women postponed families only to discover that when they wanted to become pregnant, it was too late. (I saw some of the risks associated with this strategy after I had my own child under the wire in 1982. I touted the advantages of late motherhood on a couple of television shows, until I realized that many of my friends over forty were unable to conceive.) And millions of women don't feel that being a man is the way they want to live their lives. Increasingly, young women are saying that they don't want to put off children until they almost qualify for membership in AARP.

An alternative strategy is followed in countries like France and Sweden, where the government, private employers, and/or husbands share much more of the costs of raising children. This makes it far easier for women to be mothers and to work. In France, for example, families with two preschool-age children receive about $10,000 worth of annual subsidies, including free health care and housing subsidies and excellent free preschools.[44] As a result, child poverty is unusual, and the pay gap between mothers and others is much smaller in France than in the United States or the United Kingdom.

Whenever Europe is singled out as a model, the usual response is that Americans would never support such generous social policies. But in fact, the United States already does have an extremely generous social welfare state. But unlike the welfare states of western Europe, the American government doesn't protect mothers; it protects soldiers.

Men who postpone or interrupt civilian employment for military service pay a tax on their lifetime earnings that is quite comparable to the mommy tax. White men who were drafted during the Vietnam War, for example, were still earning approximately 15 percent less in the early 1980s than comparable nonveterans.[45] This "warrior wage gap" is strikingly similar to the family wage gap, again indicating that mothers' lower earnings are not entirely attributable to gender discrimination.

But there is unquestionable discrimination in the way the government has responded to the financial sacrifices that soldiers and parents, particularly mothers, make. All Americans are asked to "make it up" to veterans of the military: The damage to a caregiver's pocketbook is unmitigated, while the damage to a veteran's wallet has legitimized a massive relief effort.

To illustrate this double standard, let's look at two men with identical characteristics. One works as a computer technician, is married to a woman in the same occupation, and has two children. He is a conscientious father, making sure to be home for dinner every night, even helping to cook it. He takes his kids to sporting events, attends teacher conferences, and tries to limit his travel and outside commitments.

This man is legitimately worried about what his dedication to family will do to his career. Let's say he does get fewer promotions and over the years earns 15 to 20 percent less than he would have had he not shared the family obligations. We can realistically say that he pays a significant daddy tax.

Now take a man with the same education and imagine that he spends three or four years in military service. He is worried that these years out of his active professional life will affect his economic future, and they might, although his boss believes that his service was good leadership training. But whatever career losses he suffers will be cushioned by the generous thanks that the nation pays to its ex-servicemen. He discovers that his warrior tax is lowered by these benefits, which are available to him even if he never got near a battlefield:

- He can stay in the military for twenty years as a *part-time reservist* and draw half pay for the rest of his life.[46]
- He will get special preference for government jobs. Extra points will be added to whatever civil service exams he may take, and some rules are written so that he will be chosen over closely ranked non-veterans. In government layoffs, he will have extra protection. Unlike mothers or fathers who find that after a few years out of the job market their credentials are downgraded, his are given a major boost by veterans' preferences.
- If he decides to go back to school for more education, he can qualify for thirty-six months of cash payments worth more than $17,000.

• He also qualifies for a government-guaranteed housing loan, financed at interest rates usually half a percentage point below the going market rate.

• He can make use of a hospital system costing the federal government $17 billion a year.

• He will have access to special low auto insurance rates, available only to individuals with some connection to the military. These come in especially handy when his teenage son begins to drive.

• As long as he remains in the military or works on a military base as a civilian, he can enjoy subsidized child care provided by the best day-care system in the country. For only $37 to $98 a week (in 1997), depending on his income, he can enroll his children in infant and toddler care and preschools staffed by expertly trained and licensed teachers. In the private sector, the fees would be two to four times higher, for often inferior care.

None of these benefits is contingent on service in combat. In 1990, 6.3 million of the 27 million veterans eligible for benefits served only during peacetime. Millions of ex-servicemen, who do not even have a hangnail to show for their harrowing experience in uniform, enjoy the same government largesse that flows to the veterans who were once put in the way of danger.

The benefits paid to military veterans are so lavish that they are now second only to Social Security in terms of government payments to individuals. And they do an excellent job of reducing the warrior tax. The educational benefits in particular help veterans overcome many of the economic disadvantages they suffer by leaving the workplace for a few years.

A congressional study in the early 1990s concluded that the veterans of World War II who took advantage of the G.I. Bill to earn a college degree enjoyed incomes of up to 10 percent more than they might otherwise have earned. Society was also the beneficiary, for the additional taxes paid by the college-educated veterans during their working lives more than paid for the program.[47]

It hardly needs to be said that there is no G.I. Bill, no health care, no subsidized housing, and no job preferences for mothers. As things now stand, millions of women sacrifice their economic independence and risk economic disaster for the sake of raising a child. This says a lot about family values, the nation's priorities, and free riding.

A third way to reduce the mommy tax would be to expand the antidiscrimination laws to cover parents. Joan Williams, a law professor at American University's Washington College of Law, argues that the design of work around masculine norms can be reconceptualized as discrimination. As an example, Williams suggests that if a woman works full-time, with good job evaluations for a significant period, then switches to part-time because of family responsibilities and is paid less per hour than full-time employees doing similar work, she could claim discrimination under the Equal Pay Act. Williams believes that disparate-action suits could also be filed against employers whose policies (including routine and mandatory overtime, promotion tracks, resistance to part-time work) have a disparate impact on women, producing disproportionate numbers of men in top-level positions.[48]

The essential point is that existing laws, and new laws preventing discrimination against people with caregiving responsibilities, could go a very long way toward improving mothers' lifetime earnings.

The Ultimate Mommy Tax: Childlessness

The cost of children has become so high that many American women are not having children at all. One of the most striking findings of Claudia Goldin's survey of white female college graduates is their high degree of childlessness (28 percent). Now that the baby-boomer generation is middle-aged, it is clear that more than one-quarter of the educated women in that age group will never have children. Indeed, the percentage of all American women who remain childless is also steadily rising, from 8 to 9 percent in the 1950s to 10 percent in 1976 to 17.5 percent in the late 1990s.

Is this rising childlessness by choice? Goldin thinks not. She found that in 1978, while in their twenties, almost half of the college-educated boomers who would remain childless had said that they did want children.

Goldin calculated that almost one-fifth of this entire generation (19 percent) of white college graduates was disappointed in not having a child. This is the ultimate price of the "be a man" strategy that has been forced on working women. For women in business, the price is staggering. A recent Catalyst survey of 1,600 M.B.A.s found that only about one-fifth of the women had children, compared with 70 percent of the men.[49]

Educated black women have had, if anything, an even harder time combining children with their careers. Many of the most accomplished black women now in their forties and fifties, including Oprah Winfrey, Anita Hill, Eleanor Holmes Norton (the congressional representative for the District of Columbia), and Alexis Herman, secretary of labor in the Clinton administration, have forgone motherhood. These women apparently discovered that the price of success included the lack of parental obligations. And educated black women face an additional problem—an acute shortage of eligible black men.

Americans have a hard time realizing that such deeply personal choices as when or whether to have a child can be powerfully circumscribed by broader social or economic factors. American women, in particular, are stunningly unaware that their "choices" between a career and a family are much more limited than those of women in many European countries, where policies are much more favorable to mothers and children.

Swedish women, for example, enjoy benefits that American women can only imagine in their wildest dreams: a year's paid leave after childbirth, the right to work a six-hour day with full benefits until their child is in primary school, and a stipend from the government to help pay child-care expenses.

And guess what? These pro-family policies dramatically reduce the mommy tax on Swedish mothers; enable a higher percentage of Swedish women, vis-à-vis Americans, to have children; and permit more Swedish mothers to stay at home while their children are young.

Germany is an altogether different story. Before the fall of the Berlin Wall, women in East Germany enjoyed many of the same policies that benefit Swedish women, including yearlong paid maternity leaves and free public child care. It was so easy to combine paid work with children that almost every woman had a baby and almost all mothers worked. In 1989 about 91 percent of East German women were biological mothers.

West Germany, on the other hand, offered much less support to working mothers. As a result, only about 80 percent of West German women became biological mothers, and significantly fewer mothers worked.

After German reunification, subsidized child care—and subsidized jobs—were eliminated in East Germany. As a result, birth rates plummeted. Berlin now has one of the lowest birthrates in the world.

In sum, an individual woman's decision whether to have a child or not, and whether to stay home or not, is heavily influenced by her country's willingness to help her bear the costs. In Germany, as in the United States, the official message is *caveat mater,* or "mothers beware": you're on your own.

CHAPTER 6

The Dark Little Secret of Family Life

> There is overwhelming evidence that mothers channel much more of their income to expenditures on children than their husbands do.
>
> —Lawrence H. Summers, former chief economist, World Bank, and former U. S. treasury secretary

Because of the mommy tax and the marginalization of mothers in the workplace, the great majority of American women with children are dependents. For all of the work they do, at the end of the day most mothers have to rely on the financial support of a spouse. And as we shall see, that is not good for women, or for children, or for economic prosperity. Yet this dependency is pervasive. Married working mothers in the United States earn on average only about half of what their husbands earn. More than one-quarter of the wives in American families with children at home earn nothing at all. They are completely dependent on their husbands.[1]

Another conspiracy of silence surrounds this uncomfortable anachronism. Wifely dependency within marriage is hidden. It is not revealed in official poverty statistics or discussed in polite company. It doesn't appear in data on income inequality, which are based on total family income, not on the income of individuals. As one of my female acquaintances puts it, this is "one of the last little secrets that no one wants to admit or talk about."

Privately as well as officially, everyone pretends that spouses are perfectly equal. Asking a woman to what degree she depends on her husband for money is like asking her whether she turns tricks. It is especially below the belt for an unmarried, childless woman to say to a mother's husband, as an acquaintance once said to mine, "I wish some man would support *me* while *I* write a book."

Economists simply define mothers' economic dependency away. Classical economic models assume that the family is a single indivisible unit, a black box that cannot be pried open. The family is presumed to act as one, pooling all resources and pursuing one common interest, determined by consensus or the benevolent dictate of a dominant family member. In these "unitary" models of the family, who earns what and who controls the money are irrelevant. Money does not convey power, and power is never used or abused.

Public policy is based on this fairy-tale version of household dynamics. The "family wage" paid to the "head" of a household is assumed to flow through automatically to all other family members. "His" or "hers" is understood as "theirs," and all income going into the household is, according to this view, perfectly shared, no strings attached. These assumptions lie behind the calls for "family tax cuts." It is simply taken for granted that all tax cuts will benefit all family members, not just the wage earner who gets a bigger paycheck when taxes are lowered.

But is this picture really accurate? The law does not take such an egalitarian view of family finances. Under current family law, "He who earns it owns it." A breadwinner's income is legally his alone, and he can do whatever he wants to with it: share it, spend it on himself, or stash it away in a secret bank account. A married spouse has no legal claim on the other spouse's income, nor do the children, aside from the obligation of both parents to feed, clothe, and shelter minors from gross neglect. In short, if one member of the family makes most of the money, it is his to "give" to the others, not theirs by right. Everyone else in the household just has to hope that the primary breadwinner has a responsible, sober, and generous spirit.

Very little is known about what actually happens to money once it goes into a household, and even less is known about the really interesting question of how "who earns what" affects family relationships. Family financial arrangements are like snowflakes in their infinite variety. The few empirical studies that have been done reveal that in some families there is indeed complete income sharing, while in others the partners have totally separate bank accounts. Some households accept the economic leadership of one partner; others are in egalitarian harmony; still others haggle over every decision. The lower wage earner may pay all the bills, spend most of the money, and make the investment decisions, or she may be completely ignorant of family finances and kept on an allowance.

Despite these uncertainties, we can safely say that most breadwinners *do* share the bulk of their income and their standard of living with their spouses and children. If not, why would the old story of the poor girl who marries the prince—now the millionaire—have such widespread appeal? In Canada, one researcher calculated that pooling of income within families raises married women's incomes from 54 percent to 87 percent of men's.[2]

But this sharing masks what we all know from experience: that the subtle balance of power in a marriage is tilted in favor of the spouse who contributes the money. In the privacy of the bedroom, who has not heard or uttered the dread cry "I make the money in this house!"

In every household a certain amount of explicit or implicit bargaining goes on: over how to spend the family's resources, who does the housework, who takes off work for a sick child. The outcome of each of these family decisions is strongly influenced by what social scientists call the "threat point"—the point at which a spouse's threats become credible. Take a young childless couple, earning roughly similar salaries. She can say, "If I ever catch you with another woman, I'm out of here," and he is probably going to believe her, and change his ways if he wants to preserve the relationship. But if they have two small children, and she has just quit her job, he may have a harder time believing that she really would walk. Her threat point has been raised. He has a little more power and a little more leeway to do what he wants in the marriage.

When fathers make much more money than mothers, and when alimony and child support are skimpy at best, the wife is likely to put up with a lot more than the husband. When the chips are down, he is more likely to have his way.[3]

This dynamic helps explain why American men still do a disproportionately small share of housework. After the first child arrives and the workload at home increases, the wife's bargaining power decreases, and with it her ability to persuade her partner to do chores he might not want to do. If he refuses to clean up after dinner, what is she going to do? Threaten to leave with the baby? Not likely.

Of course, money is not the only thing that determines the balance of power in marriage. Youth, beauty, intelligence, and strength of personality all play their part. But as one sociologist writes, "Women who are dependent upon their husbands for livelihood are in a weak position to bargain with their husbands over anything else."[4] The old adage "He who pays the piper calls the tune" is not just outdated folklore.

The power of money in marriage may be far more obvious when the dependent spouse is the man.

Over coffee in Washington, D.C., I interviewed a father who had been the stay-at-home spouse. Robert Michelson, a former corporate lawyer in New York City, and his wife had both been practicing attorneys when they realized that their three-and-a-half-year-old son needed more parental attention than he was getting.[5] Michelson, already in his mid-forties and becoming a little bored with his job, welcomed the chance to spend more time with the boy, and in 1989 he left his company to become a full-time parent. His wife, who was thirteen years younger, loved her new job as an associate at Wachtel, Lipton, one of the most high-powered law firms in the country. So she remained with her firm and went on to become a partner, pulling down more than $1 million a year. The couple's relationship thus became the mirror image of what it had been in their first years together, when Michelson had been a successful attorney supporting his pretty young wife while she struggled as an actress and then a law student.

When I asked Michelson if the role reversal had affected their relationship, he nodded emphatically. Throughout our conversation he repeatedly stressed how close and mutually supportive the marriage had always been. But "something clearly happened," he told me, when her earnings began to dwarf his, and it dawned on him that even if he went back to work he would never be as financially successful as she had become. "I felt the change in my ability to push certain points of dispute," he explained. "It was not in anything she said or did. She was incredibly nurturing. But if it was an issue where we both dug in our heels, I wasn't going to win. I wasn't the strong partner. I knew I couldn't go out on my own and replicate the standard of living I had thanks to her income.

"I'm one of the only people I know who's been on both sides of this dependency thing," Michelson continued. "I've been the source of dependency, and that feels great. And I've been entirely dependent, and it's not as good. I can't imagine a more secure relationship than ours, but I have felt very vulnerable. Never in the sense that she could—or would—walk away. But it's always there, this unpleasant, vulnerable feeling you have to deal with. It's never far from the surface of your thoughts."

In other words, he found himself in the position of the typical wife and mother.

After several years, the couple decided they had had enough of unequal parenting and the New York rat race. At the end of 1995 Michelson's wife quit her job and the family moved to rural Maine. They are now in what he calls their "third relationship": equals both financially and as parents, a development he calls "very liberating." He sounded exactly like a woman who had finally found the ideal partnership.

In some families, a caregiver's economic dependency can be more than psychologically uncomfortable. It can be dangerous. One study found that the presence of one child under age twelve increases by 50 percent the relative probability that a woman will be battered.[6] When John Fedders, a senior official in the Reagan administration, was exposed as a wife beater, his spouse was asked why she had put up with severe physical abuse for years. A stay-at-home mother of five, Charlotte Fedders explained that she and her children did not have the money to leave and survive on their own.

Similarly, the wife of Mel Reynolds, a former Rhodes scholar and congressman from Chicago, accused him of beating her repeatedly and intimidating her into cooperating in his misuse of campaign funds. She never reported the abuse, she said, because she was dependent upon him for the support of herself and their children.

No doubt the great majority of breadwinners never abuse their power, but that is not really the point. The point is they could if they wanted. As sociologist Paula England has said, spouses are neither selfish nor altruistic, mean nor generous, loyal nor disloyal. They are all of these things, depending on the circumstances. They are likely to be one thing on good days and another on bad; one thing when a marriage is working and quite another if it turns sour. The dependent partner is always aware that the wind can change and start to blow from the wrong direction.

More Mommy Taxes, on Rich and on Poor

Fortunately, mothers' degree of economic dependency is decreasing. Roughly 16 percent of married women with children now earn *more* than their husbands.[7] Only two-fifths of American wives born in 1955–59 have earnings of 30 percent or less of their husbands', compared to two-thirds of wives of an older generation—those born in 1930–34. Black women born in the 1940s and 1950s are significantly less likely to have low earnings relative to their husbands' than older black women.[8] And although almost two-thirds of women in married-couple households still feel that their partners' jobs offer more financial security than their own, that represents a drop of 19 percentage points since 1981.[9]

However, a punitive tax system cancels out much of women's progress in narrowing the marital wage gap, forcing them right back into dependency on their spouses. Married working mothers pay the highest taxes in the country on their earned income, *in addition to* the mommy tax. This heavy taxation powerfully affects their ability to preserve their independence.

Consider what happens to the salary of a woman who makes $30,000 a year and is married to a man who earns $60,000. As her income is taxed not as the earnings of an individual, but together with her husband's wages, she faces an effective tax rate of roughly 48 percent: an income tax rate of 30 percent, beginning on her first dollar earned; Social Security taxes of 8 percent; and state and local taxes of up to 10 percent in many states. This brings her take-home pay down to roughly $15,000. Child-care expenses, which are *not* deductible as a business expense, can easily cost $10,000, and other work-related expenses, like clothing, commuting, and meals, can add another $4,000 or so to the family budget.

This typical mother will soon enough hear what tax expert Edward McCaffery calls "the accountant's tale": the news that if she doesn't actually *lose* money by working, she can expect to end up with no more than $1,000 to $2,000 from a full-time job that pays $30,000.[10] What is she likely to do? Work hard at a job that keeps her away from her children all day for virtually no salary? Or throw up her hands and quit? As Michael Boskin, chairman of the Council of Economic Advisers under President George Bush, wrote more than twenty years ago, "The net effect of the [U.S.] tax system is clearly to drive female labor out of the market into the home."[11]

Among the poor, the deck is stacked even higher against the working mother. Take the case of a mother who can only find a minimum-wage job of about $10,000 a year, and whose husband's annual salary is $15,000. She faces a marginal tax rate of 50 percent: a 15 percent income tax, an 8 percent Social Security tax, 10 percent for state and local taxes, plus the loss of the earned income tax credit of $2,000 that the couple would qualify for if she (or he) didn't work—not to mention the probable loss of other government benefits.[12]

It should come as no surprise, therefore, that among poor two-parent households, two incomes are rare, for low-earning married mothers have almost no incentive to work. The tax laws, never written with the poor in mind, set up a situation that discourages two-breadwinner families among the very people who need the income the most. And once again, the woman is dependent. In these circumstances, single parenthood carries some advantage. A woman's income taxes plummet to zero, she qualifies for an earned income tax credit, and she retains her independence. It is no accident that single-parent households are most common among the poor: a man has to overcome a high hurdle before he looks good enough for a woman to undertake the risks of marriage.

The bottom line is that most married mothers, rich as well as poor, are not as economically viable as their husbands. In 1999, male high school graduates had average annual earnings of $30,572, compared with $18,415 for women. Among college graduates, men earned on average $67,434, as against women's $37,113. Only 8.4 percent of married women earn as much as $50,000 a year, compared with 31 percent of married men.[13]

Some of the most extreme marital dependency is hidden within the households of the rich. Many women might kill for the life of the trophy wife, but from Palm Springs to Palm Beach those who move among the rich will tell you, "It's the hardest money you'll ever earn."

The vast majority of the people who struck it rich during the 1980s and 1990s—dot.com millionaires, investment bankers, venture capitalists, top corporate executives, real estate developers, lawyers in the big firms, big-time entertainers, and sports figures—were men. (As of 1995, 70 percent of Americans with a net worth of more than $10 million were men.)[14] And marriage to one of these highfliers, more often than not, spells the end of a woman's career.

Husbands earning serious six- or seven-figure incomes usually work horrendous hours, which puts the lower-earning or nonearning spouse in the position of having to handle everything else in life. His workload, the tax on her income, and the fact that the couple doesn't "need" the money she could earn, operate as effectively as a mullah's edict in pushing a wife back into the home.

The affluent wife and mother often becomes the "domestic executive," married to the CEO and principal shareholder. She ends up more like a privileged employee than a true partner and peer. An exceedingly rich man I went out with a couple of times in the early 1980s summed it up succinctly: "My first wife was like my housekeeper," he thoughtfully informed me.

The *Wall Street Journal* recently discovered the high-income wife-as-housekeeper phenomenon. The business daily reported that the new economy has brought a resurgence of the old family model, as couples who were once economic equals are mutating into traditional Man-the-Provider, Woman-the-Helpmate patterns. Nearly half of households earning between $250,000 and $499,999 had just one breadwinner in 1998, for example, up from about 38 percent just six years earlier. Over 90 percent of those breadwinners were men. At higher incomes, a wife with a career is as rare as Ripple in the wine cellar.[15]

In other words, the rising *income* inequality in the United States has brought with it increasing *gender* inequality. The *Journal* reported that high-earning husbands are delighted with this development. The men interviewed adored having stay-at-home wives who supported their careers and handled all the domestic responsibilities (one executive boasted that it was like being spoiled by his mom again). The women were less euphoric. One thirty-four-year-old wife and mother, who had slightly outearned her husband when they first both got out of law school, had just had her application for a credit card turned down. Her take-home message: "I have no power in this family or in society."

Her instincts are right. Recent polls reveal that the higher the family income, the less independent power a homemaker has over major financial decisions or purchases.[16] Professionals such as decorators, real estate brokers, and psychiatrists who have a window into the private arrangements of the rich confirm that many wealthy wives who appear to have unlimited bank accounts in fact are kept on a tight leash, like an expensive pet.

Carlotta Miles, a psychotherapist in Washington, D.C., says her wealthy female patients frequently tell her that they have no idea of their husband's assets and no real control over how the money is spent. "Some of these women are living in million-dollar-plus houses and couldn't get their hands on $5,000," Miles reports.[17]

Philanthropic fund-raisers are also acutely aware of the second-class status of many wealthy wives. Hope Brock, a New Yorker who has raised money for Radcliffe College, told me about one couple in which the man gave $250,000 to Harvard and the woman donated $10,000 to her college. But "getting even $10,000 out of a woman is like pulling teeth," she said. "Women don't feel they have any control over the charitable contributions that are being made. They are not financial players."[18] This reality among the rich helps explain why only 5 percent of all foundation giving in the United States is earmarked for programs that benefit women and girls. The big money is simply not in mothers' hands.

Strong Mothers Equal Strong Children

Maternal dependency, despite its ill effects on women's equality and peace of mind, is not considered to be a problem, as long as a mother relies on a man rather than on a government. But a growing body of evidence demonstrates that marital dependency is not only detrimental to women, it's not good for children either.

In most families, two incomes are necessary for the extended financial support that children increasingly require. And a family's economic investment in its children turns out to be greater and more secure if mothers have some control over family income. This is because income earned or controlled by mothers is more likely to be spent on children than income controlled by fathers.[19]

This is the powerful finding emerging from decades of research and experience in economic development. Economists now believe that mothers are so much more likely than fathers to invest in children's health and education that the surest way to promote economic growth in poor countries is to educate and empower girls. Apparently, nothing improves human capital so much as capital in the hands of mothers.[20]

That strong, independent mothers are good for children makes common—and evolutionary—sense. In all mammals, the female is the parent who nurtures the young, who fights most fiercely to defend them, who expends the most energy to guarantee their survival. And among mammals, human females are extreme in the amount of time and energy and resources they invest in the young.[21]

Again, this was reflected in my own family. Before our child arrived and for years thereafter, I was the parent who bought the baby books, devoured their contents, and agonized over putting their lessons into practice. I was the one who felt as if I had fallen under a spell, who wanted to spend hours holding and playing with this enchanting little creature. I was the one who felt physically bereft when we took our first trip away from the baby, and I was the one who quit my job. Later on, I was the one who read the bedtime stories, who detected the colds and the ear infections, and was quicker to run to the doctor. I was the one who invested in a piano, insisted on a reading tutor, researched the summer programs, and dragged us on Sundays to the zoo and the science museums.

Now that our son is a teenager, my husband is far closer to him than before and has backed him wholeheartedly in his creative projects, proving every day that two parents are better than one. But I am still the one who keeps track of developments in school; who insists on more evenings at home; who fights the centrifugal forces.

Families, of course, are not all alike, but this division of labor is apparently so typical that at a school meeting one night, Richard Moll, the head of admissions at Vassar, declared that "when it comes to getting a kid into college, mothers are the engine, and the rest of us are the train."

This intense maternal concern offers a powerful rebuttal to the argument that a traditional, male-dominated family is the best arrangement for children. Even today, the economic dependency of mothers is justified "for the sake of the kids." Social conservatives still maintain that what children really need is a full-time mother at home, completely at their disposal, and a father who is the primary breadwinner and "head of the household."

This belief depends on several assumptions: first, that father knows best; and second, that he will act on that knowledge to everyone's advantage, putting his own personal wishes aside.

Even those who cannot swallow such paternalism tend to take it for granted that both parents are equally devoted to their children's welfare; that as far as offspring are concerned, it doesn't matter who brings home the bacon or controls the family purse strings. But unfortunately, these assumptions appear to be highly questionable.

Studies conducted on five continents have found that children are distinctly better off when the mother possesses enough income and authority in the family to make investing in children a priority. As one survey put it, there is "considerable empirical evidence, across diverse cultures and income groups," that women have a higher propensity than men "to spend on goods that benefit children and enhance their capacities."[22] Even more provocative is the considerable evidence that children's welfare is enhanced not just when mothers have their "own money" but when no man is able to challenge maternal priorities. Two researchers summarize this potential dynamite in the dry language of social science: "Evidence is growing that the internal distribution of resources in female-headed households is more child-oriented than in male-headed households."[23] In other words, matriarchy, the original family arrangement, may turn out to be the optimal one after all.

Researchers in Africa, Latin America, the Caribbean, Asia, and the Indian subcontinent have all found that when mothers are educated and have some control over the family income, children are healthier, get more schooling, and will eventually have a greater earning capacity, with all that implies for economic prosperity. The sad truth is that quite a bit of income in the hands of men seems to find its way into bars and the pockets of cigarette companies, among other fleeting pleasures.[24] "It is widely perceived," one report notes, "and supported by a mass of case study material that, relative to women, men spend more of the income under their own control for their own consumption. Alcohol, cigarettes, status consumer goods, even 'female companionship' are noted in this literature."[25]

The different value that mothers and fathers may attach to children was dramatically, if inadvertently, highlighted by a series of *New York Times* articles on the effects of the 1998 Asian economic crisis on the poor. In the first story, a thirty-two-year-old Thai mother faced the excruciating choice between a lifesaving operation for herself and food for her four-year-old daughter. She chose to spend the money on her child.[26]

In the second story, the same reporter talked with an Indonesian family with two daughters, ages ten and four, who appeared to be malnourished. The wife explained that "when we get some meat, my husband eats it." The head of this household also habitually spent one-sixth of the family's meager cash income to buy tobacco and betel nuts, a mild narcotic.

"When the fathers are asked why they smoke cigarettes instead of buying food for their hungry children, they say, 'We can always make more children,'" said Dr. Anugerah Pekerti, the chairman of World Vision Indonesia, an aid organization.[27]

Similar stories span the globe:

- In Kenya and Malawi, researchers have found that among sugarcane farmers, the more income controlled by women, the greater the household caloric intake, whatever the overall household earnings. The reason: in Malawi, female-headed households spent 25 to 50 percent less on alcoholic beverages than male-headed households.[28]
- In Jamaica, female-headed households consume foods of higher nutritional quality and spend a larger share of their income on children's goods and a significantly smaller share on alcohol than male-headed households.[29]

• In Brazil, $1 in the hands of a Brazilian woman has the same effect on child survival as $18 in the hands of a man.[30]

• In Guatemala, the higher the share of total household income earned by a child's mother, the better nourished the child. Using this data, based on a sample of children, one scholar estimated that an additional $11.40 per month in a mother's hands would achieve the same weight gain in a young child as an additional $166 if earned by the father.[31]

• A study of fourteen typical poor villages in South India found that the men retained up to a quarter of their earnings for their own personal use—five to six times the proportion of their own income that women spent on themselves.[32]

• In the Ivory Coast, household expenditure data indicate that a doubling of the income under women's control would lead to a 26 percent decline in the budget share going to alcohol, as well as a 14 percent decline in household expenditures on cigarettes.

According to Muhammad Yunus, founder of the Grameen Bank in Bangladesh, which pioneered microlending to poor female villagers, women are far more responsible with money than their husbands. "Women have plans," he said during a visit to Washington, D.C., in 1994, "for themselves, for their children, for having children, for the home, the meals. They have a vision. A man wants to enjoy himself." To illustrate his point, Yunus pointed out that the Grameen Bank had a payback rate of 98 percent on small loans to dirt-poor women, in contrast to the $9 billion the big commercial banks of Bangladesh had lost in defaulted loans to male-owned enterprises.

These findings are so compelling that when Mexico decided to establish an assistance program to alleviate the extreme poverty in rural areas, it focused the effort on those who would spend the money most responsibly: mothers. The $800-million-a-year Progresa program makes cash payments of $26 a month on average to women, provided they keep their children in school and take them for regular medical checkups. According to observers, the program is working, despite some mothers' complaints that their husbands are pressuring them to take the kids out of school to help in the fields.[33]

In light of this research, it is worth mentioning that the United States abandoned plans in the 1970s to convert welfare into direct cash payments to all poor families because the money threatened male control over the family. Experiments with a negative income tax—a cash stipend for low-income families—were conducted in several U.S. cities, including Seattle and Denver. They showed that poor families getting moderate grants from the government tended to break up significantly more often than families not receiving such grants.

Apparently, the money reduced wives' financial dependence on their husbands and increased the probability that an unhappy wife would pack her bags, scoop up the kids, and leave. The project leader of the Denver-Seattle experiment labeled this the "independence" effect, and there was much anxious discussion of how greater female independence could cause a decline in the morale of the male family "head." There is no record of any equivalent concern over the morale of mothers or children.

One scholar at the University of Wisconsin's Poverty Institute even suggested that to prevent the independence effect, perhaps the payments should be added to the husband's paychecks instead of mailed to the home, where the wife could get her hands on them. In any event, once southern congressmen found out about the independence effect, the possibility of a cash payment to poor married couples was dead.[34]

Years later, Congress did approve something very close to the negative income tax: the earned income tax credit, a cash bonus paid by the federal government to low-wage workers. By then the divorce rate had already risen to roughly 50 percent, and the EITC, if anything, has apparently helped stabilize poor, two-parent families. But a cash stipend paid directly to mothers—a commonplace in Europe—is still unthinkable in the United States.

Critics of the research linking maternal resources with healthier, better-educated children have argued that it may simply reveal that the mothers who are clever enough to obtain their own resources are also the kind of competent people who invest more heavily in their offspring. (This is called the "better mother" effect.) To be really conclusive, a study would have to distribute extra money to a *random* sample of mothers and then see if those families subsequently spent more on the children.

As it happens, such an experiment did take place, quite by accident, in Britain. In 1946, the country's new Labour government introduced a family allowance, a direct cash payment for families with children. The original legislation proposed to pay the allowance to the father, but protests by women's groups defeated that idea, and the payment was sent directly to married mothers. Since World War I, English feminists such as Eleanor Rathbone had dreamed of a "mother's wage," paid by the state, that would reimburse women for their work as mothers and end their overwhelming economic dependency upon men. The new allowance was inadequate by that standard; it was not enough to eradicate child poverty or secure the economic independence of mothers. But many British mothers did come to rely on it and regard it as their due.

A more important source of financial support for families was a child tax credit, which reduced the taxes withheld from the family breadwinner's paycheck. In 1977 another Labour government decided to merge the child allowance and child tax credits into a single payment called a child benefit. This nontaxable weekly sum for each child would be paid directly to mothers. The government's explicit intent was to increase economic equality within the family by reallocating income from a father's wages to a paycheck from the government for the mother.

Men, from conservative Tories to trade unionists, reacted with alarm. There was a fierce parliamentary debate about the transfer from the male "wallet" to the female "purse." As one parliamentarian put it during the uproar, "Far from a new deal for families, it will take money out of the husband's pocket on the Friday and put it into the wife's purse on the following Tuesday. Far from being a child benefit scheme, it looks like . . . a father disbenefit scheme."[35] Some government ministers were so concerned about a possible male backlash that they decided at one point to defer the whole plan.

But the change did go through, and the much-feared backlash never materialized, perhaps because overall benefits to low-income families actually increased.

The new and larger payment to British mothers amounted to a vast random experiment, testing the hypothesis that money in the hands of women benefits children more than money going into a general "pool" of family money via the breadwinner's paycheck. The sums involved were not insignificant. In 1980 a woman in the United Kingdom with two children was receiving an annual "wage" from the government of £500 for her unpaid caring work, worth the equivalent of about 8 percent of average male earnings.[36]

A thorough study of this "natural experiment," comparing data from before the benefit went into effect (1973–76) and after (1980–83) concluded that paying the money directly to the mother did change spending patterns slightly. For example, in families with up to three children, expenditures on women's and children's clothing, relative to expenditures on men's clothing, increased.

The authors of the study admit that there is no way to "prove" that the changes in expenditures were caused by the policy change. But they do believe that their findings are evidence "that 'kids do better' when their mothers control a larger fraction of family resources."[37]

Robert A. Pollak of Washington University, a coauthor of the study, told me that the moral of this story is that children gain when their mothers have greater earnings opportunities; that is, when both the mommy tax and maternal dependency are reduced. In his view, if societies make it easier for mothers to combine work and family (by providing paid maternity leaves, a shorter working day, and subsidies for good child care), children will be better off.[38]

More systematic research on the effect of mothers' income on child welfare has not been conducted anywhere in the industrialized world. But what little information there is is consistent with studies in the Third World. In the United Kingdom, Jan Pahl, a sociologist at the University of Kent in Canterbury, concluded from her research in the 1980s that "compared with men, women hold less [income] back, both absolutely and relatively, for their personal use." Pahl drew the same policy conclusions that development economists have reached: "The best way to raise the living standard of poor children is to increase the amount of money over which their mothers have control. This would also have the effect of increasing the power of women within the family."[39]

Perhaps the best evidence we really have that mothers in rich as well as poor countries are more willing than fathers to invest in their children surfaces when mothers lose their influence over fathers' income. In the United States, fathers, who can effectively disinherit their children, frequently do so after divorce. This happens so often that one legal scholar was prompted to comment that divorce has created the modern-day equivalent of the old-fashioned bastard: the child "claiming a blood tie to the father but cut off from the share of paternal affluence that falls to the child of the intact family unit."[40]

Divorced fathers are much less willing to finance their offspring's higher education than mothers—even though they are in a much better position to do so. A 1992 study by the Department of Education found that only 6 percent of custodial parents (almost all of them mothers) expected help from their former spouses in paying their children's college bills. College financial aid directors report that they are seeing more and more cases of "degree default" by fathers "who act as if they have divorced their kids as well as their spouses."[41]

In most states parents are required to support their children only to age eighteen. This gives the divorcing parent who is less concerned about a child's education a bargaining chip to force the other parent to accept a lower financial settlement. I have two friends whose husbands threatened during the divorce process not to pay for the children's college education—even though both men had graduate degrees themselves. Divorce lawyers confirm that fathers often use blackmail to reduce child support. As Gary Skoloff, a divorce attorney in Livingston, New Jersey, explained to me, "Men say to their wives, I won't pay for college unless you accept lower support."

To prevent this kind of blackmail, several states have laws making both divorced parents responsible for their children's college expenses. According to Skoloff, fathers' rights groups in New Jersey have lobbied to overturn such a law. They want to bar family court judges from ordering both parents to contribute to higher education.

One other piece of evidence suggests that women in the developed countries are more willing than men to invest in children. Female politicians are clearly less reluctant than their male colleagues to spend money on social programs that benefit the young. In Scandinavia, where approximately 40 percent of the national legislators are women—more than three times the proportion of women in the U.S. Congress—governments spend far more per person on family-support programs than the federal government spends in the United States. And within the United States, social expenditures on children tend to be higher in states like Washington, where women make up a large proportion of state legislators, than in states like Pennsylvania, where women in the statehouse are as scarce as peach trees in Alaska.

NONE OF THESE findings proves that mothers inherently care more about children than fathers do. Caring for children is a mother's moral obligation and prescribed social role in virtually all societies, and for that reason alone mothers would be more inclined than fathers to meet children's needs. A mother's standing in the community depends on how well she performs her assigned "job," and how well her children turn out, giving her an enormous personal stake in their future.

Still, the maternal preference for children does seem to be firmly rooted in some fundamental differences between the sexes. In a masterly work on maternal behavior, *Mother Nature: A History of Mothers, Infants, and Natural Selection,* primatologist Sarah Blaffer Hrdy explains these distinctions in terms of "quantity" versus "quality." From data on the behavior of the great apes, the earliest hominids, and traditional foraging cultures, which provide the best window we have into the world of our prehistoric ancestors, she concludes that females are programmed to maximize the well-being of each child, with the goal of raising offspring who will survive to reproduce. This desire for "quality"—for well-spaced, healthy children who can be provided for and have a good chance to make it to maturity—is in age-old tension with a male desire for "quantity"—to sire as many children as possible.[42]

From this inherent conflict between the sexes—"build the nest" versus "scatter the seeds"—Hrdy draws several conclusions. One is that having a *strong mother* is all-important to a child. Hrdy describes females as active, ambitious players in the game of life as they, no less than males, seek the power and social dominance that can contribute to their reproductive success. She cites data from various primate studies documenting a positive connection between female status and infant survival rates. She describes how Flo, the Gombe chimpanzee observed by Jane Goodall for many years, used her high status to provide ample food for her offspring and protect them from harassment by other mothers. Eventually Flo's high social rank made it possible for her daughter Fifi to inherit her mother's territory, instead of having to move off to join a new group at puberty, as most female chimpanzees do.

According to Hrdy, these data strongly suggest that status and motherhood were totally "convergent" in the distant past. The problem for mothers (and children) today, she says, is that a woman's ambition has to be played out in male-designed realms that have no tolerance for children, putting her toughness, aggression, and zeal to succeed in direct conflict with the young child's need for constant care and attention.[43]

As for primate males, they—like their human cousins—are highly variable in their interest in offspring. Hrdy reports that only 40 percent of primate species exhibit some form of male care, and that within those, *only monogamously mated males with a high probability of being the father exhibit direct and extensive care.* "Ethnographic information for different human societies . . . similarly suggests," she writes, "that paternal care is most intensive where monogamously mated men have a high certainty of paternity."[44]

In traditional foraging societies, where sexual alliances are often quite fluid and paternity uncertain, men do not necessarily invest significant resources in their offspring.[45] Studies of the Hadza tribe in northern Tanzania, for example, revealed that the men preferred to go after big game, even when their chances of success were lower than if they sought smaller and easier prey. If a hunter succeeded, he tended to give much of the meat to new potential mates, rather than to his existing offspring. His own family didn't end up with any more food than anyone else.

In Hrdy's words, "Hominid fathers have been choosing between investing in the children they already have and finding new mates with whom to sire more for as long as there has been a division of labor between hunters and gatherers."[46]

Even when fathers have certain knowledge of paternity, they do not necessarily invest in their children unless mothers have enough influence to persuade them to do so. Among the Dogon of West Africa, a patriarchal, polygamous society that keeps women under strict subordination, almost half of all children die before the age of five. Across cultures, the chances of a child dying are seven to eleven times higher if the mother is living in a polygamous family than if she is in a monogamous union.[47]

In contrast, in societies where women have significant status, men are more likely to be engaged with their children. In virtually *all* of the many subsistence societies in which there are close bonds of affection between fathers and their children, women wield authority in the community.[48]

After an analysis of premodern societies from all over the world, sociologist Scott Coltrane of the University of California, Riverside, concluded that there was a strong and statistically significant link between men's responsibility for taking care of children and women's participation in community decisions and access to positions of influence.[49] "Close father-child relationships are associated with greater public power and prestige for women in virtually all types of societies," Coltrane found.[50]

Similarly, in contemporary Scandinavia, where women have greater income equality and more political power than virtually anywhere else in the world, married men are more involved in caring for their children than almost anywhere else in the world. Mothers' relatively high earnings are so important to the family that fathers are able to share the unpaid work of child care without jeopardizing the family's income. And the more time a man spends with his young child, the more he discovers, as generations of women have done, that this can be one of the most rewarding experiences in life.

A link between strong maternal influence and a people's propensity to invest emotional and financial resources in children has also been uncovered by historians. In a massive study of the "wealth and poverty of nations," David Landes, a professor emeritus of economics and history at Harvard, states flatly that "in general, the best clue to a nation's growth and development potential is the status and role of women."[51] Literate, empowered women, Landes argues, have enabled some nations to invest more heavily in human capital than others, and therefore to become more prosperous. In other words, when it comes to the creation of wealth, mother matters.

THE IMPLICATIONS OF this research, encompassing so many disciplines and cultures, cut deep. If it is true that mothers really are children's greatest advocates, and a major force in economic development, we have failed to grasp the import of the social changes affecting families.

The emergence of women as independent economic actors is not depriving children of vital support; it is giving them more powerful defenders. Depriving mothers of an income and influence of their own is harmful to children and a recipe for economic backwardness.

Conservatives often object that strong, independent mothers make fathers irrelevant. The implication is that it is impossible to have paternal involvement without paternal control. As we have seen, the facts suggest the opposite: men are more likely to share the increasing responsibilities involved in raising children if mothers have more leverage to convince fathers that the children come first.

This is why reducing the mommy tax, by making it easier for married as well as single mothers to maintain their own income, is so important. It is also an argument for strengthening the hand of mothers in marriage. Who is really served when mothers are dependents in marriage and impoverished if a marriage ends?

Thirty years ago, sociologist Jesse Bernard described women's unpaid work as the infrastructure on which the entire superstructure of the economy rests. What family caretakers need more than anything else, she argued, is an economic base that reflects their very real value to society.[52] But the terms of marriage, just as much as the terms of employment, deny mothers a solid base on which to stand.

CHAPTER 7

What Is a Wife Worth?

> If a conservative is a liberal who's been mugged, a liberal is a conservative woman who's been divorced.
>
> —Carol Tavris, author

In 1997, Americans were treated to the spectacle of one of the most closely watched marital battles since Charles and Diana. This was a high-profile Connecticut divorce involving one of the country's most lavishly paid business executives and his homemaker wife of thirty-one years. Much of the husband's fortune (his estimate, $50 million; her estimate, roughly $100 million) was tied up in separate little gift-wrapped boxes labeled "Do not open until retirement." The key to the financial settlement was how the judge would rule on these future sources of income, including deferred compensation, which Connecticut law does not automatically consider marital property.

That was *Wendt v. Wendt* on one level: a *Dynasty*-like property dispute between Gary Wendt, the head of GE Capital, the most profitable division of the General Electric Company, and Lorna Wendt, the fifty-three-year-old wife he had decided to discard. But the Wendt case wasn't featured on *20/20,* discussed by Oprah, covered by every major newspaper, and the subject of its own Web site just because it promised to set a precedent on the distribution of future stock options. On the deepest level, the case was really about the status of mothers in contemporary marriage.

The Wendt case posed *the* question for women who devote much of their lives to raising their children: Is caregiving really valued equally with moneymaking in a marriage? If a woman chooses to set aside her own income and ambitions to become the primary parent in a family, supporting her husband's career in the process, will she be considered an equal partner? Or, despite all the lip service to the importance of family, is a wife an equal only if she contributes an equal amount of money to the partnership?

The press, in covering the trial, gave its answer. The story was labeled "What is a wife worth?" as if a wife were her husband's employee, and the only question was what he would have to pay to buy out her contract. But the journalists were simply reflecting a persistent cultural attitude that families are like an Orwellian animal farm, where everyone is equal but some are more equal than others. Why, for example, even on joint accounts, is the husband's name always printed first on the checks? Why do income tax returns always assume there is one "head of household" and a "spouse"? And why do people still talk about a long-married woman "asking" for "his" money in a divorce?

Gary Wendt's view of his marriage could have been lifted out of a novel by Trollope. "I know what Lorna's needs are, and I want her to be able to live very, very comfortably after we're divorced," he declared in a pretrial deposition, as if he were arranging for the dignified retirement of a faithful retainer whose services were no longer required.[1]

Wendt's attorney, Robert Epstein, made the equation of a wife with a servant even more explicit. Lorna Wendt's labor over three decades was worth roughly $2 million at the going rate for a nanny-cook-housekeeper, Epstein calculated, putting her value at just under $65,000 a year. This was considerably less than the $9 million in assets and $250,000 a year in alimony Gary Wendt had offered his wife, and much more than she could have earned had she pursued a career as a music teacher. What was her problem? What more did she want?

Lorna Wendt's answer was simple. She wanted half. "This isn't about money," she told everyone who asked. "It's about fairness." She believed that marriage was a mutual journey through life, for better or for worse. Each partner was an equal, in her view, and entitled to half of the fruits of their union, whatever their division of labor. She had raised two daughters and shouldered every domestic responsibility while her husband had concentrated on his eighty- to ninety-hour-a-week career. She wanted half the family property, not 10, 20, or 30 percent, and she thought she had earned it.

I was intrigued by the Wendt case because Lorna Wendt was the first prominent woman to speak up publicly for the important principle of equality of women, not just in education or the labor market, but also in marriage. In 1997, this was still a radical claim.

In the 1970s and early 1980s, the joint property claim first put forward by mid-nineteenth-century wives finally became, for the most part, the law of the land. All assets accumulated during a marriage were deemed to be marital, or jointly owned, property, subject to division in the event of divorce. (In most states, property that is inherited is excluded from divisible property.) But as Lorna Wendt discovered, just because a wife is entitled to a *share* of the marital assets, doesn't mean she is entitled to *half*. In most states, marital property only has to be divided "equitably," which in practice can have a wide range of meaning.

Moreover, in many courts of law, it is still considered unnatural for a wife and mother to claim a material reward for her labors on behalf of the family. This makes wives the only workers in the economy expected to work for no remuneration, which is obviously why women as a group are still so much poorer than men.

Judges, and according to numerous studies the entire legal establishment, are still so in thrall to these attitudes that most wives undergoing divorce usually just settle for whatever they are offered. (Fewer than 5 percent of divorce settlements are ever brought before a judge in a public courtroom.) Several attorneys told reporters that Lorna Wendt was being unusually "aggressive" in going to court with a claim for half the couple's assets.

To this day, many judges still view marital property as "the guy's net worth" rather than "the family's assets." As a rule, the more financially successful the marriage, the greater percentage of family wealth the major breadwinner can keep as his own. Rich men have to share a far smaller fraction of a married couple's net worth than other men. If there are substantial assets, the man's attorney will ask the wife's, "How much does she *need*?" The judge will then "give" her "enough."

Neither "need" nor "enough" is defined. Some judges interpret "need" to mean only the most basic necessities, while others see need when the former spouse can no longer live in the luxurious style to which she has become accustomed. But numerous attorneys have told me that judges are satisfied if the wife is "given enough" to go forward with a not too diminished standard of living. This concept—"enough is enough"—is not normally associated with an equal, contractual partner.

In Connecticut, a common-law state, things are even worse for family caregivers than in most other states. In 1987 researchers for the Connecticut chapter of the League of Women Voters found to their surprise that the only marital sharing required by the state statutes is a joint responsibility for family debts. The family assets are presumed to belong to the spouse whose income earned them.

Eight weeks into the Wendt trial, on January 29, 1997, I attended the proceedings at the small redbrick civil courthouse in downtown Stamford. Four television photographers were huddled outside the entrance in a cold winter drizzle, waiting to pounce on the two principals in their miserable moment of notoriety. Upstairs, in windowless courtroom number 3, more than a dozen observers were crowding into their seats as if for a screening of the film *The First Wives Club*. Most of the spectators appeared to be women who either had been or were going through a divorce, Lorna's friends, or female journalists writing about the well-publicized case.

"We think she's wonderful," one middle-aged blond woman confided to me. "I don't know her, but I've been through a divorce, and my lawyer told me, '[Your husband] doesn't want you anymore; take what you can get and get on with it.' I think it's just great she's doing this."

Another woman, who identified herself as a close friend of Lorna Wendt's for twenty years, had brought along an acquaintance who was in the midst of a divorce from a "wealthy" man. The friend confirmed a story I had already heard: that Gary Wendt had refused to pay part of the cost of a piano that Lorna had recently purchased for one of their daughters. "She put up with a lot," she leaned over and whispered to me. "He's ruthless."

Lorna Wendt sat with her legal team at one end of a long table facing Judge Kevin Tierney. In her bright canary yellow jacket, she stood out from the drab surroundings like a tropical bird in a wintry forest. By all accounts, she was not a woman who was comfortable being a crusader.

The daughter of a rural Wisconsin schoolteacher and a Lutheran minister, she seemed the embodiment of an unpretentious Midwestern matron, albeit one with a weakness for designer clothes. She sang soprano in the local Lutheran church choir and still made her trademark peanut brittle every Christmas. Her friends had described her as an "ordinary person" who, like Anita Hill, had been reluctantly dragged into the limelight. "She is not any kind of revolutionary," said Christine Lodewick, a childhood friend and the president of the League of Women Voters in Ridgefield, Connecticut. "She just opened her mouth about something we should have opened our mouths about a long time ago."[2]

At the other end of the witness table sat Gary C. Wendt, a ruddy-faced fifty-four-year-old man of medium height. His well-cut gray suit did not quite hide a slight paunch. Although both Wendts had come a long way, they were still recognizable as the milk-fed high school sweethearts they had once been in Rio, Wisconsin (population 600), he the star athlete who played the trombone and she the pretty fair-haired girl who sang and played the oboe.

During testimony that day, it came out that Gary Wendt had written a new codicil to his will, leaving $2.5 million to a person he described as a "companion," the same term he had used to characterize his wife. In a departure from the usual scenario, his new friend and companion was an older woman in her sixties—and one of Lorna's acquaintances. When I asked Gary Wendt why he thought things had come to a public trial, he shrugged and said, "A woman scorned." Shortly after the divorce was final, he married the other woman.

As in many states, Connecticut law does allow judges to grant wives some compensation after a divorce for their unpaid family labor. But because no precise weight is put on nonmonetary contributions to a marriage, they can be and are often ignored altogether.* This meant that Lorna Wendt had to bolster her claim to half the family's assets not by

*The Uniform Marriage and Divorce Act (UMDA) provides that courts, in dividing marital property, should take into account the contributions of each spouse. Contributions as a homemaker are named as one factor among many to be considered. But no guidance is included to direct courts on how to balance the numerous factors enumerated. Studies have found that courts are overwhelmingly influenced by monetary contributions alone.

proving she had been a good mother and fulfilled her half of the couple's marriage bargain, but by arguing that she had played a significant part in the couple's financial success.

She could cite several studies showing that managers and professional men with wives at home actually earn more than men with wives who work—even after controlling for other differences among the men. One study, of 231 men who received M.B.A. degrees in the late 1970s, found that all else being equal, those married to stay-at-home wives earned from one-quarter to almost one-third more than men married to working women.[3] By Gary Wendt's own admission, the fact that Lorna had managed the family virtually single-handedly had enabled him to rise as high as he had. "Perhaps I should have spent more time with the children, and perhaps I shouldn't have made so much money," he swore in a deposition. "I wouldn't have if I had spent more time with the children."[4]

Lorna Wendt's legal team played up this angle, feeding the press numerous stories about Lorna's role as a "corporate wife." She had typed Gary's papers while he was at Harvard Business School, and along with the other B-school wives, had been given a framed P.H.T. degree ("Put Hubby Through") when he graduated. During his career she had moved the household four times to five different states before they had finally settled in 1975 in Stamford, where the GE Capital division is based.

Wendt herself swore that she "took [her] job very seriously," including frequent entertaining to further Gary's business interests. One of Lorna Wendt's lawyers, Sarah Oldham, told me that eight days after the couple's first child was born in 1968, Gary Wendt's secretary had called and said, "Your husband has decided to have a dinner party tonight. There will be twelve people arriving at seven P.M." In December of 1995, about a week after Gary told her he wanted a divorce, she played hostess at her last black-tie GE Christmas party.

To counter this picture of the stalwart helpmate, Gary Wendt was forced to depict his wife as lazy or worse. Epstein, his attorney, tried to insinuate that because she didn't do her own ironing or make her own clothes, she was an indifferent homemaker. This of a woman whose husband was bringing home $1.6 million in aftertax dollars. If she had done her own ironing, she would have been the only person in her income bracket who did.

One witness on the day I attended the trial had the unenviable task of denigrating Lorna Wendt, whom he had known for twenty years. Angelo Astone, a longtime employee of GE Capital, blurted out in response to one question, "I don't know what I'm supposed to say." But he did know how to play his assigned role.

Astone testified that Lorna's only useful role on the numerous GE trips she had taken with her husband was to suggest where the wives could shop. "She's a great shopper, this lady," he enthused.

He explained that "she had nothing to do with" the much-publicized dinner parties for ninety. The invitations to the company's annual Christmas party had been addressed at the office; the big-name entertainment had been arranged by consultants; food and decorations had been provided by florists and outside caterers. As for Lorna's part in the transformation of GE Capital from a small corporate division into a major financial institution, Astone had this to say: "I haven't seen anything that she contributed to the company, no."

I glanced over to see how Lorna Wendt was reacting to all this. She was wiping her eyes with a tissue. It was immediately and excruciatingly clear why so few wives are willing to challenge their husbands in court.

One of the most painful moments came when Arnold Rutkin, Lorna Wendt's other attorney, asked Gary Wendt if he had had any idea, when he started out, how successful he would be.

"I had dreams," Wendt replied.

"Did you have any idea how much money you would make?" Rutkin inquired again.

"I had dreams."

The singular pronoun rang out through the courtroom, like a wake-up call to every married woman present. When do "our dreams" become "*I* had dreams"?

"You had no idea it was an equal partnership with Lorna?"

"I can't ever recall that being discussed or thought about."

"You never thought about your marriage as a partnership?"

"In economic terms? No, I didn't."

"Did you ever tell her that?"

"No, and she didn't ask."

"You didn't think of your marriage as a team effort?"

"No, I didn't."

There was an audible gasp in the courtroom.

Gary Wendt testified that he had been "totally responsible for all creation and value of the assets. . . . I cannot find anything close to [justifying] an equal distribution of these assets." This led to the crucial exchange of the trial:

"Is it your view that making money is more important than raising a child?" Rutkin asked.

After several objections, Rutkin rephrased the question: "You have testified that the financial contribution to the marriage was almost all yours. . . . Do you believe that raising children is less important than making money?"

"Raising children should not be measured by anywhere near the same standard as making money. I don't believe they should be measured in any way next to each other; they are two different things."

As Wendt had put it in a deposition, "My rewards were financial, and I think her rewards were perhaps emotional . . . the satisfaction of being with the children."

This, of course, was the heart of the matter. Gary Wendt was restating the old idea of separate spheres in marriage, which is still alive and well. This ideology says in effect to mothers: your caring contribution is not economic, and don't imagine for a minute that it entitles you to any economic consideration. Your work on behalf of other family members is a labor of love, and we all know that love is its own reward.

Feminist legal scholars argue that this nineteenth-century view of "women's work" as entirely outside the material realm operates to this day to keep married women in a subservient position. Lorna Wendt was up against the reality that every day, in courts all over the country, judges decide that husbands' paid work gives rise to financial entitlements in marriage, but wives' unpaid caring work does not. If the law reflects a society's values, then family law in the United States says that child-rearing is a second-class occupation. As Ann Laquer Estin, a professor at the University of Colorado School of Law, puts it, "Within the law, there is a remarkable disregard for caregiving—the norms of nurturance, altruism, and mutual responsibility that are usually thought to characterize family life . . . [are] almost entirely irrelevant when courts resolve the financial incidents of divorce."[5]

"The current statutes suggest that ultimately self-interest and autonomy matter more than connection and interdependence," Estin has written. "Perhaps this is the wrong message to send about families."[6]

"This is the pervasive issue in divorce," says Joan Entmacher of the Women's Legal Defense Fund. "Most states ignore the value of a parent's contributions to the care of children, and the costs of providing that care. This puts women at a huge disadvantage."[7]

When Lorna Wendt emerged from the courthouse during the lunch break, she was mobbed by television camera crews, who chased her briefly as we hurried to a nearby delicatessen. Over lunch I asked her why she had decided to undergo this ordeal, against the odds of any success.

"I thought Gary's offer wasn't fair," she repeated. "I believed we had a partnership . . . that we were a team. Don't teams share their ups and downs? I believe that half of what we had is fair."

She paused. "Isn't 'team' a word GE uses?" she asked Sally Oldham. "Remember that magazine ad for GE Capital? You know, the one showing a man with his wife and kids, and it says he's a team player, and his wife is part of the team?"

"We have it somewhere," said Oldham. "Let's use that tomorrow."

SOME FEMALE REPORTERS writing about the Wendt case seemed to think that Lorna Wendt, corporate wife and homemaker, was something of an anachronism. Betsy Morris of *Fortune* magazine, a baby boomer, commented that reporting the story was in some ways like a "time warp." After she finished the story Morris called her mother "and told her I'd never understood until now how different the rules and expectations were for the generation that came before us."[8]

Morris implied that a more contemporary woman, with a good education and some professional experience, is surely not as vulnerable as a woman in a traditional marriage. Even if something happens to her marriage, God forbid, she can always take her M.B.A. or her teaching or nursing or writing experience and go back to work. With much of the family property hers by law, and the help of child support, she'll be just fine.

This is the public story in the postfeminist age. In fact, most thirty- to forty-year-old mothers are in the same implicit marriage bargain as Lorna Wendt. As we have seen, the typical married-with-children family in the 1990s still has a semitraditional arrangement, with the husband the primary breadwinner and the wife the primary homemaker—even if she also works outside the home. And these typical wives are the very ones who, if anything, are hit hardest by divorce. The middle-class professional mother who has "done the right, responsible thing" and cut back on her career for the sake of her family quickly discovers that when it comes to divorce, no good deed goes unpunished.

Divorced women rarely discuss this and married women try not to think about it. But I was able to elicit this truth from numerous women, including the following two professionals, one in her fifties, the other in her thirties. Both of these women, who were kind enough to reveal intimate details of their lives, requested that their names be changed.

The older woman—we will call her Kate—was a brilliant young international economist when she married a man, also an economist, who was her junior professionally. In the 1970s they had two daughters, who were cared for by a nanny during the day and primarily by Kate in the evenings and on weekends.

By the time the younger child was five, Kate had risen to within reach of the upper ranks of the prestigious World Bank, hitherto an almost all-male preserve. But the pressures of a demanding job and a young family became intolerable, and she decided to take a year's leave of absence to do research and spend more time with the children. She was shocked to hear that a German coworker had said to one of her friends that she had probably committed career suicide.

He was more or less right. Soon after her return to the bank, she realized that despite her six-figure salary she had been shunted off the fast track and would never become one of the top officers of the organization. She decided to turn a negative into a positive by moving to a nonprofit think tank where the stress—and the salary—would be less. The family needed a flexible parent more than it needed the extra income.

All this time Kate's husband had been slowly rising at the bank, and after she switched jobs, he became the bigger breadwinner. This was irrelevant at the time. The scarcest family resource was parental time, and she could now contribute more of it to the family enterprise.

Then, while still in her forties, she had a serious illness, forcing her to take medical leave and eventually stop working altogether. She made a full recovery, but she decided that life was too short to go back to work full-time. She became a consultant, working from home on various international projects. The younger daughter was in high school, applying to colleges, and still needed a support system that included a parent on duty. It couldn't be her father, because he was now traveling overseas much of the time. Kate had to pinch-hit for him, even to the extent of buying birthday presents for a daughter's sixteenth birthday and pretending that they had come from him.

It was at this point that he announced, after twenty-five years of marriage, that he wanted a divorce. Of course there was another woman.

Their marital property by law in the District of Columbia, as in most states, had to be divided "equitably." But "equitable," like "need," is an elastic concept. Above all, property valuation is critical. As Kate explains, "You each are supposed to be getting 50 percent. But 50 percent of what? If the value of the stuff going to him is set too low, you're not getting any 50 percent. . . . If one partner handled the investments and the finances, as he did in our case, while the other was primarily responsible for the children, the mother will be playing catch-up in trying to challenge his valuations—and she is playing catch-up at $400 an hour, which is what she will be paying for a lawyer."

Kate believed that her husband's estimates of the value of his pension benefits and of rental property that he had managed were improbably low. Even a sports car he had purchased a couple of years earlier showed up on the list of assets valued at $23,000, although she knew he had paid $38,000 in cash for the vehicle.

She decided to do an asset analysis of her own and hired accountants to help her. But she believes that her attorney, one of the most high-powered divorce lawyers in Washington, D.C., didn't take her suggestions seriously. The car became a symbol of her frustration. At every meeting she would point out that its valuation was wrong, and every time her lawyer would brush the topic off as "too small" to worry about. Finally a young associate in the firm looked the car up in the Blue Book and found it had depreciated by only $1,000. The lawyer never apologized.

"It was a small point," she said later, "but it was indicative of their attitude. The wife's own attorneys have the attitude that she should take what he 'gives' her, not what she properly owns. It made me wonder about the whole system. It's a male thing—the lawyers, the judges, the mediators. I'd say something, and they'd dismiss me. I can't imagine how anyone without my background in finance could begin to cope with the complexities."

Kate is angry that after a quarter-century of marriage between two peers, her soon-to-be ex-husband is going forward with at least twice her income, what she is certain is more than half of the family assets, and the female companionship that eased him out of the marriage in the first place. As she puts it, "I'm having a hard time accepting the fact that I'm the one who got shafted, and he's the one who's rewarded." She is especially angry that none of this unfairness is even slightly relevant under the law.

At the beginning of settlement negotiations, she had informed her attorney that she wanted some financial compensation for her contributions of time and care to the family. He told her that this would be impossible; that alimony, or "spousal support," is rarely granted to someone who isn't hard up after a divorce. She was particularly bothered by the fact that the two court-appointed mediators, both married women in their thirties with young children, seemed to accept the withholding of compensation as a given.

"Both of them told me, 'Don't try to go for any spousal support; what you'll have in a property settlement will be adequate. You won't get anything more from these judges—don't even try,'" Kate reported to me during one of our Sunday hikes. "One of them had been a hotshot attorney in New York City and moved down here because of her husband's job. She took a huge salary cut. . . . I wanted to say to them, 'The chances are that one of the two of you will be in my place in a few years; don't you want to fight to change this?' But obviously they didn't see it."

I decided to call the "hotshot" attorney and find out whether Kate was right; whether it was true that an intelligent, informed married mother in her thirties really didn't realize that she could end up in the same boat. It turned out that she already had. In fact, her boat had almost sunk.

Pamela, as we will call her, had indeed left her law firm in Manhattan to move to Washington with her husband. The two had met in New York City while he was clerking for a judge and she was still in law school. Both had eventually joined big firms, and both had worked the notorious hours of young associates, even after their first child was born. It was the 1980s, and they were an upwardly mobile young couple on their way to having it all in the Big Apple.

Pamela was eight months pregnant with their second child when her husband received an offer from a federal agency in Washington, offering him a chance to join the Bush administration and practice the kind of securities law he loved. She agreed to follow him, and as a second-year associate weeks away from giving birth, she joined her firm's new Washington office.

The work turned out to be lobbying, which she disliked, and after the baby was born, she dropped back to part-time at the firm. But the relocation, the stresses of two young children, and the change in her work were all too much, and one year later, the seven-year marriage was over. The children were ages one and three.

Pamela moved into a spare bedroom in the basement, while her husband stayed upstairs, where the children slept. After a few weeks, he informed her that he had decided not only to sue for divorce but to seek custody of the children. He claimed that he had become the primary parent in the last few weeks of the marriage and could prove it.

He later presented the child psychiatrist who was to make the final custody decision with a multihundred-page, single-spaced diary detailing how he had become the children's principal caretaker in the weeks before the split—a document he had worked on late at night at home, while she thought he was just bringing work home from the office.

She claims that until the end of the marriage she had still been the primary parent, the one who got the kids up in the morning, dressed them and brushed their teeth, prepared them for bed at night, and read the bedtime stories. She had no proof, however; it had to be her word against his diary.

I asked if he had shared much of the parenting before those final weeks, and she dryly replied, "Absolutely not. He used to call from the office to make sure the kids were in bed before he came home at night. He worked a full day in the office and a half day at home on weekends."

Facing divorce, she left her part-time job, put the children in day care, and took a full-time position with a smaller firm. She thought this would enable her to survive financially and to cope with what became a full-scale custody battle. In the end she won custody of the children, but because her new salary was higher than her husband's government salary, she was awarded no alimony and very little child support.

During the custody dispute, her new firm had issued an ultimatum: she would have to increase her hours or leave. She was briefly able to boost her billable hours, but now she was a single mother of two small children, who could not afford to lose their mother as well as their father.

She finally gave up. She left the firm, and for two years she scraped by, barely supporting two children on occasional consulting and mediation work for the family court. The brisk, promising young attorney from Manhattan was now too poor and too afraid of the outcome to spend money on a lawyer to go back into court to ask for more child support. She never had to go on welfare, but she came close. (Today, of course, after welfare "reform," she couldn't qualify for public assistance anyway.)

In the end Pamela climbed out of near-poverty the age-old female way: she married another man. When we met, in the summer of 1995, she was in her late thirties and had just started working as the deputy CEO for the Washington affiliate of a national nonprofit housing organization. Her hours were 7:30 A.M. to 3:00 P.M., a schedule that allowed her to pick up her two children, now ages eight and ten, from school every day. The job paid less than half of her previous full-time salary, and much less than either her current or her former husband earned. But she was thankful that she had a stable, flexible job at all.

Her new office was in the gritty, largely Latin neighborhood of Adams-Morgan, bustling with bodegas and street vendors and cheap ethnic restaurants. It was a long way from the polished offices of the big New York law firm where Pamela had started her career. I thought of that cigarette ad campaign aimed at young women in the late 1970s: "You've come a long way, baby." She certainly had.

I asked Pamela if it was true that she had counseled women like Kate not to try to fight the antimaternal bias in the family law system.

"Change has to start before things fall apart," she said, toying with her fork and evading the question. "Somehow *work* has to allow for parenting."

My next stop was the office of Armin Kuder, one of the most prominent family lawyers in the Washington, D.C., bar. Kuder was still tied up when I arrived, so I spent a few minutes chatting with one of his junior associates, a pretty, petite woman in a tightly fitted suit who appeared to be in her early thirties.

I asked her what was likely to happen to a long-married wife and mother who gets divorced in the nation's capital. It turned out that the firm had just settled such a case in suburban Virginia, involving a twenty-eight-year marriage. The wife had never worked outside the home—she had "no skills," as the attorney put it—while the husband earned more than $90,000 a year. The wife had been awarded half of the property and compensation of $2,000 a month, leaving her with $24,000 a year to live on and her former husband more than $70,000.

The young lawyer interpreted this outcome as a fine, healthy recognition of the woman's contribution to the marriage. "There was never any discussion that she wouldn't get at least half of the assets," she said, as if that settled the matter. But what about the fact that the woman would now have to live on one-third of the income her husband would have? Even if she could find a job, she would still end up with a standard of living far lower than she had had during the marriage, while his lifestyle could continue more or less as before.

"There is *no* presumption in the law that there should be an equal standard of living between the two parties after divorce," she said, seemingly impatient with the very idea. "I don't think you're ever going to see that."

Kuder, a tall, lean man in his fifties, arrived and continued the lesson in Divorce 101. "If the wife is under fifty, and there are no kids to take care of, and she's not drooling or otherwise totally incompetent, the court will say this person has to become self-sufficient. You can forget long-term alimony."

"But what if she has spent twenty years or more raising children?" I asked. "Isn't there any credit for that?"

"When there are no kids at home anymore, the courts aren't offended unless there is a big disparity in income. . . . It is definitely true that the economically dependent person is still going to be economically disadvantaged. But it'll be manageable," Kuder said with a comfortable smile.

"What if the wife is in her thirties or forties and there are still kids at home?"

"The judge will ask two questions: How much money is involved? And what was their deal? Did they agree that she'd raise the kids while he made the money? If so, and there's plenty of money, she'll get some alimony.

"Otherwise . . . I had a client, a husband, who said the deal was that the wife would go back to work eighteen months after their first child was born. Then they had a second child, and after thirteen or fourteen months they looked at day-care centers. The husband subsequently left the marriage, and she decided not to go back to work at all. We proved they had looked at a day-care center, and that she had changed the deal when she decided to stay at home. So she got less money."

I pointed out that the typical arrangement left the husband with more income than all of the other people in the family put together. Was this fair?

Fair was not the issue. "The courts will consider *his* standard of living; *his* accustomed lifestyle," Kuder explained.

"What about her standard of living?"

"There is the expectation that someone else will take [care of that]. These things aren't said outright, but they are part of the calculation."

Kuder added that whatever a wife's contributions to the family, she would still be punished for adultery. He represented the husband in a case involving another twenty-eight-year marriage with two older children, in which the wife had kept the books and otherwise contributed to the family business. But the husband had obtained love letters proving that she had been having an affair for twenty-four years. These were read in court.

"One said, 'I love you even though I am carrying someone else's child.'. . . You could see the judge turning white as this [was] read. In the end she got only 26 percent of the property."

I thought of two of my friends who had been Kuder's clients. Both of their husbands had left them for younger women. Both men had broken up long marriages and decamped with more than half of the family assets and the great bulk of the former "family" income. Apparently extramarital adventures are punished only when wives have them.

These nasty little unwritten rules of divorce go a long way toward explaining the phenomenal success of *The First Wives Club,* a movie that grossed $100 million within two months of its release in 1996—thereby proving that female revenge fantasies can sell at least as well as men's.

Kuder and a number of other divorce attorneys in the nation's capital told me that two or three years after a divorce, an upper-middle-class mother and her children would probably be living at about half the level of their father—unless she could find another man. Thirty years after women's liberation, this is how far mothers have gotten.*

AND WHAT ABOUT Lorna Wendt, who posed the first serious challenge to the concept that family money is "his money"? After mulling over the case for months, Judge Tierney awarded her half of the family's hard assets of cash, stocks, and real estate. Going further, he expanded the definition of marital property to include deferred compensation, awarding the aggrieved wife a portion of her ex-husband's unexercised stock options and future pension benefits, plus a Macy's credit card entitling the holder to a 45 percent lifetime discount. All on top of alimony of $250,000 a year.

Both sides claimed victory. She increased her take-away portion of the family's wealth to roughly $20 million, more than twice what she had originally been offered. And he was still able to keep well over half of the fortune that he had amassed.

---

*White women often do regain their previous standard of living within a few years by remarrying. Five years after divorce, women who remarry on average enjoy a living standard that is 125 percent of their living standard in the year before the divorce.[9] But five years after divorce, those who do not remarry have still not regained their former living standard. And divorced *men* average 130 percent of their predivorce living standard five years later—whether they remarry or not.

The case had an immediate impact on divorce among the rich and famous. It sent a signal that the fancy new forms of compensation flowing into the coffers of the corporate elite would not be immune from serious sharing with a spouse. "*Wendt* will leave its fingerprints all over America," predicted Raoul Felder, a Manhattan lawyer who represented Elizabeth Taylor's latest husband.[10]

Within weeks of the verdict, wealthy wives were telling their lawyers, "I want to fight like Lorna Wendt." And in April of 1998 a New York judge, reportedly influenced by the Wendt case, granted the largest courtroom divorce award in New York state history to longtime homemaker Vira Goldman. Mrs. Goldman received half of an estimated $90 million in family assets. (Her former husband, Robert I. Goldman, the chief executive officer of Congress Financial Corporation, died a few months later, no doubt coincidentally.) When the former Mrs. Goldman met the former Mrs. Wendt six months later, they immediately became fast friends, according to an associate of Mrs. Wendt's.[11]

Lorna Wendt also had an answer to the frequently heard objection to serious property divisions: What would she *do* with all that money? She would become a philanthropist. She promptly created a new Institute for Equality in Marriage, designed to promote divorce reform.

CHAPTER 8

Who Really Owns the Family Wage?

Of course the husband owns his wage vis-à-vis his employer, but this does not determine whether he owns it vis-à-vis his family.

—Joan Williams, American University

In 1995, the divorce trial of a couple more typical than the Wendts ended in a small town in Ohio. The husband and wife, a truck driver and a homemaker, had been married for fifteen years. They had four children, including a newborn, but very little property or assets. Neither one had a college degree, and they had agreed early on that theirs would be a traditional marriage, with the wife working as a full-time homemaker.

The reason that the two were divorcing was also fairly typical: he had fallen in love with someone else. There was no custody dispute; he was happy to leave the children with their mother.

I heard about the case from Robin Bartlett, a professor of economics at Denison University in Ohio, who had been approached by the wife's attorney to be an expert witness at the trial. The lawyer wanted Bartlett to answer this question: How much money would the husband have to transfer to the wife each year so that everyone in the family would have the same standard of living after the divorce?

Bartlett was teaching a course at the time on women in the labor force. She thought the divorce case would be quite revealing about the economic prospects of women in the real world, so she asked her class of senior economics majors to come up with a fair financial settlement for the couple, whom she called "Jack and Jill."[1]

What's a Fair Divorce for Working Families?

Jill, like the great majority of married mothers, was financially dependent on Jack. He earned $49,774 a year as a truck driver, and she made about $4,500 a year from baby-sitting. She had never had any other paid job during the marriage. Bartlett's class calculated that the family's pre-divorce standard of living was 2.5 times the poverty rate for a family of six. They figured out that after the couple separated, Jack's standard of living—one person living on $49,774—would be 5.88 times greater than the poverty level. Jill and the children—five people living on $4,500—would have a standard of living only one-fourth (.26) of the poverty level.

The students figured that Jack would have to transfer to Jill three-fifths of his income—that is, $30,000 a year—to equalize the two households' living standards after the divorce. He would be left with $19,774, putting him at 1.98 times the poverty level (for a single individual). The children and Jill would have $34,500 and also be at 1.98 times the poverty level (for a family of five).

This exercise immediately demonstrated an important point about divorce: everyone ends up worse off financially if the costs are distributed evenly. This is primarily because two households are much more expensive than one. In Jack and Jill's case, an equitable distribution of the family's income would leave everyone with a standard of living 21 percent lower than they had enjoyed during the marriage.*

Bartlett told me that her class was particularly impressed with this stark fact. They got the message: divorce is incredibly costly. This is the principal reason why so many children of divorce are poor. No matter how well intentioned the parents may be, after a divorce they may not be able to afford their children anymore.

Almost everyone in the class, men and women alike, also believed that it was only fair that all members of a family should share the financial pain equally. Most of the students identified with the children in the case,

*In one study researchers found that after divorce a family will need about one-third more income in order to maintain its previous standard of living. According to another researcher, if a family's total income stays the same, "the couple can expect a drop in standard of living between 21 and 26%, depending on the number of children and how they are divided between the parents."[2]

possibly because many of them were from divorced families themselves. They wanted to protect the children from the consequences of a breakup they hadn't caused.

None of the students thought that Jill should have to leave the home and try to get a full-time job while the children were small. They recognized the value of her presence at home and realized that after so many years out of the job market she would be unable to find any work that would pay more than a bare minimum anyway. "They all figured that this was the way Jack and Jill had decided to run their little enterprise," Bartlett told me. "When two people form a union, it's like a partnership. Any income or wealth that's generated belongs to both, and so do any liabilities. In the end, if the partnership fails, nobody should pay a higher price than the other."

The class didn't believe that a financial partnership between two divorced individuals should last forever. They thought that as each child reached eighteen, Jack's transfers could be reduced and the equal standard of living still maintained; and that when the last child reached a majority, Jack's obligation should end. Jill should use the intervening years to prepare to support herself once her job of child-rearing was over.

Bartlett presented all of these findings in testimony during the divorce trial that spring, with her students sitting in the courtroom. Jack's attorney proposed a standard settlement: an equal division of the couple's assets and liabilities, no alimony, and child support of less than $10,000 a year, which was in accordance with state guidelines. This proposal would have left Jack with almost $40,000 a year, and Jill and the four children will less than $15,000 a year. Like roughly 40 percent of all divorced women in the United States, Jill would tumble into poverty, probably have to go on welfare temporarily, before going to work full-time, provided she could find child care.

This would have been the usual outcome in a very typical American divorce. Bartlett's students were shocked to learn that no law in Ohio—or any other state—requires an equal standard of living for all members of postdivorce households. They were surprised to discover that no lawyer in their county had ever even utilized the kind of basic economic analysis they had done. They were even more surprised when one lawyer told them that Jill and the children stood almost no chance of receiving as much money as the class had calculated they needed.

The lawyer turned out to be right, but just barely. The court, demonstrating that expert testimony can make a difference, awarded Jill a far better settlement than most women in her situation usually get. She received $15,000 a year in child support for the four children, plus $7,200 a year in spousal support, giving her a total income of $26,700, counting her own earnings of $4,500. That left Jack, assuming he continued to earn the same income, with $27,574 a year. He would still have a far higher standard of living than other family members, and far more than the impartial college class felt he deserved, but surely less than his new sweetheart had hoped. At last report he was contesting the settlement.

The case gave Bartlett's students, especially the men, plenty of food for thought. "I now realize that women get the short end of the stick in divorces, especially if they keep the children," commented one male student. "I had always thought it unfair that the man had to give up so much money. Now I can't even imagine a woman not receiving what she needs." Another student wrote, "It became increasingly apparent that the number one rule in life was 'Don't Get Divorced.'" The case taught a third student that "divorce is a messy and complicated process, especially when children are involved. I have learned to avoid divorce at all costs." Still another male student wrote that the exercise would make him "extremely careful" about his future plans.

The female students were especially struck by the implications of a mother's dependency when marriage fails. "I can understand now why so many divorced women and children are poor," one of them commented.

AS THE CASE of "Jack and Jill" illustrates, in most broken families, the principal asset is not property but the two adults' earning power: the diamond of marital property. Unless this jewel—the couple's joint income—is shared for some fixed period after divorce, children and their caregivers will continue to pay by far the heaviest price.

This realization has spawned a new generation of family law reformers, who are trying to find persuasive justifications for postdivorce income sharing. Their ultimate goal is for all family members to emerge from a marital breakdown with roughly equal standards of living, so that no one, specifically children and those who care for them, suffers disproportionately from the failure of a marriage. This was the intuitively fair solution recommended by Robin Bartlett's students.

From Alimony to Compensation

In February of 1994, I attended the symposium "Divorce and Feminist Legal Theory," sponsored by the Georgetown University School of Law, in Washington, D.C. It was my first exposure to the new ideas buzzing around the movement for equality in marriage, and for two days I sat like a fly on the wall, listening to discussions that reminded me of the revolutionary ferment of the late 1960s. Change was in the wind.

The speakers included several dozen female law professors and a few men. Interestingly, the fierce pressures that have driven so many women with children out of the major law firms have attracted some of the best and brightest female attorneys into university teaching. Outraged by the continuing inequities in modern marriage, these women have mounted a massive intellectual campaign on behalf of economic equality in the family. In dozens of articles and at gatherings like the one I attended, these reformers are talking about bringing the women's revolution home at last.

One of the most formidable speakers at the symposium was Joan Williams, a professor of law at American University in Washington. The key problem for mothers, Williams argued, is the fundamental assumption that the income flowing into families does not belong to all family members, but only to the individual who earns it. In her view, both parents' earnings should instead be considered joint marital property belonging to everyone in the family, including the children—a true "family wage."[3]

Traditionally, under English common law—which became the basis for marriage law in the majority of states in the United States—a husband had sole ownership of all family property and income, including any wages the wife might earn. This was the legal doctrine of coverture, hich a wife was legally subsumed under her husband after marriage. s literally did not exist as independent citizens, able to make contracts or own property of their own. As we have seen, American wives did not win the right to own their own property and keep their own wages until the mid–nineteenth century, although most still had neither. To this day, mothers have no legal right to the greatest single financial asset that most families possess: the primary breadwinner's income. Nothing exposes this truth more starkly than divorce.

As Williams pointed out, "a man can overinvest in his career with the secure social knowledge that if his marriage fails, he can walk away with his wallet and enter the secondary marriage market largely unimpaired."[4] Women, on the other hand, invest heavily in their children but have nothing like the same security.

Despite the obvious inequity, most legal scholars doubt whether the concept of marital property can be expanded to cover income. In an effort to help family dependents devastated by divorce, the notion of joint property has already been stretched to include pensions, stock options, a share in any business started during the marriage, personal injury awards, even frequent flyer miles. In some states the future value of advanced degrees and professional licenses, including a professional athlete's contract and a stock exchange seat, have also been considered divisible marital property. (My own favorite example is a divorce settlement that gave Rita Lucas an equal share of any Nobel prize money her husband might receive in the future. Seven years later, in 1995, Robert E. Lucas did win the prize in economics, and as agreed, he split the $1-million prize with his ex-wife. "A deal is a deal," this excellent man told a reporter.)

But appellate courts in the majority of states have consistently rejected the argument that degrees and licenses are marital property, and they are even less likely to swallow the idea that an individual's income is not his personal property. Most of the discussion at the Georgetown conference therefore centered on another justification for postdivorce income sharing: the idea that a caregiving spouse deserves some *compensation* for her financial sacrifices.

The new theory gaining acceptance is this: if one spouse incurs a loss of earning power during the marriage because she or he has fulfilled the family's obligations to care for children, then she or he has earned the right to compensation from the other spouse in the event of divorce.*

In other words, if one partner incurs a mommy tax, the other spouse is obligated to reimburse her (or him) for part of the loss. Rather than charity, based on need, alimony is morphing into compensation, or something earned. According to June Carbone, a professor of law at the University of California at Santa Clara, this is the "emerging model" of alimony.

The American Law Institute, a group of prominent jurists, legal scholars, and attorneys, has issued a set of recommendations on family law that calls for compensation for caregivers. Noting that lost earnings during marriage are both significant and common, and "cannot be ignored by the law," the ALI's *Principles of the Law of Family Dissolution* recommend that the caregiving spouse—typically the wife—should be awarded compensation if she can prove two things: first, that she has a lower income at the time of divorce than when she married; and second, that she performed "substantially more than half of the child care."[5]

Spouses in childless marriages of short duration would not qualify for compensation. As one lawyer pointed out, "It's the parenting that creates an entitlement to marital earnings."

ALI recommendations are not binding unless they are incorporated into law by state legislatures. But a number of states have already amended their laws to make it easier for courts to award compensation to primary caregivers. The new state laws allow the following factors to be considered in spousal support: "periods of unemployment" as a result of performing "domestic duties"; "contributions to child care"; "the care and education of children"; "the well-being of the children"; "impaired earning capacity"; and "lost income production capacity."[6] In Canada, the Supreme Court has also reconceptualized alimony along these lines.

That is the good news. The bad news is that many judges and practicing divorce lawyers are still either unfamiliar with the new principles or dead set against applying them in favor of ex-wives. Although one study found that 80 percent of women assume they will be able to get alimony

*This concept of compensation is based on the theory that if one spouse's human capital (that is, experience, skills, earning capacity, etc.) deteriorates during the marriage because of service to the family, then that person is entitled to some recompense for the loss.

if they need it (or earned it), in fact only about 8 percent are actually awarded any.[7]

Indeed, the emerging consensus in support of compensation for caregivers is virtually unknown outside academia. Judges and attorneys in several states assured me that "theoretical" debates about justice in divorce were so much Sanskrit to family court judges, administrators, legislators, mediators, and attorneys—not to mention the public. Apparently, the legal profession doesn't read the journals the way the medical profession does, even though the consequences of ignorance can be just as devastating to clients.

Leslie Spillane, a domestic relations judge in Hamilton, Ohio, told me that only after she started researching a master's thesis on spousal support did she discover that a state statute had been amended in the 1990s to allow compensation to a caregiving spouse who has suffered a loss of earning capacity. When she interviewed the very legislators who had passed the law, she discovered that "the guys didn't know what it meant. The literature had seeped into the statutes, but no one understood it."[8]

(An alternative explanation is that "the guys" don't want to grasp the fact that divorced mothers have the right "to bargain in the shadow" of laws that strengthen their hand.)

Judges have also demonstrated a deep fear of "commercializing" marriage by putting a price tag on caring labor and requiring husbands to pay part of that price, even though it is increasingly clear that "women's historic poverty stems in significant part from the way successive legal regimes have turned their labor into love, leaving property the province of men," as Joan Williams cogently puts it.[9]

Courts all over the United States still require a wife to show that she needs alimony, not that she earned compensation. In order to claim any share of a breadwinner's income, a wife has to paint herself as a charity case that her husband is morally obligated to assist. This mentality was vividly expressed by Craig McCaw, the multimillionaire entrepreneur, during his divorce case—the largest ever filed in the state of Washington. In rejecting his wife's financial claims, McCaw noted, "I have a lot of other goals and aspirations and if I were picking places to charitably expend my money, this would not be the first."[10] (McCaw's attitude did not prevent his wife from receiving a huge share of the couple's business.

The Best and Worst States for Divorced Mothers

Divorce is like a lottery, but in some states, the odds are better for the parent who is the primary caregiver.

Besides child support (which I address in the next chapter), the financial outcome of a divorce is dependent on two factors: the division of property and alimony (or spousal support, maintenance, or compensation, as it is more often called today).

In most states, the divisible property includes everything acquired during the marriage, excluding personal gifts and inheritances. (Fourteen states, however, are so-called kitchen sink states, where everything, no matter when or how it was acquired, is considered joint property and divisible in the event of a divorce. These fourteen states are Washington, Oregon, Montana, Wyoming, North Dakota, South Dakota, Kansas, Mississippi, Michigan, Indiana, Vermont, New Hampshire, Massachusetts, and Connecticut.)

In only three states—California, New Mexico, and Louisiana—does marital property have to be divided fifty-fifty. These are therefore the safest places for a wife and mother of substance. In six other states—Idaho, Nevada, Arkansas, West Virginia, North Carolina, and New Hampshire—judges start with a presumption that property should be split fifty-fifty.

In most states, marital property must be divided "equitably" by the courts. This is supposed to mean "fairly" but in practice can mean anything from giving a caregiver more than half the marital property to giving her only a fraction, as often happens in cases involving great wealth.

If stock options are part of the assets, the wife would be best off in the few states, including Maryland and Wisconsin, that are more likely to divide options between spouses. Corporate wives who can should avoid Oklahoma, which tends to allow the breadwinner to keep all of his stock options—though since the Wendt decision the treatment of options is changing.

Alimony is more important than property in divorces where the breadwinner's income is relatively high but the couple has not been married long enough to have accumulated much property. Yet, if anything, alimony is even more of a crapshoot. The laws vary from jurisdiction to jurisdiction, and a caregiver is subject to the whims and vagaries of whatever judge she happens to draw. The only generalizations are these: the great majority of awards are of short duration, and alimony is generally awarded only after a long-term marriage. It is also safe to say that a wife who has an affair has kissed her chances of alimony good-bye.

In Texas, alimony was against the law until quite recently. In Washington state, in contrast, alimony can be used to equalize the postdivorce income of the two parties. In Georgia, alimony can be lowered or terminated if the recipient has a live-in lover of either sex.

Even within the same jurisdiction, alimony awards are generally unrelated to the husband's income, the wife's share of the property, the couple's average net worth, or the wife's unpaid contributions as a mother and homemaker. The overwhelming impression one gets from reviewing judicial decisions on spousal support is their striking arbitrariness. This wild unpredictability makes divorce acrimonious and expensive. In almost every state the outcome depends on who has the better lawyer. This is rarely the wife.

A handful of states are relatively generous to long-term homemakers. Courts in Massachusetts, Minnesota, Montana, Vermont, and Washington have stressed the importance of a similar postdivorce standard of living for both spouses after lengthy marriages, although exceptions abound.

Some judgments are gratuitously mean to long-term homemakers. An appeals court in Wisconsin reduced an alimony award of $6,000 a month to a wife in her midfifties after a thirty-three-year marriage. The husband earned $260,000 a year as a lawyer, and after taxes and alimony still had almost $10,000 a month for himself. But the judges decided that the wife could be "comfortable" on $3,600 a month.

In Kentucky, a judge denied any maintenance to a wife in her late fifties who had been married for thirty-four years and couldn't find a job. He reasoned that she could live just fine off her marital property of $533,000, noting that she could invest the money at a 9 percent yield and have a more than adequate annual income of $48,000.

At the time of this sage advice, interest rates on treasury bills and savings accounts were roughly 3 percent, and stock dividends were at historic lows. If this woman knew how to earn a safe 9 percent on her money, she could've found a job on Wall Street.

In the end, the best state for divorce is a state of affluence. Most wives and mothers don't live there.

She is now worth about $1.5 billion, making her one of the wealthiest women in America, and a major philanthropist.)

Usually only the oldest, most helpless long-term homemakers are "awarded" any compensation for their caregiving services, and even then for a limited time. In most states, if a mother has been married for less than ten years, is relatively young and able-bodied, and has any ability to support herself, she has about as much chance of getting compensation as she has of winning the lottery.

In a typical case, a New York appeals court in 1989 threw out an alimony award to a schoolteacher-mother who had been married twenty-three years. The woman, who was in her forties, had an income of $28,000 a year, and her husband, roughly the same age, earned $40,000. Her salary was lower because she had taken ten years out of the job market to raise their children. The court conceded that had she remained in teaching throughout the marriage, their salaries would have been approximately the same. But the judges saw no reason to balance out the penalties of divorce by ordering the husband to compensate the wife for her financial sacrifice of one-third of her earning capacity. Since she didn't need more than $28,000 a year, the court reasoned, she would have to get along on that.

Law professor Ann Estin discovered the systemic refusal to compensate for caregiving after two of her friends in their midthirties called her for advice on their impending divorces. While one woman was an ex-schoolteacher and the other a former interior decorator, both had been at home with young children for about five years. They wondered what financial consideration they could expect for having quit their jobs in order to raise their children.

Estin, the mother of two young daughters, had already paid a hefty mommy tax herself. Her first child was born just as her term as a clerk to a federal district judge was ending. She had then joined a small law firm as a litigator but found the work "incredibly hard" to combine with motherhood. While on maternity leave with her second child, she accepted a teaching job. Her family's income fell to a fraction of what it once was, but Estin describes herself as "incredibly fortunate" to have found such a satisfying alternative to the practice of law.[11]

Estin's research on behalf of her two friends ultimately produced an article summarizing what young mothers in the 1990s who put their children first can expect in the way of compensation: virtually nothing. "My friends were shocked when I told them they would get no alimony," Estin told me. "And I was taken aback. I thought, 'Why is this work of child-rearing so invisible? Isn't it socially valuable?'"

In her study of appellate court decisions around the United States, Estin found few cases of alimony awards to caregivers with children at home, except in Missouri.[12] And even in Missouri, a separate survey conducted in the mid-1980s discovered that in no case did a custodial parent get enough alimony and child support to keep a standard of living comparable to that during the marriage.[13]

Even if a woman relinquishes her career entirely in order to care for her children and support her husband's career, he will not necessarily have to reimburse her. Her unpaid services to the family are considered a "gift." In fact, a California study, looking at a large sample of divorcing couples with at least one child under sixteen, found that well-educated women who had worked and supported themselves before they married and had children were especially unlikely to receive alimony—even if they had left the job market years before.[14]

If the mother is working at the time of divorce, her chances of compensation are even slimmer. A study of alimony awards in a relatively affluent suburb of Detroit in the 1980s revealed that even the judges who most often awarded alimony did not give it to working mothers, although their income was less than one-half that of their husbands.[15]

Lynne Gold-Bikin, a family law attorney in Norristown, Pennsylvania, describes the no-win situation mothers typically face: "When a mother of three comes into court, the judge will say, 'Do you work?' If she does, no alimony. She doesn't 'need' it. If she is at home, the opposing lawyer will say, 'You don't work, do you?'—implying that she is lazy. No one is saying, 'What is the value of this woman's work as a parent?'"[16]

In this regard, middle- and upper-income mothers are in exactly the same boat as poor mothers. If they lose the financial support of their children's father, and don't immediately go to work full-time, they are branded as parasites trying to live off the toil and sweat of others. The only difference between "alimony drones" and "welfare queens" is their social status.

"You can't imagine the level of bitterness and hatred there is toward alimony in this country," says Diane Dodson, an attorney formerly with the Women's Legal Defense Fund. "It is almost impossible to sell."[17] Despite the new theories justifying compensation for unpaid caregiving, between 1990 and 1994 alone there was a 9.5 percent drop in the number of people reporting income from alimony.[18] When alimony is awarded it is almost always designed to tide the dependent spouse over until she is "rehabilitated," i.e., self-supporting—prompting Ann Estin to suggest that it is family law that needs to be rehabilitated.

Divorced mothers who are raising children, like welfare mothers, are not supposed to "sit around at home all day"; they are expected to go out and get a "real" job. In 1995, when Estin presented a proposal to the American Bar Association for "alimony for children," calling for enough compensation so that divorced mothers with young children would not necessarily have to go back to work full-time, the general reaction was "No judge will buy it."[19]

This leaves only one other rationale for distributing joint family income to mothers and children after divorce: child support. Women's and children's advocates have concluded that the battle for postdivorce fairness simply cannot be won in the name of mothers. It has to be fought in the name of the children.

CHAPTER 9

Who Pays for the Kids?

> Mothers have always understood that having children decreases future freedom. Fathers need to learn the same lesson.
>
> —Joan Williams

The boy had been a handful all his life. Severly emotionally disturbed, he had had problems as early as grade school, and in junior high he was caught bringing a weapon to school and was expelled. At that point his mother made him her first priority. She transferred him to a special private school and quit her job as a manager at Roy Rogers. This enabled her to drop him off in the mornings and pick him up in the afternoons and make sure that he got the help that he needed. Over the next six months the boy thrived in this new environment and showed marked improvement both in his schoolwork and in his conduct.

With the mother's reduced earnings, however, money was tight, so she petitioned for an increase in child support. She and the boy's father had never married, but paternity had been established and the father had been ordered to pay a small amount of support. When the order came up for review, the judge did increase it, but he did not require the father to pay half of the rising costs of the child's schooling, tutoring, and medical bills. The judge held that having a mother at home was a luxury that the father should not be expected to underwrite.[1]

As this case indicates, the child support system has been heavily influenced by the growing cultural norm that mothers as well as fathers should work outside the home. The value of the work they do in the home, on behalf of their families, can't compete, despite the that children need care just as much as money, or maybe even r

Welcome to the child support system, American style. Always catch-as-catch-can, varying from state to state, one thing holds true: support is viewed as monetary, almost never in terms of parental time or care. Indeed, the working mother who decides to care for her offspring, rather than maximize her income, should expect to see her child punished with lower support from the father if divorce or separation occurs.

This is not a trend many people see, because child care is largely absent from discussions of child support. The official news is that child support is improving as the federal government pushes the states, kicking and screaming, to take enforcement more seriously. But as we shall see, there is much more to the story.

An initiative to improve the collection of child support was indeed launched in the mid-1980s, after the inadequacy of the system finally became a nationwide scandal. The drive for tougher enforcement was instigated by an odd-couple alliance between fiscal conservatives in the Reagan administration and liberal advocates for poor women and children. The Reaganites wanted to reduce government spending by "privatizing welfare," that is, by making fathers pay more of the cost of supporting their offspring, who often ended up on welfare. The liberal advocates were anxious to increase mothers' share of the postdivorce family income as a means of reducing maternal and child poverty.

As is often the case in such campaigns, an enemy was created to whip up popular enthusiasm. The "deadbeat dad" became the target of countless articles and speeches, joining the "welfare mom" as a new folk figure, scapegoat, and national disgrace.

The first step toward his eradication was taken in 1984, when Congress ordered every state to establish numerical, statewide guidelines to be used to determine child support awards. Numerous studies had shown that support awards varied drastically from state to state, from county to county in the same state, and even from judge to judge within the same county. Parents had no idea what they could expect when they went to court, and support levels were often totally unrelated to the parents' income, not to mention the actual expenditures on children.

According to Maureen Pirog-Good of Indiana University, an authority on child support, "the feds were brought in" because "there were so many grossly inequitable and varying awards."[2]

The states themselves were to set the proper level of child support, and to assist them, the federal Department of Health and Human Services developed a set of model guidelines. The template that was produced, and eventually adopted by more than thirty states, was based on "income shares," and it required both parents to share the cost of the children in proportion to their relative incomes. Thus, if a noncustodial father earned two-thirds of the parents' total income, he would be expected to pay two-thirds of the "cost of the child." That would be his child support.

Note that according to this formula, both parents have to contribute money proportionately, but not care. Time and care do not count. The formula is called "income shares," not "care shares." The custodial parent—the one who gets the children ready for school and sends them off with breakfast and a kiss, who takes time off work for school conferences, doctor's appointments, and sick days, who arranges play dates, leaves work in time for dinner, talks over the day's events, spends evenings helping with homework, and reads the bedtime stories—gets no credit for any of this under the child support guidelines used in most states.[3]

In general, custodial mothers earn less than their former husbands, often precisely because of their parenting responsibilities. But the guidelines expect them to devote the same proportion of this lower income to the financial support of their children, *and* to provide most of the care. In other words, the child support formulas in most states are deeply regressive, and in effect, discourage care.

"Guidelines are based on a percentage of income, and fathers always say that mothers should kick in the same percentage," states Marilyn L. Ray, an expert on the issue. "But they do this and more. Typically, a mother makes one-third to one-half of what the father makes, and has all the overhead—the house, the car, baby-sitters, et cetera. Her contribution to those kids may be 100 percent of her income—far more than his."[4]

The "income shares" formula also grossly underestimates the actual costs of raising a child. It leaves out savings for college, or the expense of a house in a suitable neighborhood, or any number of unexpected costs that may confront parents. Above all, it omits the single biggest cost of a child: the loss of income of the primary caregiver. In other words, the child support guidelines, from the very beginning, made sure that divorced and single mothers would continue to pay most of the steadily rising costs of rearing a child.

In effect, the child support levels for the majority of American families are based on little more than guesstimates, and not on any survey of actual expenditures. When I realized this, I decided to find out what a child really costs.

MOST NEW PARENTS have no idea what they are getting into. Recently, while looking at the Web site Hipmama.com, I found an on-line conversation in which people were telling a prospective mother that all she had to worry about was the price of diapers and an occasional baby-sitter.

I didn't have the heart to chime in with the naked truth: a baby is ferociously expensive. So expensive, in fact, that inner-city schoolteachers sometimes use the government's estimates on the cost of children to scare teenagers away from pregnancy.

"They tell me it works," says Mark Lino, an economist at the Department of Agriculture who calculates these sums every year. "Kids usually guess that a baby will cost them a few hundred dollars a year. They're shocked to find out it's several thousand in the first year alone."[5] According to Lino's estimates, a middle-income family (with an average net income of $43,094) in the urban West would have to spend about $850 month, or 19 percent of the family budget, on one child, and $1,355 per month, or 37 percent of family expenditures, on two. In an upper-income family (with an average net income of $81,700 a year), one child would cost $1,210 a month and two children $1,910 a month, including health and child care. None of these estimates, Lino notes, includes college expenses or the value of a custodial parent's time.[6]

By the time a child finishes high school, even a low-income couple can expect to have spent roughly $170,000. Middle-income parents can easily spend twice that before a child is college age, and among high-income families direct expenditures can reach $1 million on top of forgone earnings of another $1 million. In the early 1990s *Town & Country* magazine reported with no detectable irony that the cost of raising a child just to age eighteen would run about $679,483, or more than $37,000 a year. (*T&C* threw in a "learning psychologist" at $3,000 a year and a $10,000 teenager's "utility car.")

Another way of looking at the cost of children is to ask the question this way: How much more money would a couple need if they had a child and wanted to preserve the same standard of living? According to the Department of Labor, families would need a 26 percent increase in income to stay even with one child and a 46 percent increase with two. But what generally happens when a child arrives is that the family's income goes down just when it needs to go up, because one parent, almost always the mother, usually decides to cut back on paid work.

Women's and children's advocates understood the implications of the government's recommended guidelines immediately. They knew the "income shares" formula would ensure that divorced women and their children would continue to bear the economic brunt of divorce, except in the relatively few cases in which the father had custody or the custodial mother earned more money. They knew that even if the new guidelines were 100 percent enforced, and all the noncustodial parents conscientiously paid their support obligations in full, their payments would still amount to no more than a fraction of the real cost of raising a child.

But the federal government put its enormous weight behind "income shares," essentially because it was the only approach to child support reform that would be politically acceptable to male-dominated state legislatures. By 1989, when the use of guidelines became mandatory for all states, the "income shares" formula had become the dominant basis for determining child support in the United States.

"Basically, the states took a theory that allowed them to codify the status quo, which forced divorced mothers to pay most of the costs of raising their children," says Marilyn Ray Smith, chief legal counsel of the Massachusetts Office of Child Support.[7] "One thing we've learned is that in spite of all that has been done on strengthening enforcement, the situation of divorced women and their children has not dramatically improved," Richard R. Petersen of the Social Science Research Council told me in 1996, years after guidelines had been adopted. "The kinds of awards they'd need to get are fairly huge, and probably deserved, but judges just aren't going to give them."[8]

The Great California Mommy War

Just how difficult it has been to improve the child support system was made clear in California, where divorce rates were higher, and support payments lower, than almost anywhere else in the country. A move in the early 1990s to make California fathers pay more of the costs of their children unleashed a massive backlash that took everyone by surprise. It was led, not by angry white men or by a million black men marching on Sacramento, but by women—the divorced fathers' second wives.

The California mommy war began in 1988, when state senator Gary Hart (no relation to the former senator and presidential aspirant) was watching a late-night talk show about the devastating effects of divorce on women and children. Hart, who had been in the California legislature for almost twenty-five years, was something of an expert on family law, but he was unaware of the economic fallout of marital breakup.

The next morning Hart instructed his staff to verify the information he had heard on TV. His office quickly learned that empirical studies in such diverse states as Vermont, Maryland, Utah, Oregon, and Alaska had found that the economic penalties of divorce fell disproportionately on women and children. According to Drew Liebert, one of Hart's staffers, the legislator became convinced that the state had a serious problem and he made up his mind to fix it.*

California in 1988 was an exemplar of the chaos that the congressional guidelines were intended to remedy. "The levels were set by county, and

---

*The most in-depth study on divorce outcomes in California subsequently found that child support awards to mothers in California in the mid-1980s were actually somewhat higher than awards to mothers in a national sample. But given the "sharp disparity in economic well-being between divorced mothers and fathers," the authors of this study concluded that most fathers in their sample could afford to pay more. The report revealed that the immediate drop in the income of divorced mothers was almost twice that of fathers. Four years after the divorce, mothers' median annual earnings were still only about 60 percent of fathers' ($21,596 versus $37,887), even though 82 percent of the mothers were working. When child support was factored in, the disparity was reduced only slightly, even assuming full compliance. The average child support payment was only 10 percent of the father's gross income for one child. If a father shared custody, child support was even lower. Only two-thirds of California fathers who shared legal and physical custody were ordered to pay any child support, and among those who did, the average payment for two children was only 8 percent of the father's income—even when fathers earned considerably more than the mothers.[9]

they varied wildly," Liebert explained to me. "Kern County, for example, was substantially lower than the county next door. In many counties the average support order was around $50 a month, regardless of the man's income."[10] Even high-earning fathers in 1988 were required to pay no more than $300 a month in a state with one of the highest costs of living.[11]

"It was hard to debate the fact that something had to be done," Liebert said. "And then the federal government passed a law saying that every state had to follow a uniform child support guideline."

Diane Dodson of the Women's Legal Defense Fund was among the experts brought in to advise Hart's staff on the issue. She saw the California situation as a golden opportunity. Her own research had concluded that California was among the bottom nine states in terms of providing children with a decent standard of living and achieving equity in postdivorce households.[12] If new statewide guidelines were written right in California, the country's most populous state, they could set a progressive precedent for the nation, Dodson reasoned.[13]

To satisfy the new federal requirement, the California legislature ordered the adoption of a temporary statewide guideline, raising support levels. Then in 1990, Hart introduced legislation establishing permanent guidelines.

His proposal defined child support as a simple percentage of the noncustodial parent's net income—the second most popular formula after income shares. But fathers in California were used to receiving substantial reductions in support payments if they had custody for more than the typical one-night-a-week, one-weekend-a-month arrangement. This "discount" was justified on the grounds that the father's expenses went up the more custody he had.

The trade-off between time and money—or "time shares"—was a major reason that the state's support payments had been so low. It was also blatantly unfair, for a mother didn't receive an equivalent "credit"—an increase in payments—if the father failed to honor his custody commitments. The law never equated mothers' time with money, the way it did fathers' time. As one woman's advocate put it, "a mother's time is a freebie right off the top."

Hart's attempt to eliminate the discount unleashed a firestorm of protest from divorced fathers. The hearings on the bill were incendiary, and Hart's staff were suddenly aware that they had touched a political third rail. "We were into something big and difficult and scary," Liebert recalled. "We felt the pressure. We learned that these family law issues are the most volatile things that you can get into."

In the 1992 legislative session, a compromise was reached. The final formula for the new state child support guideline was murderously complex, but its impact was clear enough: it raised support levels by 25 percent on average. The California legislators, few of whom fully understood what they were doing, according to several of their own staffers, approved a bill that catapulted the state from the bottom to near the top in terms of child support. By one calculation, the new guidelines placed California fourth among the states in average per capita child support payments required of noncustodial parents.[14]

The bill was signed into law with some fanfare by Republican governor Pete Wilson in May 1992. It was heralded as emergency welfare reform legislation, intended to reduce the state's budget deficit. California, like the federal government, hoped to cut its welfare expenses by shifting more of the cost of children onto their dads. The postdivorce playing field was going to be leveled, and fathers were right in front of the steamroller. No more moms scrimping on food money while dads polished their sports cars. California fathers were about to learn the lesson that mothers already knew: children do not come cheap.

As word of the new guidelines spread, divorced mothers began hauling their former husbands into court for modification of their support orders. Many men's payments doubled, even tripled. Lori Sanders-Crabb, a housewife from Bakersfield, was in the courtroom when a judge more than tripled her husband's monthly support payments for a child from his previous marriage. Stunned, she went straight home from the courthouse to write a petition to repeal the law. It was the beginning of a grassroots movement.

"The new guidelines were the genesis of fathers' rights groups in California," Liebert recalled. "I remember we agreed to meet with this fledgling group out of Bakersfield where some of the biggest jumps in support were taking place. That was when we saw for the first time how angry the second wives were over this."

Thus was launched a war on first wives. The protesters, calling themselves COPS (Coalition of Parent Support) quickly attracted support from mostly white, middle-class Republican men and their second wives, often mothers themselves. COPS soon had chapters all over the state, offering emotional support and resources for fund-raising and lobbying. By 1995 the group claimed 3,000 to 4,000 members, about half of whom were women.

COPS recognized early on that the second wives could make a more compelling case than fathers trying to wiggle out of child support, and the women eagerly took up the cause. A group of COPS activists left hundreds of balloons plastered with their children's pictures in legislators' offices, after testifying in tears that first wives' children were taking food from their own babies' mouths. They picketed the Los Angeles offices of NOW with signs reading "Second wives are women, too," and informed the American Association of University Women that the AAUW's support of increased child support did not represent the views of all women. They disrupted rallies of divorced women and staged protests outside courthouses in Los Angeles, Orange, Riverside, and San Bernardino counties. It made a great story: mothers against mothers, forcing the law to choose one child's welfare over another's.[15]

With the Republican party's backing, COPS won several victories, including legislation to exclude second wives' income from calculations of child support, and a gradual phase-in of the higher support levels for fathers who had been keeping up with their payments. But the moment of truth was scheduled to occur in January of 1996, when a COPS-supported bill to roll back child support by some 25 percent was up for a key vote in the assembly's Judiciary Committee. If it passed in the full assembly, California would fall below the middle ranks of states in terms of support guidelines. Similar bills had been defeated in 1994 and 1995, but this year the Republicans had a majority in the assembly, and the bill was given an excellent chance of passage. A nationwide grassroots rebellion of fathers against the new child support guidelines had already scored some notable victories elsewhere. A fathers' rights group called POPS—Parents Opposed to Punitive Support—had succeeded in rolling back support guidelines in Indiana, and guidelines for payments by upper-income fathers had been lowered in Washington state.

I decided to go out to Sacramento for the big showdown. California has long had a reputation as a bellwether state, and I was curious to see whether one of the country's boldest efforts to make the costs of parenting more equitable could survive there. I reasoned that if tough child support could make it in California, it could make it anywhere. The state's unruly denizens had rolled back property taxes, curbed the premiums of auto insurance companies, fought to eliminate social services to legal immigrants, and all but rioted in the streets to protect their pocketbooks. Tax rebels and citizen activists are among the state's native fauna. If California could sustain a substantial transfer of income to children and ex-wives then a similar redistribution of the costs of care might prevail in the country as a whole.

On the day of the Judiciary Committee vote, I headed for the ornate state capitol, set in a forty-acre palm-filled park in the middle of the old city of Sacramento. Constructed soon after the gold rush began to fill the state's coffers, the classical revival-style building has been the scene of countless reshufflings of the state's wealth ever since. But this week the principal protagonists were not giant industries or powerful interest groups but families, fighting over how their resources would be divided among their children.

The hallway outside hearing room 444 was jammed with COPS supporters. Most of them appeared to be in their thirties and were milling about like excited classmates at a reunion, handing out cards and exchanging greetings. I tried to imagine a similar scene of mothers, backed by their second husbands, enthusiastically lobbying to reduce their financial support of their firstborn. I couldn't.

I sat down next to Irene Villapardo, a thirty-six-year-old clerical worker who had married her husband, Fred, after his wife had found him in bed with Irene and kicked him out. Dolores, the first wife, had hacked up the bed with an ax, burned Fred's clothes in the backyard, and sworn to kill him if she ever saw him again. Dolores had not hesitated to invoke the new child support guidelines in order to have Fred's payments increased in 1992 from $380 to $963 a month for his two sons, Aaron (fifteen) and Eric (ten). Irene, the pretty, dark-haired second wife, was afraid that the increase would prevent her from having children with Fred, a meat cutter. She and Fred had a combined income of $62,600, compared to the $30,000 Dolores earned working for a grocery store chain.

Both women had told their side of the story to a *Los Angeles Times* reporter. Dolores had described how she and the children had lived on rice and beans at times before the increase in support, and how she had to share a house with seven others before she could save enough to make a down payment on a house of her own. "When they got married, Irene knew Fred had two sons," the first wife had told the journalist. "He needs to help raise these children. These children were both planned."

Stepmothers like Irene weren't hard to figure out. They were lobbying for their own future offspring, as opposed to the other woman's. But what about the fathers? In effect, these men were demanding their "right to reproduce" at the expense of their existing children.*

In search of some insight into this mentality, I visited Bill Morrow, the Republican legislator from Orange County who had introduced AB 180, the COPS bill to roll back support. A hefty man with the look of an ex-athlete, Morrow opened the conversation by boasting of his sponsorship of a bill to repeal California's helmet law for motorcyclists. He was also supporting a bill allowing schools to paddle students. His district was a bedroom community of Los Angeles, and many of his constituents had lost their jobs in the defense industry. Divorced men were telling him that when their income went down, they couldn't readily go to court for a modification lowering their child support. "The state just treats them like walking wallets," he said; it collected their money but wouldn't enforce their visitation rights. Interestingly, these complaints echoed those of custodial parents, who say that they too have trouble getting modifications when their income goes down or the fathers' goes up. Mothers say they get scant help locating deadbeat dads, and fathers can't get help against recalcitrant mothers who won't let them see their chil-

---

*American states vary widely in their accommodation of this male desire to reproduce with different women at little additional cost. But judges in many states do frequently lower a child's support so that a man has more disposable income for a second family. In Massachusetts, for example, a 1993 review discovered that the most common reason for deviating from the child support guidelines was "the expense associated with subsequent families." In those cases, the average judicial deviation was 36 percent below the guideline.[16]

dren. Clearly, the cumbersome family law system wasn't working well for anyone.

Morrow told me that he had received a lot of mail supporting his bill, so I decided to take a look. Sure enough, most of the letters were from women and the steam rising from the bulging files of mail would have scalded the thickest-skinned lawmaker. What was most striking was the bitterness the second wives seemed to feel toward the first. On its face, this anger was puzzling. According to a national study by the American Bar Association's Center on Children and the Law, most families paying child support are better off financially than the families receiving it. And the second wives have the husband as well. Why were they so mad?

Many of the letter writers were seething with resentment over the imagined luxuries enjoyed by first wives, courtesy of their child support checks. Vacations to Hawaii were a particular sore spot, as were new cars. One second wife, whose husband was paying $700 a month to his child, was tormented by the knowledge that her predecessor "has a house TWICE the size of ours with a new built-in pool . . . [and] a new Volvo. We drive nine- and seven-year-old cars."

Perhaps these women represented the relatively few second wives who weren't better off than the first, a status that seemed to them to violate the natural order of things. They had married only to discover that the future was mortgaged by their husbands' prior procreations. The rules had changed in the middle of the game, and they were taking out their rage and frustration not on their husbands but on a safer target: the other woman.

Often, the second wives were divorced mothers themselves. Dianna Thompson, a member of the Orange County chapter of COPS, told me a long and involved story about her husband's ex-wife, who she claimed had left the state with their two children, gone on welfare, remarried, and made visitation difficult out of a fear that her kids might never come back.

Thompson herself had five young children, a daughter by her own previous marriage and four children with her current husband. She is home with the children all day, while he works twelve-hour days at two jobs, as an operator in a power plant and doing data entry at a hospital.

"In fourteen years I never received any child support from my ex. When I was a single parent, I was never on welfare. But my husband's ex has been on welfare for years. Because she shows no income, her child support is higher. So I had no money coming in from my ex-husband, and now money is going out to my husband's ex-wife. We live from paycheck to paycheck. I don't see it. I believe that both biological parents should support their children financially."

Ironically, the lives of second wives like Thompson would have been much easier if tougher child support had been in place years ago. But not one—not even among those with several young children—saw that they too might have been grateful for a solid safety net of child support or still might be if they are divorced again. "I have asked some of these women, 'Don't you see that as many as half of you will have this same problem sometime in the future?'" said Barbara Grob, of the Public Media Center in San Francisco.[17] "But they don't see it."

Fathers' rights activists take the position that no child is entitled to a fixed percentage of their income. Just as family law holds that a divorced man only has to provide a long-term wife with what she "needs" of "his" money, fathers' rights groups argue that a noncustodial father's income is his alone. His children are entitled only to what they "need" in terms of bare-bones expenses.

When I asked Bill Morrow whether he believed that children had a right to share in both parents' standard of living, his answer was an unequivocal no. "My parents were children of the depression," he explained. "They didn't have anything, and they got ahead. You don't have to be middle-class to succeed. We can't guarantee that every child can be middle-class or upper-class even if Dad is. That's not necessary or even desirable."

Many divorced men in California seemed to equate child support with welfare. When I spoke with Jim Stivers, a member of the Orange County chapter of COPS, he called child support "the largest privately funded welfare system in the country." I saw one letter from a father who deplored the "most tragic result" of child support: the "children who learn at a very young age to wait for the check in the mail signed by 'Daddy.' This is just a prelude to the day when the same kids will be waiting for a check signed by 'Uncle Sam.'" The irony, as one Sacramento family lawyer told me, is that "these men would rather pay a day-care center to take their kids all day than pay their former wives enough to enable them to stay at home even part-time."

The only participants in their battles whose voices had been strangely silent were the first wives and their children. Their sole advocates appeared to be a couple of lobbyists for nonprofit children's groups, a few legislative staffers, and a freshman Democratic assemblywoman from southern California named Sheila James Kuehl.

Kuehl was the first openly gay legislator to be elected in the nation's most populous state. A former television star (she had played Zelda Gilroy in "The Many Lives of Dobie Gillis," a popular sitcom in the early 1960s) and a graduate of Harvard Law School, Kuehl, as cofounder of the California Women's Law Center, had drafted more than forty pieces of legislation on violence against women, child support, child care, and sex discrimination. In Kuehl, COPS had a formidable opponent. Why, I asked her, were there almost no letters, no demonstrations, not a peep from divorced women on an issue that literally meant bread on the table for hundreds of thousands of families?

"Many of these women are at the edge of survival," she shot back. "They're not privileged enough to be able to organize and influence their representatives."[18] Kuehl patiently explained that most divorced women with custody of children work full-time. They don't have the freedom to stake out courthouses recruiting disgruntled mothers as they emerge, a favorite tactic of the fathers' rights groups. They don't have computers, so they can't network through the Internet and organize on office time, as many fathers do. They don't have legal and economic experts among their ranks to help them define the debate with their chosen facts and figures. And they don't have second husbands who demonstrate, attend hearings, and visit representatives' offices. First wives, in short, are seriously outgunned, which may be one reason why a movie depicting them as glamorous victors was such a smash hit.

In response to Morrow's bill to slash support, Kuehl had introduced her own bill, to increase support by slightly less than the rate of inflation. On the crucial afternoon of January 17, 1996, both bills were up for consideration by the assembly's Judiciary Committee.

As yet, the legislators had little knowledge of how the 1992 support guidelines were working. According to Judge James D. Garbolino, superior court judge of Placer County, the most basic information was lacking: how much money was actually being transferred from one parent to the other, what kinds of sacrifices were being made by either parent, or what the actual cost of raising children in California was. Pending a study of the situation, the state's Judicial Council and the American Bar Association had recommended that the guidelines remain unchanged.

The absence of this information made no difference to Kuehl's core argument: child support, like other transfer payments such as Social Security, should be indexed to inflation. Since it is not, she proposed a slight increase in support. "The issue," she concluded, "is are we doing what's needed for these children?" The committee voted against her bill, nine votes to two.

When Bill Morrow's turn came to appeal to the committee, he cited the "sudden and drastic consequences" of the new laws. "People can't even maintain their own lives, much less pay child support," he alleged. His bill to cut child support across the board by roughly one-quarter was approved. As we left the hearing room, Leora Gershenzon, a lobbyist for poor women and children, whispered that they had taken a "woman off the committee to make sure they'd win." But the bill never got any farther. Editorials in the big-city dailies blasted the idea of rolling back child support, and when the proposal came up on the state assembly floor, only two people, one of them Bill Morrow, stood up to defend it. It was defeated by a more than two-to-one margin. The following November the Democrats regained control of the state assembly, and higher child support guidelines were safe for the moment.

Deadbeat Dads

Raising the level of required child support is an important step, but after the judges have ruled, the fathers are supposed to pay—and a lot of them don't. Thus enforcement was a key part of the nationwide effort of the 1990s to squeeze more child support out of noncustodial parents. Enforcement significantly improved over the course of the decade, as the federal government went on a manhunt for the deadbeat dad. The states were ordered to institute immediate wage withholding for most support orders issued after January 1, 1994, and in 1996 it became a federal felony to cross state lines to avoid child support arrearages of $5,000 or more. Also in 1996, Congress ordered the states to deny drivers' and professional licenses to parents in arrears.

The tightening had an effect. Child support collections rose from $8 billion in 1992 to $12 billion in 1996 and $14.4 billion in 1997, when improved computer systems helped the states track down more than 1.2 million delinquents. Nonetheless, according to the Census Bureau, in 1997 more than 7.4 million parents—almost all of them men—still owed more than $43 billion in past child support.

These figures have been challenged by fathers' rights advocates on the grounds that they are based on surveys of custodial mothers, who probably exaggerate the degree of nonpayment. Sanford Braver of Arizona State University, for example, has found that noncustodial fathers report much higher levels of compliance. He concludes that "the truth lies somewhere in between."[19]

But even "in-between" points to systematic underpayment by millions of delinquent fathers. They may not all be "deadbeat dads"—Braver found that the single most important factor relating to nonpayment was unemployment—but they aren't providing for their children the way mothers are, either.

While in Sacramento in 1996, I met with Shirley Craig, a heavyset woman of forty-four who arrived at my hotel with two bulging blue binders containing the record of her struggle to get her ex-husband to pay something toward the support of their two daughters. According to Craig, her husband still owed more than $50,000 in arrearages, although she had been in and out of the Placer County courthouse nine times.[20]

Craig had worked for a local savings and loan but had suffered a recent back injury and was now unable to hold down a full-time job. She earned an average of $300 to $500 a month as a temporary bookkeeper, plus Social Security disability assistance of $500 a month. That income, plus $300 a month in welfare for her two daughters, kept the family barely afloat.

Until 1991, she had been a stay-at-home mother while her husband ran his own construction company, a business that had generated $5,000 to $6,000 a month. He began traveling more and more, ostensibly on business, and she finally had to face the fact that he had built a whole other life, complete with girlfriend. She filed for divorce, and in early

1992 her husband was ordered to pay $1,004 a month—$355 in spousal support and $649 in child support.

No checks ever arrived. Craig's husband, and all evidence of his business, evaporated. He had been charged with contempt for nonsupport. According to Craig, he finally lost his contracting license in the state of California. At that point, he left the state. "He'd call and say they can't do anything to him—he'd never have to pay all that money," Craig told me. She was forced to sell the family house and move into a small two-bedroom apartment on the outskirts of Sacramento.

How had all this affected her daughters? I asked.

Craig immediately became more animated. She pulled out pictures of two tall blond California girls, both almost six feet tall, thin, with stunning good looks. According to their mother, they had seen their father only once in the last four years. Looking at the photos, I thought his absence from their lives defied reason.

"Both lettered in three different sports," Craig said proudly. "The oldest is now working at Godfather's Pizza, and they're going to make her a manager. She's a senior, and she's changed her schedule to permit outside work experience. She eventually wants to go into law enforcement, to the police academy and maybe on to the Secret Service. She once said to me, 'If I ever had to pull my dad over, he'd get a ticket.'

"The younger one just started working at Godfather's too. She wants to be a physical therapist—she's in a special program in her high school, with all her classes having to do with health."

Craig said her older daughter pitched varsity softball, and her younger girl had qualified for a basketball travel team that could attract the attention of college recruiters. To help pay their expenses, their mother had donated time coaching, driving players to games, keeping score. She said the girls had asked her why she was doing all that; they didn't realize she was being paid for the gas to get them to games. But she couldn't afford the expenses of having her daughter on that travel team.

"My ex-husband is now in Reno—we know because he sends them letters off and on. My younger daughter asked him for the money for her uniform, and he said no. It made her want to quit." She hesitated, and started to cry. "It's been very hard. They were hurt, and angry, and bitter. They ask me, 'Why doesn't he want to see us? What did we do?'"

Because Craig's husband had crossed state lines and owed more than $5,000 in arrearages, he had violated federal law, and the U.S. attorney could have stepped into the case and had him arrested for a crime that carried a jail sentence. But she was up against the hardest animal in the world to track down: the self-employed deadbeat dad. He had no reported wages that could be garnished. And the authorities don't like to go after these particular outlaws; for one thing, they're much too much work. The fathers' rights groups have a point when they charge that the government would rather crack down on the guy who misses a payment or two, or pays a portion of his support order, than go to the trouble of locating a determined lawbreaker.

Shirley Craig had the additional disadvantage of living in Placer County, which ranked fortieth of the fifty-eight counties in California in overall child support performance. Placer County had a record of locating (that is, finding a computer data match on) fewer than 30 percent of the noncustodial parents it was required to locate, compared with a national average of 93 percent. The performance of the state's most populous county, Los Angeles, is even worse.

Double Jeopardy

Deadbeat dads are clearly criminal, easy to stigmatize, if not to locate. More subtle, and more difficult to confront, are the relatively affluent fathers who are able to reduce their child support to a minimum by using a perfectly legal loophole. The woman who is most vulnerable to this stratagem is the typical educated mother, the one who has voluntarily cut back on her career in order to have more time for her children. Judges who never heard of a mommy trap often assume that such a woman can just breeze back into the full-time job market and pick up where she left off. So they award a mother who once worked full-time less child support than a woman who never worked at all during her marriage.

Rebecca Leet found herself in such double jeopardy. Leet, a consultant in northern Virginia, worked full-time for a national environmental organization until she had two children in rapid succession in the mid-1990s. With a new baby and a one-year-old, she decided to leave her

$80,000-a-year position and set up shop as a freelance consultant working out of her home. Hers was exactly the sort of decision taken by hundreds of thousands of new mothers who can afford to make it.[21]

"I still worked," she explains, "but not flat out; I was able to make about half my old salary, and my husband never complained. On one level, yes, I wasn't using my earning capacity to the maximum. But we made the decision that it would have been harmful to the children if we both worked full-time out of the house while they were so young; that they were more important than my earning another $30,000 or $40,000."

In other words, Leet was in the most common American marriage bargain: both spouses worked, but he became the primary breadwinner, she the primary homemaker and caregiver. Then, as she put it, "came the awful year. We had some deaths in the family, and the marriage fell apart." As the couple began divorce proceedings, Rebecca's husband charged that she had been "voluntarily underemployed." He asked the judge to impute an income of $80,000 to her; that is, to assume that she could be earning the $80,000 she had once made, instead of the $17,000 she had actually earned during the previous year. If the judge did this, the husband's support payments would shrink drastically.

The judge complied. Rebecca ended up with less child support than if she had never worked at all. The following year, she says, "I had to crank my income back up, or we wouldn't have had a house over our heads. The children had to go into full-time day care."

The weapon used against Leet is called "imputation of income." The original idea was to prevent a noncustodial father from avoiding his proper child support level by deliberately understating his income. For example, in a case involving an acquaintance of mine, a man deliberately quit his six-figure job and transferred his assets to his mother during his divorce. He was hoping that feigned penury would reduce his child support payments. The judge saw through the ruse, imputed his former salary to him, and ordered his payments to be set accordingly.

But in some states, a rule designed to prevent child support evasion is being used to produce the opposite effect. Judges are imputing income to custodial mothers, thereby reducing fathers' obligations.

A seminal case illustrating this trend involved two married doctors in Missouri. In 1990, after twelve years of marriage, Linda Gail Stanton and her husband, Elliot Abbey, divorced. Both were making approximately $100,000 a year. He didn't seek custody of their four children, then ages ten, eight, five, and three, and he agreed to pay monthly child support of $2,250.[22]

Stanton had worked full-time since graduating from medical school, putting in sixty- to eighty-hour weeks. Both she and her husband were often on call and frequently worked weekends. The children were cared for by a husband-and-wife team; a man who worked the first six hours of the day and a woman who came in the afternoon and stayed as late as necessary. "I saw my kids just before bed," Stanton told me during a long telephone conversation. "Me being a doctor meant that kind of commitment." After the divorce, she continued at the same pace.

Then in 1992 she remarried and moved with her new husband to northern California. Her ex-husband had no objections to her moving to the West Coast with the children, but he sought major modifications in their financial settlement, asking, among other things, that his child support payments be cut in half, now that she had remarried. He also wanted his ex-wife to pay the children's transportation costs between California and Missouri on all of their school vacations.

Stanton objected to these demands, and the case went to court. Stanton did not plan to go to work immediately after the move to California, in order to get settled and help the children make the adjustment. Neither she nor her lawyer dreamed that her decision to become a stay-at-home mom would be held against her. They couldn't have been more mistaken.

Elliot Abbey's lawyer, Margo L. Green, depicted Stanton in court as a creature of utter privilege. Green showed the judge pictures of Stanton's new $2-million home. She argued that this was "a wealthy woman who chose not to work," a woman whose husband's "astronomical" income (i.e., $225,000) permitted her that choice.

"This woman was never a full-time mother," Green said to me over the phone. "She didn't even do her own housework after she stopped working," she added. (Child support, for the record, is totally unrelated to housework. It is supposed to be based on the costs of raising children.)

As Stanton explained her reasons for deciding to stay home, they centered on her third child, a boy in the second grade. He had always been extremely shy and had had a rough time during the divorce, tuning out the world and withdrawing into himself. He had improved markedly, but in California he had been put in a class somewhat behind his previous level, and he was "major-league bored," according to his mother. She spent hours with his teacher, devising extra projects for him, and within six months a decision was made to switch him to the next grade.

This turned out to be one change too many, and the boy shut down, often refusing to go to school. One day, after she had dropped him off, he turned around and walked home again. For the next three weeks, she went to school with him every day until he had overcome his painful shyness. "If I had been working," Stanton said, "who knows what would have happened to him?"

There were other matters requiring her attention: finding new pediatricians and dentists; arranging physicals for four children, an orthodontist for one, and an eye doctor for another; and child-proofing the new house. Stanton didn't even have a license to practice medicine in California. But the judge imputed an income of $100,000 to her and ruled that her ex-husband (a doctor with a six-figure income) was entitled to some financial relief. The judge agreed to virtually every one of Abbey's demands and reduced his monthly child support payments almost in half, to $1,232, or about $300 per child.

The decision was the first case in Missouri in which the income of the custodial parent was imputed in determining child support, and the first case in which a new husband's salary was a factor in the decision. In effect, the decision said to divorced mothers: if you remarry, and take on a greater personal obligation to your children, their father can reduce his obligations to them.

The couple appealed the decision, which they estimated would cost them $18,000 a year, on top of the roughly $40,000 they spent on litigation. On March 8, 1994, the appeals court upheld the lower court decision. By this time Stanton was pregnant with her fifth child and even less likely to return to work as a doctor.

Stanton v. Abbey set an important precedent. According to Joe Jacobson, the attorney who handled Stanton's appeal, several other custodial mothers in Missouri subsequently had their child support reduced because they were "not working," and numerous fathers were reopening their cases in hopes of lowering their payments. Margo Green told me that she had gotten "calls from all over the country" from professional men, asking her to represent them in cases against wives who once worked full-time. "They want to impute income to the custodial moms, so they can reduce their support payments," she said. "I hear judges saying they are going to impute income to wives. I know the case is influencing judges' thinking."[23]

According to Green, this new development in divorce law reflects judges' evolving perception of men and women as joint breadwinners. She argued that because judges for years had been imputing incomes to noncustodial parents, now they were just "equalizing the picture."

"The time has come . . . to recognize that it is the mother's responsibility, as well as the father's, to support the kids," she declared.

I asked Green how equitable it was to expect Stanton's household to provide almost all the care as well as most of the financial support of four children?

"[She] was not a woman who stayed home to nurture her children," Green replied. "If she'd *always* nurtured her children, I don't think any court would have done this."

In other words, Stanton was being punished both for having once had a career and then for giving it up. I asked Green if she thought this was a message to married working mothers to "forget about ever staying at home with your children."

"I think so," she replied, "so you're not ever dependent on another human being for your survival. These ladies who think that he's there to take care of them for the rest of [their] life . . . it just isn't so anymore. Any woman in the workforce who thinks she might quit and stay home with her children down the road has to think long and hard about what's going to happen to her and the kids if she gets divorced."*

---

*The states vary enormously in their treatment of income imputed to the custodial parent. In Colorado, the child support guidelines require a judge to impute potential income to a parent who is "voluntarily unemployed," unless she is "physically or mentally incapacitated or is caring for a child two years of age or younger."[24] In Massachusetts, on the other hand, a judge cannot impute income to a custodial parent with a child at home who is under the age of six. But, according to Laura Morgan, an authority on child support, the practice is spreading. "A lot of states give a nod if the child is under the age of five," Morgan told me. "But once that kid hits five, all bets are off."

AS BOTH THE Stanton and the Leet cases illustrate, the child support system in the United States punishes mothers for doing the right thing for their kids. The system deprives children of parental care as well as money by discouraging caregivers from staying at home even on a part-time basis.

These two cases also show that relatively wealthy men are often the exception to the rule that divorced fathers are now paying more of their income toward child support. Many states' guidelines are very specific in requiring fathers to pay a fixed percentage of income for each child. But some of these states waive the support guidelines altogether for high-earning fathers because a fixed percentage of their income amounts to more than a child "needs."

Even in states where high-income fathers are subject to percentage-of-income guidelines, several state studies have found that judges routinely make substantial downward revisions in the guidelines to reduce the obligations of affluent fathers. This research shows that high-income husbands pay a much lower percentage of their income for support of their children than do poor or middle-class men.[25]

"The system is unfair to lower-earning men, who are subject to strict support guidelines, and to women and children in high-income families," says a court mediator in Washington, D.C. "In families where the husband has high earnings, there is a situation of ambiguity. Women don't know what kind of child support they're entitled to, so they trade off support for other things, like custody or college tuition." Jerilyn Borack, a California family lawyer, notes that "someone making $36,000 a month can end up paying less than someone making $3,600 a month."[26]

Borack represented the wife in a case in Sacramento, California, in which a noncustodial father with a several-million-dollar estate and annual earnings of roughly $300,000 was ordered to pay about $400 a month in child support for his ten-year-old son.

The father, a developer, had described his son in court as a "T-shirt, tennis-shoe type of kid," that is, low maintenance. The judge apparently agreed. He set child support at $859 a month, with the comment that that "would buy a lot of pizza." The parents—the father with his $300,000 income and the mother with less than $25,000 in annual earnings, plus the custodial responsibility—were ordered to split the financial support of the child fifty-fifty.

According to Borack, the judge assumed that because the boy's mother was living with another man, her real income was higher than $25,000. He ruled, in effect, that the man who was enjoying the sexual services of the mother had a greater obligation to support her children than their biological father had.

Meanwhile, at the other end of the income spectrum, poor men, including unwed fathers, are being hounded to "pay up." The states are now required to try to establish the paternity of all newborns, under the controversial principle that a biological parent has an obligation to support his children even if he never intended to become a parent.

Unmarried teenage boys, visiting the young mothers of their new babies in the hospital, can find themselves cornered by a government worker and persuaded to sign a document committing them to supporting that child for the next eighteen years. This development, largely propelled by the federal government's desire to reduce spending on welfare, has led some unmarried men to complain that they have a "right to choose" fatherhood, just as women have long demanded the right to choose the awesome obligations of motherhood.

But mothers, at every income level, continue to pay the bulk of the steadily rising cost of raising a child. In the end, then, the answer to the question "who pays for the kids?" in the United States is whoever has the least power and money. This is why between a third and a half of all divorced women ended up on welfare before the program was terminated as an entitlement—perhaps the best final comment on the fairness of the American system of support for children of divorce.

CHAPTER 10

The Welfare State Versus a Caring State

> No government has attempted to attach a significant value to the unpaid work of caring that women do in the family.
>
> —Jane Lewis, scholar of the British welfare state[1]

Divorce is a financial disaster for mothers and children not only because fathers don't pay for or provide their fair share of care. The government, instead of being part of a solution, is part of the problem. Quite simply, although unpaid caregiving is the ultimate social safety net, caregivers themselves are expected to perform without a net.

The problem for mothers may be framed this way: contrary to popular perception, the United States does have a welfare state, but it is designed to ameliorate the economic risks of paid workers only. Unpaid workers, including those who care for dependent family members, are excluded from the system. Work at home does not qualify a person for the same social programs that insure everyone else against the risks of the market economy. As Nancy Folbre has written, "While motherhood is idealized as the most fulfilling work a woman can perform, public policy continues to define it as though it were not really work at all." The welfare state has thus played a major role in the "feminization of poverty," or what Folbre calls the "pauperization of motherhood."[2] The welfare state has never really been a caring state.

A Tale of Two Mothers

On a hot summer day in Washington, D.C., in 1996, I interviewed a former "welfare mother," a pretty woman in her late fifties with smooth gray-streaked hair cut in a perfect pageboy. She was wearing a pale blue suit with a crisp white blouse; the picture of a well-groomed upper-middle-class white woman who looked like her only connection with welfare was through volunteer work.

Thirty years earlier, this woman had been the twenty-nine-year-old wife of a successful stockbroker, living what she described as a "Leave It to Beaver" existence in a big house north of San Francisco with three children all under the age of six. She was playing a good role in a perfect script—until her husband became manic-depressive, lost his job, and effectively deserted his family. Overnight, the stay-at-home mom became a single mother with no college degree and no visible means of support. (She had dropped out of college after two years to marry and put her husband through school.)[3]

She sold her Marin County house just two weeks before it was scheduled for foreclosure, ending up with $300, a washer, and a dryer. She exchanged two big cars for a beat-up old Volkswagen and moved with the three kids into a two-bedroom bungalow. She hated the prospect of leaving them to go to work, and when she went to an employment agency, she flunked all the tests. When the agency representative asked her what the problem was, she said she didn't want to be there and really didn't want to work full-time.

They sent her out on a trial interview, telling her to lie about her situation. She told the interviewer that she was happily married and had a live-in housekeeper who could handle all the problems that might arise at home. She got the job, as a secretary to a vice president of an electronics company. The pay—$580 a month—was barely enough to cover the bills for a family of four, but not enough for decent day care. In that first year, she recalls, she had thirteen different baby-sitters. Her ex-husband never paid a nickel in child support.

She tried to get a second job as a waitress in a nearby restaurant, but when she admitted that she had no experience waiting tables, she was rejected. Finally, a friend told her about AFDC: Aid to Families with Dependent Children, a.k.a. welfare. She had never heard of it, but she applied and was approved for just enough money to cover a full-time caregiver. With that, and the food stamps and health care that came with the assistance, she had enough income to scrape by on without having to work nights as well as days. She remembers the assistance as something that enabled her to hold her family together.

She stayed on welfare for three years, from 1968 to 1971. A job promotion finally gave her enough income to handle things on her own, and she left welfare, remarried, and persuaded her mother to come down from Seattle to take care of the children after school.

"My kids were never latchkey," she relates with some pride. "They wanted to be at home, and I was able to arrange it. But it took all that to enable me to get on my feet: some college, a 'good' job, the welfare, a new marriage, and a family able to help. And I was a very assertive person. . . . I don't know how somebody with less education, who is less assertive, who doesn't speak English well, can cope."

Her three children survived their brush with welfare dependency. When we spoke, one son was a highly successful wine merchant, the daughter was president of a Web-page production company, and the younger son had just graduated from college.

This former welfare mother, Lynn Woolsey, is now a Democratic member of Congress from Petaluma, California. Every year, with conservative Republican Henry Hyde, she cosponsors legislation that would create a federal system of child support collection. With most child support experts, she believes that if the country had one national collection system, and all Americans had to pay their child support as routinely as they pay their federal income taxes, as many as 800,000 mothers and children would no longer need any public assistance. Every year the proposal is defeated.

Another onetime welfare mom is a black woman in her late forties who grew up in poverty in rural Georgia with an aunt, who raised her after her mother died. She successfully finished high school, worked for a few years, then married and had three children. In 1973, when the children were all still under six, her husband deserted the family. Up to this point, her story is just like Lynn Woolsey's.

But Emma Mae Martin had to take two minimum-wage jobs to stay afloat—the very thing that Lynn Woolsey was able to avoid because she lived in a state with far more generous levels of assistance. (Welfare, like child support, does not have national levels; the payments are set by each individual state.) Martin worked in a senior citizen's home during the day, came home for a few hours "to make sure the kids were OK," and then went back to work in a crab factory in the evening. Another aunt watched the children while Martin was away at night.[4]

Then the beloved aunt who had raised her suffered a stroke, and Martin quit work so that she could care for her. That was what finally forced her to go on welfare, although quitting also enabled her to devote more time to her children. She was the only able-bodied adult in a household with five dependents, counting a fourth child she had had after her husband's departure. For her work of caring for five people, she received a welfare check of $169 a month. When I asked her how she managed to survive, she said, "It was necessity."

She never received any child support. Only once, when her youngest child was three, did she try to have it collected. "I think I got one check, but that was all," she recalled.

After about four and a half years on welfare, Martin finally had to put her aunt in a nursing home, and she started working again at the minimum wage, earning $135 every two weeks. That was enough to disqualify her for welfare, and, she told me, "I haven't been back on since."

About the time she was working two minimum-wage jobs, her younger brother, who had been raised by a better-off uncle, was in Yale Law School. He became an attorney, and in 1980 the ambitious young black man made a speech before a conference of black conservatives in which he criticized his sister for having taken assistance from the government. "She gets mad when the mailman is late with her welfare check," he told the audience. "That's how dependent she is. What's worse is that now her kids feel entitled to the check, too. They have no motivation for doing better or getting out of that situation."

The brother omitted a few details from his welfare horror story. He failed to mention that his sister's children never had any support from their father. Then as now, welfare mothers were the more popular target in conservative circles. It is an old, sad story: blame the weak and kick the dog that can't bite back.

But Emma Mae Martin had done exactly what a woman is supposed to do: graduate from school, get a job, work hard, get married, care for your family, and bring up your kids as best you can. She had accepted the responsibility of caring for a sick and aged relative, in addition to raising children whose father had declined the honor. A true conservative might have praised her, and all other women who take on unpaid, unsung family obligations. Instead, her brother criticized her in public.

Clarence Thomas's speech attracted the attention of the Reagan administration, which was recruiting right-thinking blacks. The young lawyer was offered the chairmanship of the Equal Employment Opportunity Commission, which led to a federal judgeship and eventually to a seat on the Supreme Court. Which all goes to show, as one black journalist later wrote, that "a little scapegoating can take you a long way in politics, even when you use your own sister."[5]

I was curious about what Thomas had called the "worst" part of the story: the fact that his nieces and nephews were growing up as "welfare dependents," virtually trained to become permanent wards of the state. In the summer of 1996, I called Emma Mae Martin, who was still living in rural Georgia, south of Savannah. She said that both her youngest child, Leola, then twenty, and Christine, twenty-five, were planning to attend vocational school in Savannah in the fall, one to study draftsmanship and the other "still undecided." The next child, Mark, twenty-seven, had been working for more than five years as a carpenter, and the oldest, a boy named Clarence after his uncle, had a career in the navy and had served aboard the battleship *Wisconsin* during Operation Desert Storm. Like Congresswoman Woolsey's children, Martin's seemed to be well on their way to repaying society for the extremely modest investment that taxpayers had made in them.

Martin herself, at the time we spoke, was working full-time for $9 an hour at a hospital not far from her home—the same hospital where her mother had once worked as a nurse's assistant. But she was looking for additional part-time work. There were going to be layoffs, explained the sister of the Supreme Court justice, and she didn't know what would happen to her job.

I asked Martin what she thought about her brother's disparaging comments so long ago. "We haven't talked about it for years," she said warily.

Pitied But Not Entitled

Reading numerous newspaper stories about the struggles of welfare mothers, I have been struck that in virtually every case, the woman—like Lynn Woolsey and Emma Mae Martin—would have been self-supporting if she had not been trying to meet her family obligations. If she had just given in to the temptation of running away from it all, like a heroine in a Joan Didion novel; if she had decided to travel light, carry no baggage, and never look back when she heard the sound of broken glass; if she had just behaved, in short, like so many men, she wouldn't have become that dread, demonized figure, the welfare mom.

One such story described a thirty-nine-year-old black woman who was determined to hold it all together for her own two children and four nieces and nephews, the offspring of a drug-addicted sister. This woman received $35,136 a year to help support six dependents, including $28,800 for the care of the four foster children. The article explained that because she had lupus, she wasn't being asked to enroll in job training for work as a secretary or clerk.

But as the article made clear, this woman *already had a job*—the job of rearing six children. Her constant vigilance was helping these children, including two teenagers, stay off the streets and out of serious trouble. "You may be *in* the projects," she bellowed at them, "but you don't have to be *of* the projects!"

By any measure, this woman's efforts to keep half a dozen children in a stable environment and in school were worth $35,000 a year to society. Obviously, mistakes had been made. Her sister should never have had four children or succumbed to drugs, and neither mother should have lost the help of the fathers of their children. But these things had happened, and six children still needed to be given a decent start in life. What would have happened to them if they hadn't had their welfare mother? What would have happened if she was able to do something really useful, like working at a supermarket checkout?[6]

The same newspaper also ran a story about a mother in Norway who received a salary of $18,000—80 percent of her previous income as a secretary—to stay at home with her newborn for a year. Her salary as a mother, mailed from the government, is treated like any other paycheck, with income and social security taxes withheld.

This woman had just returned to her secretarial job—held open for her by law—and her husband was about to begin his year at home with their daughter. The parental payment for this second year was considerably smaller—a little less than $5,000—but the story pointed out that parents who didn't choose to take the second year at home could go back to work and put their child in subsidized day care.

"We have decided that raising a child is real work, and that this work provides value for the whole society," Valgard Haugland, the minister of children and family affairs, told the reporter. "And that the society as a whole should pay for this valuable service."

The American journalist, T. R. Reid, was obviously impressed. "Politicians in Norway love to talk about 'family values,' and in that they're no different from politicians almost everywhere else," he wrote. "What's different here is that Norway has put its money where its mouth is."[7]

Maternal dependency and second-class citizenship for wives and mothers were built into the Anglo-Saxon welfare state from the beginning.[8] In the American and British welfare states that evolved in the mid-twentieth century, social insurance was provided on two tracks: one for people who were employed full-time, and another for everyone else. Only the former were permitted to qualify for the "first tier" benefits, such as Social Security, unemployment insurance, and workman's compensation. These programs are perceived as rights, or entitlements that are earned. They are paid to "beneficiaries" who "deserve" their checks from the government.

Historically, the beneficiaries of these programs have been disproportionately white male wage earners. Social Security insures working men against the economic dependency that comes with old age; unemployment insurance reduces the dependency that occurs after a job loss; and workmen's compensation alleviates the dependency caused by workplace accidents. Even the most vociferous antigovernment ideologues—also disproportionately white and male—have never called for the elimination of these programs that keep the wolf from their door.

The second tier of the American and British system is what has become known as "welfare." Welfare is based on "need" and is not an entitlement. It is perceived as charity, as a handout given to "recipients" who are not thought to have done anything to earn or deserve their payments from the government.

Historically, welfare offered the only public protection against the economic dependency incurred by caring for others. Most caregivers, it was assumed, would be supported privately, through their association with a spouse. In this respect the welfare state perpetuated the legal doctrine of coverture, which denied that wives and mothers were full citizens in their own right, who were entitled to the fruits of their own labor. Only if a married mother lost the income of a breadwinner did she qualify for public assistance, but solely in the form of welfare. Instituted early in the twentieth century, these payments were originally designed to enable "deserving" poor mothers, mostly widows, to stay at home with their children, instead of having to give them up to foster families, orphanages, or the streets. Even these worthy recipients, however, were never allowed more than a pittance. Welfare has always been grudgingly given, and only to those who can prove they are destitute. Since its inception in 1936, Aid to Dependent Children (or Aid to Families with Dependent Children, as it was called after 1962) never amounted to more than .5 percent of the GDP. In the memorable phrase of one feminist scholar, mothers could be "pitied but not entitled."[9]

Welfare's second-class status emerges clearly from a comparison with Social Security. Unlike Social Security, welfare benefits were always conditional. For example, if a recipient was living with a man, it was assumed that she should be dependent on him, rather than on the government. This led to the infamous searches of women's apartments for "a man in the closet." If one was found, she was summarily cut off.

Also unlike Social Security, welfare was never indexed to inflation. In the quarter-century between 1970 and 1996, when AFDC was terminated altogether, welfare stipends lost almost half of their purchasing power, or to put it another way, between 1969 and 1996, the real value of government cash transfer payments to single parents declined by 40 percent.[10] This was devastating to children. When the value of AFDC payments rose, as it did by roughly 30 percent between 1960 and 1970, childhood poverty declined by nearly 60 percent. In the next quarter-century, as welfare failed to keep up with inflation, poverty for children under age six climbed back up almost to 1960 levels.[11]

In sum, the American welfare state has never acknowledged that the caregiver of a young child incurs a huge risk of losing income in a competitive market economy, and deserves some insurance against that risk, just as workers are insured against the other major risks of old age, involuntary unemployment, and injury on the job.

A closer look at Social Security, the keystone of the American welfare state, shows just how disenfranchised mothers are. A person can only qualify for Social Security as an employed worker or as the "dependent" spouse or widow of an employed worker. Years spent caring for others, unpaid, are calculated as zeroes. I had a dramatic reminder of this when a Social Security statement arrived recently, informing me of my estimated benefits when I retire. The statement was full of zeroes—each one representing a year in which I earned nothing because I was making a home and raising a child. For full-time mothers in the American welfare state, their only hope of Social Security is derivative, based not on their own unpaid labor, but on their husband's paid work. The only contributions to Social Security that count are monetary. To be covered, a person must pay the Social Security tax on wages. Years spent raising the next generation don't count even though the entire Social Security system depends on mothers, who produce the future taxpayers who will finance the country's pensions. (A person's retirement and medical care in old age are not paid for by their own lifetime contributions to the system, but rather by the Social Security taxes collected from succeeding generations of workers—that is, other people's children. The economic beneficiaries of productive children are not their parents but their parents' entire generation.)

Here's how the system works: Benefits are calculated on a forty-year work history, with the five lowest income years removed. Thus a person must be employed for thirty-five years to earn full benefits. At retirement age (sixty-two to sixty-five), women can choose between their own benefits or an amount equal to *half* their husband's—whichever is greater. In the eyes of the government, caregivers thus deserve half the retirement income of wage earners. This penalizes almost two-thirds of American women. In 1993, only 36 percent of women drew Social Security benefits based on their own work records. Even by the year 2030, it is estimated that only four out of ten women will be earning more Social Security in their own right than as "dependents."[12]

All of this sends some strange social messages. A professor at the University of Illinois who raised three sons on her own after an early divorce was forced by her family obligations to stick to relatively low-paying but flexible teaching jobs. Her three children are now all working and paying taxes into the Social Security system. Yet she receives less Social Security than her ex-husband, who paid only negligible child support, and her unmarried brother, a diplomat who never had children.

Similarly, a couple who each make $65,000 a year all their lives, and produce no children, will each receive more from Social Security than a blue-collar couple who jointly earn $25,000, accepting a lower income so they can care for two children. The first couple pay more taxes into the system, but the second contribute the children whose payroll taxes will actually pay for both couples' retirement. Do we really believe that the first couple is making a more valuable contribution to the economy or to society?[13]

At the 1997 annual benefit for the Children's Defense Fund, the leading national advocacy group for poor children, I was reminded of the invaluable contributions a good mother makes to society, and by extension, to Social Security. One of the speakers was Charles Reed, Jr., the son of a black single mother. "From most accounts, my family should have been a statistic," Reed told the audience, gathered in the National Pension Building in Washington, D.C. "I came from a broken home, and my mother supported five children on her salary as a bank teller and a part-time real estate agent." But instead of grim statistics, the Reed family—a "female-headed household"—produced Reed himself, then the special assistant attorney general for the state of Georgia, two college students, and a 1997 "Who's Who Among High School Students" national honoree.

By my very rough calculation, Reed and his siblings will probably earn more than $10 million in their lifetimes. They will contribute roughly $3 million in tax revenues, and at least $1.5 million to the Social Security Trust Fund—not to mention whatever nonmonetary contributions they will make to their communities. None of this will entitle their mother to a bigger retirement check, but their contributions to Social Security will support the retirement of people who never spent an hour or a nickel on a child.

The Social Security system's disregard for caregiving is reflected in other ways as well. No insurance is provided against the loss of a primary parent. The children of a stay-at-home mother who dies or becomes disabled receive no benefits. Even though someone will surely have to spend an enormous amount of money to pay for the services a mother once performed, or lose income to provide those services him- or herself, caregiving is not insured. The loss of a breadwinner, on the other hand, does initiate Social Security payments (although not in every case). The system treats the widows and children of men who die like princes, and the families of men who divorce or desert them like paupers. Yet, as scholars have observed, "nothing distinguishes the two types of women and children except their prior relationship to men. The determination of the life chances of women and children on the basis . . . of their relations to men is patriarchal culture at its most insidious."[14]

If a man dies, for example, his widow and children automatically and immediately qualify for Social Security survivor's benefits. (The children receive a benefit through the age of nineteen and two months, provided they are still full-time students in high school, and the surviving spouse receives a caretaker's benefit until the child reaches sixteen or the caretaker remarries.) These are entitlements, whatever the family's income, and they are reduced only gradually if the caregiver decides not to stay at home full-time with the children.

But if a man abandons his family, or if there is a divorce for whatever reason, his wife and children have no protection under Social Security. If they are desperate, they may be able to secure some temporary welfare, but the children will be much worse off than if their father were dead.

This double standard is particularly insidious because it denies insurance for a risk that is quite common and protects people against a risk that is rather rare. By the mid-1990s, of the almost 30 percent of children being raised by a single parent, those being raised by widows and widowers accounted for only 1 percent. The remainder were in the homes of never married (58 percent) or divorced or separated (42 percent) mothers and fathers.[15]

Caregivers also fail to qualify for the other first-track programs of the welfare state. Take unemployment compensation. If a breadwinner loses his job through no fault of his own, he may be eligible for unemployment benefits. Admittedly, the program has been seriously eroded as the states, in a competitive race to the bottom, have tightened their eligibility provisions. In 1995, only 38 percent of American workers in covered employment actually received benefits during a spell of unemployment, compared with 80 percent in 1947. (As a point of comparison, 98 percent of French and 89 percent of German workers who are out of work qualify for benefits.)

But the great majority of people whose unemployment is a consequence of caregiving responsibilities are not eligible in the first place. Most states don't extend unemployment benefits to part-time workers, a large number of whom are mothers. And many working mothers are ineligible because their work is intermittent or their wages are too low. Thus the very people who most need protection from job loss are left out of the system altogether.[16]

Even if a mother is eligible for unemployment insurance, to qualify for payments she has to have a "covered" reason for leaving her job, such as being laid off or elimination of the job. Yet the situations that most frequently force mothers out of the labor force—the lack of child care or a change in work schedules that interferes with family responsibilities—disqualify them from unemployment insurance. Their departure from their job is deemed to be "voluntary."

If the government insured unemployment due to parental responsibilities, a huge percentage of "welfare mothers" would never have had to go on welfare. A study published in 1995 by the Institute for Women's Policy Research revealed that almost half (43 percent) of all single mothers receiving welfare during a two-year period used it as if it were unemployment insurance, as a temporary income between jobs.[17]

Then there is workmen's compensation. When someone suffers a job-related illness or is disabled "on the job," that person becomes eligible for compensation. But when a mother working at home becomes disabled by, say, burning her hand on the stove, or tripping down stairs while carrying a load of laundry, there is no entitlement program to cushion her fall. And even when she has a serious accident at home that's clearly related to paid work, the injury does not qualify for any compensation. Mothers are among the few American workers who toil entirely at their own risk.

Another egregious example of the welfare state's discrimination against mothers occurs in the field of job training. In 1989, 15.6 million women were "displaced homemakers," defined as women whose primary job had been homemaking and who could not find a full-time job after losing their husbands' income, usually to one of the four "D's": divorce, desertion, or his death or disability. More than half of these women were in or near poverty, and roughly one-fifth had children under age eighteen to support.[18]

These former homemakers, many of whom had been out of the labor market for years, need job training as much as any other "dislocated worker." But they have a much harder time getting it. States have discretion on whether to offer job training to displaced homemakers, and most have opted not to serve them at all, even with the federal funds that are available for dislocated workers.

The few states that do make some allocation for homemakers blatantly discriminate against them. In some states, for example, displaced homemakers can be accommodated only after all other dislocated workers have been offered training. In other states, homemakers can constitute no more than 5 percent of a program's recipients.[19] In Arizona in the mid-1990s, even if a former homemaker was living below the poverty line, she could not qualify for certain kinds of adjustment assistance or job training if her income in previous months, *before her marriage dissolved,* was "too high."

These days, more and more men figure among the displaced homemakers applying for training assistance: either single parents with custody or men who were laid off and stayed at home with a child for a time. But the overwhelming majority are women, whose difficulty in receiving retraining is yet another reason that so many divorced and separated mothers end up on welfare.

The Geriatric Gender Gap

One of the upshots of mothers' exclusion from the social safety net is poverty in old age. Elderly women are more than twice as likely to be poor as old men. This single, stark truth puts the lie to all of the claims that the United States truly honors mothers.

The American pension system is often referred to as a "three-legged stool," with the legs consisting of Social Security benefits, private pension benefits, and individual savings. Although the system is ostensibly gender-neutral, it works well only for those relatively few women who follow a male pattern of uninterrupted, full-time paid work. Once women become mothers, their family commitments weaken all three legs. As we have seen, because of their work patterns women earn fewer Social Security benefits than men. Because so many mothers tend to move in and out of employment or work part-time, the great majority also have no private pensions. Only 29 percent of all women in the workforce and 15 percent of part-time female workers participate in a private pension plan. And because of their lower lifetime earnings, mothers also have fewer personal savings than men.

The effects of all this are clear: a geriatric gender gap. In 1997, 14.7 percent of women over the age of sixty-five were poor, compared with 8.2 percent of men. The poverty rate among elderly widows was 20.3 percent, and for single and divorced women it was 27 percent.[20] It is still true that if a woman wants to eat well in old age, she had better find a seat at a man's table.

"As a reward for raising our children and serving as caregivers for our leaders," a congressional report wrote in 1992, "millions of today's working women will become destitute in old age as the beginning of the baby boom generation retires. They have done everything that our families and society have asked of them, only to discover that the nation's retirement system . . . actually penalizes them for serving as the nation's caregivers."[21]

Thanks, Mom.

Unintended Consequences

The other result of mothers' exclusion from social insurance programs is, of course, child poverty. As we have learned, income in the hands of mothers is more likely to be spent on children than any other income. Yet the only risks to loss of income that are not insured by the American welfare state are those incurred by mothers.

The consequences are devastating for kids. Almost one-fifth of all American children under age eighteen lived in poverty in 2000, despite the longest economic boom in history. The American lack of compassion toward children and their mothers stands in stark contrast to other rich capitalist countries. The incidence of child poverty in the United States is more than twice as great as in Canada, nearly three times as great as in the United Kingdom, and roughly eight times as great as in Germany.[22] In the Nordic countries, there *is* no child poverty, thanks to generous family supports. There is a direct causal connection between these shameful comparisons and the failure in the United States to bring mothers under the same kind of insurance umbrella that protects other workers.

This record reached an all-time low in August of 1996, when Congress abolished AFDC, the unloved federal guarantee of cash support for poor children and their caregivers. By the end of the twentieth century, some states were forcing mothers of infants and toddlers to leave their children all day, anywhere, while the mothers worked a full-time job.

The welfare reform bill was unquestionably the single biggest betrayal of children in the history of American social policy, perpetrated by a Congress that couldn't stop prattling about "family values." It also ignored some convincing evidence from Europe that the best way to encourage mothers to go out and get a job is to provide their children with a safe and supportive place to be. The experience in other countries clearly shows that subsidized quality child care can do far more to encourage poor women to work than any number of punitive threats.

The European countries that offer generous assistance with child care—including Belgium, France, Italy, Sweden, and Denmark—have the highest employment rates for mothers of preschoolers. Conversely, the European countries that rank lowest in the provision of subsidized day care for toddlers—Britain, Ireland, Luxembourg, and the Netherlands—have the lowest proportion of mothers of under-three-year-olds in the paid workforce. Even within one country—Sweden—the rate of maternal employment is related to the degree of subsidized child care in a given locality.

Another interesting thing seems to occur when maternal and child policies are generous. A strong safety net for single mothers and their children seems to encourage married mothers to stay home. A major multinational study, utilizing data from seven developed countries (the United States, Canada, Australia, the United Kingdom, the Netherlands, Germany, and Sweden), found that in the countries with the highest transfers of income to single mothers (through guaranteed child support and child allowances), married mothers were less likely to work. Apparently, married women feel that the risk of staying home is worth taking when the consequences of marital failure are not economically devastating.[23]

In the United States, more married women with young children work full-time than in most of these European countries. Could this be related to the fact that the United States has the lowest income transfers to single mothers in the industrialized world—and the highest rates of maternal and child poverty?

Traditional family advocates should take note of what may be an unintended consequence of welfare reform. Just as the parent who is rough on one child finds that she is also stirring anxiety in the heart of her other offspring, a hard-hearted policy toward single mothers may well affect the behavior of millions of married women who have never seen the inside of a welfare office. The rationale for eliminating the welfare guarantee was that it would encourage mothers who were dependent on government to become self-reliant. But mothers who are dependent on husbands might also get the message that their only real insurance against divorce is a paying job.

CHAPTER 11

The Toughest Job You'll Ever Love

I am not a baby sitter. I never sat on a baby!
—Sign at a child-care workers' rally

On May 1, 1996, a few casually dressed women and a couple of men gathered at Catholic Charities Child Development Center in northeast Washington, D.C. The day had been designated Worthy Wage Day for child-care workers, and the plan was to form a cavalcade of cars that would drive through the nation's capital with banners and a bullhorn, calling attention to the economic plight of the city's care providers.

It was a shoestring rally. Only a few dozen people showed up, almost all of them black women. Before setting out, they stood around the steps of an old Catholic church and listened to a send-off speech by Bev Jackson of Zero to Three, an advocacy organization for early childhood education. "This is not a demonstration; this is not a parade; it's public education," she reminded them.

Why isn't this a demonstration? I wondered. Are these women so defeated that they can't even stand up and protest? I climbed into a van and sat beside Jackson, a well-groomed, middle-aged woman. For the next hour or so we wound our way past the historic symbols of American democracy: the Capitol, the Supreme Court, the Washington Monument. Our caravan included only ten vehicles, although Bev had hoped for twenty. A voice rang out from the bullhorn in the next van. "Our teachers earn half as much as other female workers, one-third as much as male workers," the voice announced to the indifferent sidewalk crowds as we drove by. "They are better educated than other workers. Each year one-third leave to get better jobs." No one on the street seemed to be paying the slightest attention.

We had to stop frequently for red lights, separating our little string of cars. "We should have gotten a demonstration permit," Bev muttered. "Then we'd have had a motorcycle escort, and we could go through the lights and stop signs."

"Why didn't you get a permit?" I asked. For a second she looked at me as if I obviously didn't know the facts of life. "A permit costs $600," she explained. "Where are we going to get that kind of money?" So that's why this wasn't a demonstration: day-care workers can't afford one.

It is sometimes said that the United States doesn't have a national child-care system, but this isn't true. There is a system. Mothers care for their own children for free, and child-care workers increasingly care for other peoples' children for the lowest wages in the economy. These are the twin pillars of a care system based on the exploitation of women.

The myths and assumptions about day-care workers—98 percent of whom are women—are almost identical to the myths about mothers. Several months before the May Day nondemonstration, another group of child-care providers held a rally in front of the White House. The predominantly female crowd, some with their preschool groups in tow, all bundled up against a windy November day, heard Peggy Haack, a family-care provider from Madison, Wisconsin, describe four "myths" about their work: "First, anyone can do it. Second, we don't work to support a family, so it's OK if we earn almost nothing. Third, caregiving is not serious business. Fourth, we're all motherly, just doing what we do best."

The illusion is that working with small children is an innate predisposition of women—or at least some women—so there is no need to place much value on it. This is the most dangerous myth of all. For, unlike mothers, paid caregivers can walk off the job at any time, and find more lucrative ways to make a living. Once care becomes a commodity to be bought and sold, the need for better treatment of caregivers becomes obvious. Its quality becomes highly dependent on the respect and remuneration accorded the job. And more and more, early child care and education are in the market, competing for recruits against better-paid professions.

An estimated 10 million preschoolers now spend some part of their day with someone other than a parent. More than half of all three- to five-year-old children of employed mothers, and fully 44 percent of the children of nonemployed mothers, are in some form of preprimary educational program.[1]

The most common forms of paid child care are nursery schools and day-care centers, which look after about one of every three children of working mothers. Another 17 percent of these youngsters are cared for in someone else's home for a fee, an arrangement known as family day care. Twenty-six percent are watched by grandparents or other relatives, 16 percent by fathers, and 5 percent by a nonrelative in the child's own home, such as a nanny. Six percent go to work with their mothers.[2]

One of the fastest-growing occupations in the country, early education and child care is already a $30-billion industry, dominated by large chains such as Kindercare Learning Centers and La Petite Academy and megasuppliers like Childcraft, Beckley Cardy, Kompany, and Apple. During the 1995 annual meeting of the National Association for the Education of Young Children, this "toddler/industrial complex" was on colorful display at the cavernous Washington Convention Center.

The first thing I noticed as I entered the vast exhibition hall were the corporate banners flying over a forest of booths and exhibits displaying the latest products aimed at the preschool market. Counters piled high with brightly colored learning toys, videos, and computer games made the point that early childhood is now as far removed from Dick and Jane as middle age is from false teeth and rocking chairs.

But if the child-care industry has marched into the twenty-first century, its consumers and workers are still stuck decades behind. Parents are on their own in judging which caregivers are qualified and which homes are safe, which centers are stimulating and nurturing, and which are just warehouses. In no other area of the economy is something so important left to the rule of *caveat emptor:* "buyer beware."

Just as any quack or medicine man could once set up shop as a doctor and practice his trade on your body, today virtually anyone can set up shop as a caregiver and practice on your child. The commercialization of child care has created jobs for hundreds of thousands of women whose working conditions are unregulated, whose wages are bare subsistence, and whose qualifications and training may be nonexistent. Even a knowledge of the English language—the language of 911—is optional. From the point of view of parents, children, and the workers themselves, this is a scandal.

Very little of the money paid to the corporate suppliers trickles down into the hands that touch the children. In 1996, one-third of all day-care center workers were paid the minimum wage—then $4.25 an hour—and most family-care providers don't even make that, because they are self-employed and therefore not subject to the minimum wage laws. According to the Bureau of Labor Statistics, in 1998, family care providers earned an average of $3.84 an hour, compared with $6.61 an hour for teachers in child-care centers, $8.32 an hour for preschool teachers, and a national average wage of more than $14 an hour. As for benefits, only 18 percent of child-care centers offer health coverage to their teaching staff, and fewer still offer pensions.[3]

Few people realize that these caregivers, many of whom earn less than farmworkers, parking attendants, waitresses, janitors, blackjack dealers, or cashiers at fast-food restaurants, are better educated than the general population. Contrary to the popular perception that preschool teachers are glorified baby-sitters, 42 percent of them have some college education, compared with about 23 percent of the civilian labor force.[4]

These women's poor pay has less to do with their education than with the fact that they are competing with the ultimate cheap labor: mothers and other unpaid female relatives. As sociologist Paul England puts it, "We're used to getting it for free, so the attitude is, why pay for it?" In an analysis of the relationship between pay rates and types of skill required by occupations, England discovered that caring for others pays less than anything else in the economy, taking into account such factors as education, age, and race.[5]

Research has also shown that all predominantly female jobs are systematically underpaid. According to England, "The greater the percentage of women in a job, the lower the pay . . . and these nurturing skills are traditionally associated with women."[6]

Teachers of young children call their work "the toughest job you'll ever love." As economist Heidi Hartmann has written, "Child care is just about the worst women's job of all—so close to the bottom that it's almost inexplicable. You have to ask why . . . and you have to come up with the answer that there must be an intrinsic reward. Many people in this field are simply dedicated to the development and health of young children, and because of that we assume that it's safe to exploit them."[7]

I have even heard the argument that low pay for the members of a caring profession isn't necessarily bad; at least it weeds out the mercenaries. Interestingly, one seldom hears this about doctors.

But the free ride may finally be coming to an end. The child-care profession has been losing well-trained people who love children but can't afford to work with them anymore. Even altruistic people have to earn enough money to pay their rent and put food on the table.

A few years ago, the *Boston Globe* ran a story about a South Shore day-care teacher who had just been named one of the five most outstanding child-care workers in the country. Patty Onorato described how she had developed materials for a new, hands-on learning curriculum that she adapted to each child's individual needs, and how she took her preschoolers to art museums and taught them to value their different cultures. "I love this," she enthused. "I'm having a blast."[8]

Two years later, Onorato quit. She was making an annual salary of $18,000 after seven years of teaching. She became a waitress.

The teacher who took her place left after a year to take a sales and marketing job. The teacher after that, who had a B.S. in early childhood education, three years of teaching experience, and was completing a master's degree, was paid less than $18,000 a year. She was making approximately *half* as much as comparably qualified public school teachers and had to have two part-time jobs in order to survive.[9]

So many care providers need to have two jobs to make ends meet that they even have jokes about it:

Question: "Why did the child-care worker cross the road?"

Answer: "To get to her other job."

Kentucky Fried Child Care

Kathy Modigliani, a professor at Wheelock College in Boston who has studied the child-care industry for years, believes that the combination of low pay and fast growth is changing the profile of the typical day-care worker. "We're heading for big trouble," she told me. "Of all the things that threaten our society, this is right up there at the top."[10]

Modigliani explained that "in the 1970s all of these idealistic, educated people went into this field hoping to be able to do something for children. But they're getting older now and are sick and tired of not being able to afford a car or having people think of what they do as babysitting."

Modigliani showed me a poignant transcript of an interview with Annie, a talented teacher of three- to five-year-olds in Seattle:

> One morning Maia's mother said that Maia was going to another child's house that afternoon. She never does that. I could tell she was really upset about it. After her mother left, she climbed on the table. I had some rice and was serving it out for kids, and she tipped the bowl and the rice spilled all over the floor. Instead of yelling at her, I asked if she was worried about going to Sara's house. She burst out crying! She said, "I don't know what Sara's house looks like."
>
> So we sat down. I actually do know what Sara's house looks like—I'd been there for a parent conference—and so we talked about it. I said that if she was feeling worried during the day, that tipping the rice over made it harder because then it made me angry, and she didn't get to talk about being worried. Maybe she could just come up and say "I'm worried." And she did, a couple of times that day, and it just made me feel fantastic. It excited me. The talk with her and her response later in the day. That's what makes me feel good about being a teacher.

Later in this interview, Annie commented that she was probably going to have to give up working with young children because of the low pay and lack of respect for the job. She was thinking of becoming a bank teller.

Since 1975, average salaries in day-care centers have not kept pace with inflation, in sharp contrast to the dramatic jump in the salaries of teachers, K–12, in the same period.[11] According to Modigliani, as an earlier generation of idealistic, well-trained people like Annie leave, "they are being replaced by young, poorly trained workers from the low end of the labor market. What you're seeing is more and more children spending their days in Kentucky Fried Child Care, tended by unmotivated people whose turnover matches that of gas station attendants."

Cecelie Blakey, a black professional in Washington, D.C., is one of those who has left. Back in the late 1970s, as a newly minted graduate of Howard University, she worked in a private nursery school teaching two-and-a-half- and three-year-old children of the black middle class. She still considers it "the best job I ever had," but she couldn't afford to keep it.

What was she earning? "I'll never forget it. It was 1977, and I had left a job with the D.C. government paying $12,500 to take the nursery school job at $5,600. That's how much I wanted to work with children. But then I quit and went to law school. Day-care work just wasn't competitive with my other options."[12]

Blakey became one of the few black women to graduate from Harvard Law School; when we spoke she was heading a small nonprofit organization working for economic justice. She is still motivated more by helping others than by money, but her current annual salary of $50,000 is a fortune compared to what she would be making had she stayed in early childhood education.

Similar stories are commonplace. When the Center for the Child Care Workforce, a group promoting higher wages for caregivers, sent out 25,000 postcards asking parents and care providers to describe how low wages affected them, it received numerous replies like this one from a teacher in Austin, Texas: "Although I have a Master's degree in early childhood education and 20 years of experience and I love what I do, I am seriously considering leaving the field so my own children can attend college."

One-third of all child-care teachers in the United States leave their centers each year, and many centers have annual turnover rates approaching 50 percent.[13] Fully 70 percent of the teaching staff interviewed in 1988 for a child-care staffing study had left their jobs by 1992, with the highest turnover found among the lowest-paid people.[14] The exodus is, if anything, accelerating as more states, like California, move toward mandatory kindergarten and class size reduction in the primary grades. These new opportunities siphon off the better-trained early-childhood teachers, who can make two or three times as much money and many more benefits as teachers of older children than they could ever make working with toddlers.

"We're hearing many more stories about nurseries, day-care centers, and after-school programs not being able to fill their positions with qualified and well-trained people," Marci Young, executive director of the Center for the Child Care Workforce, a nonprofit advocacy organization, told me in early 2000. "They're having a hard time retaining the kind of people they want."

And what some people call turnover, children experience as loss. From a parent in Eau Claire, Wisconsin: "The turnover at my child's daycare center has caused emotional upheavals each time [it] occur[s]. Our son weeps and acts out after a change of providers." From an administrator in Boise, Idaho, an area where the turnover rate is 41 percent: "[The children express] anxiety and frustration that results in discipline and learning problems and low self-esteem." From a teacher in Madison, Wisconsin: "I worked in one center where I was the third teacher in one year in a classroom of two-year-olds. It took the children over a month to stop asking 'Are you coming back?'"

There is evidence that even slightly higher wages can reduce turnover. A recent study found that day-care centers that managed to retain highly skilled teachers paid them at least $2 an hour more than comparably educated teachers in other centers in the same area.[15] Bright Horizons, a work-site child-care organization, pays its teachers only 10 percent more than whatever the going rate may be at nearby centers, and has a rate of teacher turnover that averages only half of the industry average.

In Madison, Wisconsin, one of the few places where child-care workers are organized into a union, the slightly higher pay of unionized staff has had a measurable effect on turnover. In 1993, unionized day-care workers were earning an average of $8.72 an hour, versus $7.03 an hour for nonunion day-care workers in the same county. Turnover in the county as a whole was 33 percent (including the unionized programs), while turnover within the unionized day-care programs was only 13 percent, according to an organizer.[16]

A program in North Carolina called TEACH has had a similarly dramatic effect. Participants in the project who complete an average of eighteen credit hours per year receive an average of 10 percent increase in their wages. They have a less than 10 percent turnover rate, compared with a statewide rate of 42 percent.[17]

"When daycare centers offer higher pay, the quality is definitely better, as measured in child outcomes," claims Barbara Willer of the National Association for the Education of Young Children. "Programs that invest in staff have lower turnover and more continuity of care, which translates into better language and social skills."

Moreover, there is evidence—hardly surprising—that better-trained care providers can have a measurable effect on children's progress. After the state of Florida mandated higher educational requirements for child-care staff in 1992, children's cognitive development and behavior improved, according to a study by the Families and Work Institute.[18]

Despite this evidence, many state and Federal policies actually work to keep wages and quality low. Although most state governments require licensing for dog handlers, they will let almost anyone loose with a baby. In numerous states there are no courses required of child-care providers, no exams to measure knowledge, no certification of skills, and no experience necessary. In some states, a person can become a provider with only a high school diploma. As advocates of higher standards point out, even manicurists are typically required to have more training.[19]

Accreditation of day-care centers is also not required by any state. Of the nation's 97,000 day-care centers, only 5,000 are accredited and another 10,000 are seeking accreditation. The only rules that exist mainly have to do with "hardware" issues, like building safety, and relatively little to do with teacher qualifications, reinforcing the idea that anyone can do the job. Of course they can, but not well.

Fully 82 percent of the roughly 1 million family-care homes in the United States are unregulated by anyone. "Family day-care homes are a good deal riskier than group day-care centers," William Gormley of Georgetown University, an authority on child-care policy, told me. "They are less likely to be regulated, less likely to be inspected, and there is usually no supervision of adults by other adults." In Illinois, for example, all the provider has to do is sign a form stating that there are no unlocked guns or poisons on the premises, and no one around who has ever abused children.

The lack of supervision of and support for caregivers working in their own homes is particularly troubling in light of the removal of welfare guarantees in 1996. The new law forced millions of poor mothers to find someone—anyone—to care for their children while they went to work outside the home. Most are turning to relatives, neighbors, and friends, who often have meager resources and rarely any training in child development or early education.[20] If the relative happens to be old and tired, if the neighbor is disoriented and isolated, or if the friend drinks, so be it. Let the consumer and her kids beware.

In Connecticut, in one year alone, there were four well-publicized deaths of children who had been in unregulated care. Shortly thereafter, state legislator Ann Dandrow received a call from a probation officer telling her that a man who had just been released from prison was receiving state subsidies of $150 a week to care for two children of a relative.

This was too much for Dandrow, a Republican. She announced that she didn't want anyone taking care of children who didn't meet the same minimal standards that are applied to family-care providers. In 1996 Dandrow introduced legislation requiring that anyone caring for the children of former welfare recipients at least be checked for a history of felony or child abuse, and have first-aid training. Homes of paid providers would be checked for working telephones, smoke alarms, adequate heating and water, and sufficient indoor and outdoor play space.

Dandrow's proposal seems unassailable, yet it was immediately attacked by conservatives and advocates for the poor. "This bill would turn state government into a gigantic nanny," declared one male Republican. "We should leave the choice to the families."[21] Welfare recipients, who demonstrated against the bill, said it would only make it harder for them to find caregivers.

After welfare reform some states even experimented with the bright idea of recruiting welfare mothers as unpaid caregivers. In twenty-six states, welfare mothers who agreed to take in a few extra children would be allowed to keep their benefits. There is nothing wrong with providing unemployed but otherwise capable women with the proper training to become licensed family-care providers. But under these new laws, a welfare mother who became a care provider would receive no training, no support services, or any additional resources for the job. Not surprisingly, when I checked a couple of years later, I was told that "basically, that effort didn't get very far."

"It's a hard job," said Carol Brunson Day of the Council for Early Childhood Professional Recognition, "and some states had a really difficult time recruiting people to do it. Also, the whole point of welfare reform was to get people to be self-sufficient, and the wages in child care are too low for that."

A few states have taken even more direct measures to keep wages low. The laws against "price-fixing" have been used to prevent organizations of care providers from proposing in their literature that early childhood teachers be paid a certain minimum, i.e., as much as $10 an hour, or as much as primary school teachers. Although many family-care providers are just trying to earn a little extra money on the side while they stay at home with their children, and don't think of themselves as having a "real job," to the government they are running a business, and must be prevented from talking to their "competitors" about what they charge.

Providers are not even allowed to exchange information that would help them rationalize their finances. During a session at the 1995 annual meeting of the National Association for the Education of Young Children, a family-care provider from Minneapolis described her frustrations in trying to run an educational workshop: "There was no way we could talk about how to raise rates enough to cover expenses and a salary." When one group of providers in the city put their rates on a paper that was put up on a bulletin board, they received a cease-and-desist letter from the Justice Department. Another caregiver told the session that during a Christmas party thrown by several providers, "one guy said, 'I don't care what the rest of you do, I'm raising my rates 3 percent next year.' During the next six months all of them raised their rates—and they got cited."

These and similar stories left the roomful of some fifty people pondering the idea of the full weight of the federal government coming down on isolated individuals earning subsistence wages caring for babies. If one were looking for evidence that women and children have no power, this is it.

Does It Have to Be Mom?

Of course, not all American mothers, or fathers, support the idea of professional child care. Americans are more ambivalent about nonparental care than almost any other people on earth—which is why it is so hard to find quality, affordable child care in the United States. A huge segment of the population worries that care by anyone other than a mother herself is not only not optimal but downright harmful to children.

The passion with which these views are held, like the passions aroused by abortion, is often immune to "evidence" or persuasion. Nevertheless, there is no reason to believe that dedicated and well-trained paid caregivers cannot perform "the most important job in the world" perfectly well. If they couldn't, where would that have left the entire ruling class of nineteenth- and early-twentieth-century Britain, including Winston Churchill, who went straight from their nannies' knees to their boarding schools to the corridors of imperial power? A more thoroughgoing system of professional child-rearing, minimizing the influence of mothers, would be hard to devise.

According to Shoshana Grossbard-Shechtman, a professor of economics at San Diego State University who studied under Theodore W. Schultz, the "father of human capital theory," there is not a shred of evidence that the traditional nuclear family creates more human capital than any other arrangement. "Professor Schultz supported women's careers, including my own when he was my mentor at the University of Chicago," Grossbard-Schectman assured me. "He never believed that mothers should stay at home."

Indeed, for children from disadvantaged homes, professional early care and education can make all the difference in life. A number of studies have shown that disadvantaged children who were placed in developmental, as opposed to merely custodial, care had better outcomes than children who stayed at home with their mothers or who were "parked" with untrained baby-sitters. Moreover, the younger these disadvantaged children went into such programs, the better they did later in life. Trained, professional caregivers were apparently able to give them more "human capital" than their hard-pressed families were able to provide.

Researchers at Johns Hopkins University, for example, in a study of 867 children nationwide, found that when children from the poorest and least-stimulating homes were placed in child-care centers before they were one year old, they later performed better on math and reading tests than children who were not in day care. In another study, the Abecedarian Project, involving 111 poor African-American families in Chapel Hill, North Carolina, children placed in full-time day care from infancy to age five consistently outperformed their peers on both cognitive and academic tests and were more likely to have attended college or attained high-skill jobs by age twenty-one. The children enrolled in this project outstripped their peers by an even wider margin than children who had entered a similar program in Michigan at the ripe old age of three or four.[22]

The toddlers in the latter program, the Perry Preschool Project, were given the "essential ingredients [that] resourceful parents typically provide," including a structured day, intellectual and social stimulation, plenty of hugs and kisses, and tender, loving care.[23] By the time the Perry graduates reached age nineteen, they were much more likely than members of a control group to have graduated from high school and to be employed, and significantly less likely to have been arrested, to have had a pregnancy, or to be on welfare.[24] By age twenty-seven, the Perry group were five times less likely to be chronic lawbreakers. A similar pilot program in Syracuse, New York, found that its children were ten times less likely to be delinquent by age sixteen than children denied its services—leading an organization of top police officers to advocate more spending on early childhood education as an effective approach to crime prevention.[25]

The mounting evidence from these studies has convinced many child-care experts—and economists—that the time has come for universal early education, or at least subsidized child care for children whose parents lack educational, emotional, or economic resources. According to Arleen Leibowitz of RAND, "Children growing up in [welfare] homes are doubly disadvantaged—they lack the advantages of having greater financial resources, but they often also suffer from not being exposed to the more enriched preschool environments available to children in out-of-home care."[26]

When I spoke with Leibowitz, she told me that many economists were convinced that subsidized early education would be cost-effective if targeted at a high-risk population. "I recently attended a conference with a group of economists," she said, "and the only area in which they were willing to put more public resources was not health care, not education, but early child care. . . . They understand now that it can be quite productive, socially and culturally as well as cognitively, especially for disadvantaged kids."[27]

But no such care is given. The tragedy is not just that welfare, the subsidy for full-time mother-care, was eliminated, but that it was swept away without being replaced by a guarantee of quality care for every child.

Join the Army

Ironically, the U.S. military is one of the few American institutions that does understand that quality child care, like quality soldiering, does not come cheap. The Department of Defense provides the largest and what many consider the best child-care system in the country, by treating its paid caregivers—like its soldiers—as skilled professionals who require training and all of the support and equipment they need.

The military subsidizes day care for some 200,000 children of its personnel. In the fall of 1997, I visited a woman who was providing care to five of those kids in her home on the grounds of Ft. Meade, a huge military base located in Maryland, south of Baltimore. Elaine McCann was a civilian working under contract to the military to care for children in her own home. She loved working with children, but she had also had to complete a thirteen-unit course covering child development, psychology, and health and safety as part of her certification. If an aspiring caregiver can't complete the course within eighteen months, she has to leave the system. If she makes it, she receives a civil service–level income, roughly twice that of her civilian counterparts, plus full benefits and a chance for promotion. To top it all off, more than 75 percent of the Department of Defense's child-care programs have been independently accredited, versus 7 percent nationally.

McCann, like every other trained caregiver I have ever interviewed, told me that the instruction was invaluable. Above all, it had taught her that she was a professional, a true good-parent surrogate, not a baby-sitter or "child-minder" or "help." After observing her in action one day, I became convinced that every *parent* as well as every paid caregiver ought to be required to take the same training course.

McCann's small town house had only two rooms downstairs, a living-dining room combination and a kitchen. The space was completely given over to toddlers and their staggering array of equipment: toys, puzzles, books, not to mention strollers, cribs, and sleeping mats. Artwork and decorations covered every inch of wall space. McCann's husband, like the husbands of almost all of the family-care providers on military bases, was an enlisted man, who stopped off during the day to say hello. It occurred to me that the "fighting men" in these providers' homes live in a world of children to a far greater extent than most men or women today. Those who fret about the "feminization" of politics might ponder the fact that almost 10,000 active-duty servicemen willingly choose to live in what amount to nurseries. "My husband loves kids," another provider, the wife of a drill sergeant, told me. "In fact, when he gets out in two years, we're planning to start a day-care center together."

I had imagined that a small house containing five children under the age of five would probably be a scene of chaos and squalor. But at the McCanns' all was relaxed orderliness. Part of the secret seemed to be a plan. Both the children and their teacher were busy all day in a varied but predictable routine. Children love continuity and routine, and here everyone knew what to expect.

Military family-care providers are offered ideas on scheduling and daily activities by a monthly newsletter and by supervisors who visit regularly. Mornings after breakfast at Elaine McCann's were devoted to arts and crafts, kitchen science projects, and the like, and an outing in a nearby park if the weather was nice. Next came time with toys while "Miss Elaine" fixed a hot lunch (one protein, one vegetable, one fruit). Picking up the toys was a game, directed by the oldest girl, whom Elaine described as the group's "mother figure." Just before lunch everyone trooped down to the bus stop to meet the five-year-old, who had spent the morning at kindergarten—another chance to run and scream and let off steam.

After lunch came nap time, a snack, and more physical activity, including songs and outdoor play. Interspersed throughout the day were games to encourage children to express their feelings, to resolve conflicts, to share. (One game was "Let's talk about happy feelings and sad feelings.") Providers can borrow toys and equipment free from a lending library on the base. "If you're running short on what to do, there's plenty of help," Dorothy Huff, another Ft. Meade woman who cares for five children, told me. "I called the other day and said we're going to do dinosaurs or trucks, and they sent a whole bunch of books over to me."

I had to admit that although I had a lot of help *and* stayed home part of the time while my son was small, these children were probably getting a richer daily experience than he had had. While I was at McCann's house, Captain Pamela Pewitt came in to pay a noontime visit to her eighteen-month-old, the youngest in McCann's daytime "family." She confided that she felt the same way.

"My kid often doesn't want to leave," she said. "Sometimes at home he'll walk around and swing his arms like 'What are we going to do now, Mom? I'm bored!'" Pewitt told me she had turned down a better-paying job as a civilian systems analyst because she couldn't find any other care that came close to what the military offered—at subsidized rates.

The fees in military day-care centers ranged from $37 to $98 a week in 1997, with parents paying on a sliding scale based on income. This represents a fraction of the actual cost. What the military has done is break the link between what parents pay and what good care really costs, by heavily subsidizing the care (at an average $3,400 per year per child). Even if they could find the kind of care offered by Elaine McCann, most families could never afford it.

One of the centers that Pewitt visited when she was contemplating leaving the military "had ten infants sitting on the floor rocking, with runny noses," she said. "There were three adults there, but they had nothing to say when I tried to ask questions. . . . My neighbor is pregnant right now, and I can see the panic on her face. She doesn't know what she is going to do. She asked me, 'Do you know anyone? Can your provider take him?' I had to tell her you had to be in the military to have Elaine."[28]

A mother has to join the military in order to find decent, affordable child care? Am I the only one who thinks this is crazy?

CHAPTER 12

An Accident Waiting to Happen

> CHILD MONITOR (domestic ser.): Observes and monitors play activities or amuses children by reading to or playing games with them. Prepares and serves meals or formulas. Sterilizes bottles and other equipment used for feeding infants. Dresses or assists children to dress and bathe. Accompanies children on walks or other outings. Washes and irons clothing. Keeps children's quarters clean and tidy. Cleans other parts of home. . . . May be designated Baby Sitter (domestic ser.) when employed on daily or hourly basis.
>
> —U.S. government's definition of child care in a private home

In the fall of 1997, a nineteen-year-old English girl was convicted in Boston of killing a baby who was under her care. The girl, Louise Woodward, was a teenager who had minimal qualifications to care for an infant. And yet she had been admitted into the country for the express purpose of caring for two young children, an eight-month-old and his three-year-old brother.

The outrage on both sides of the Atlantic that accompanied Woodward's trial and conviction included criticism of the murdered child's mother, an optometrist who had had the audacity to leave her baby for a few hours a day, three days a week, to practice her profession. But the anger that was so aggressively directed at the two women never quite focused on the real issue: Why on earth was the United States allowing immature kids into the country to take responsible jobs caring for young children?

Working parents still don't realize that their enormous difficulties in finding qualified, responsible caregivers to work in their homes are the direct result of an obscure immigration law that ranks trained nannies as "unskilled" labor. This strange state of affairs began in 1990, when Congress passed an immigration bill that drastically reduced the number of unskilled immigrants allowed to enter the United States. Since nannies and child-care workers were defined under the new law as unskilled, they were effectively shut out of the country, unless they come under the au pair program, which allows foreign students to work in exchange for bed, board, and a stipend. After 1990, if Mary Poppins tried to get an American work permit, she would be denied.

The new law virtually guaranteed that there would be insufficient trained, legal caregivers to meet the rapidly growing demand for in-home child care. Since it was passed, countless working parents who need support have either had to hire unqualified people, including many of the teenagers who are admitted as au pairs, or break the law. As a result, working women face a terrible choice: they can go to work and risk leaving their children in unsafe hands, or stay at home and risk losing their livelihood and financial independence. The official disregard for child care affects every child's safety and every mother's peace of mind, regardless of income or class.

The immigration bill was a bipartisan effort, drafted by Senators Ted Kennedy and Alan Simpson in 1988. Kennedy was then chairman of the Senate Subcommittee on Immigration and Refugee Affairs, and Simpson, the previous chairman, was a passionate advocate of greater restrictions on immigration. At the time, approximately 27,000 unskilled people were entering the United States legally every year, including women who were coming to fill jobs as housekeepers and nannies. Democratic staffer Eugene Pugliese told me he remembers saying to his Republican counterpart, "'Why are we taking in 27,000 unskilled workers a year, when we get at least that many every day or every month coming in across the border illegally?' We weren't confident that there was a need for visas for these workers," he added.[1]

According to a female aide with firsthand knowledge of the negotiations, when one of the senators' male staffers asked who would be affected by the elimination of visas for the unskilled, the answer was "maids and rich matrons in Beverly Hills." In other words, no one we need worry about.

Warren R. Leiden, executive director of the American Immigration Lawyers Association, claims the senators were fully aware that such a restriction would have adverse effects on working mothers. "I was told, behind closed doors, that if women want to leave the home and go to work, then let them pay $45,000 a year for the privilege," he said. "Let them be put to that trial. There was a real hostility to working women.

"But there's also a real irony in Congress voting this in," Leiden continued. "Lots of senators, congressmen, and their staffers, who have working wives, are trying to bring in foreign home-care workers."[2]

The first step an employer has to take to bring in a worker is to apply to the Labor Department for a certification that no American can be found to fill the job. The agency then has to classify the applicant as to skill level, using the government's *Dictionary of Occupation Titles,* a compilation of more than 21,000 salaried occupations.

The *Dictionary* became infamous in the 1970s when a study revealed that it rated many "women's" jobs at the lowest possible level of complexity. Paid occupations resembling traditional women's work, like nursery school teacher, were classified as custodial or menial labor—far below such elevated tasks as marine mammal handler, barber, and bus driver. The government rankings also overemphasized formal education, so that occupations requiring "people skills," jobs like clergyman or dean of boys, received higher ratings than foster mother, a demanding job involving work with often troubled children. Jobs in the caring field, including home nursing and child care, were not even listed. There was, for example, no such thing as a "nanny."

The 1970s study had concluded that the *Dictionary* "systematically—though not purposely—discriminates against virtually all nondegreed, people-oriented women's jobs. . . . jobs suffering most are the salaried derivatives of homemaking and mothering, particularly those at the paraprofessional level in the fields of health, education, and welfare."[3]

In response to this critique, some changes were made. All job titles were made gender-neutral, so that the occupation of "governess" became "children's tutor." And many traditional women's occupations were moved up from the notorious .878 code, which had branded them as devoid of any significant skill. But mysteriously, the Department of Labor still considers even British-trained nannies with two-year diplomas from training colleges as unskilled workers for purposes of immigration. They have to be classified either as a "child monitor" whose job description (quoted above) is that of a menial, or as a "children's tutor," a job that is also given an unskilled ranking.

The new Kennedy-Simpson immigration bill didn't in the end eliminate all visas for unskilled workers, but it did reduce the annual allocation to 10,000. The change meant that after 1991, when the law went into effect, only about 4,000 to 5,000 individuals intending to work as nannies were granted permission to do so in the United States each year.

To put these numbers in perspective, in 1990 there were an estimated 325,000 nannies in the United States, including roughly 75,000 who were living in their employers' homes. According to the Census Bureau, by 1995, half a million American children under the age of five were being cared for by nannies. The demand for at-home care, not just of young children but of the elderly, is expected to skyrocket in the coming years. With most working-age women now unavailable for full-time unpaid child care, the Bureau of Labor Statistics has predicted that residential care will be the fastest-growing industry in the country in the next decade.

In short, the decision to shut off the legal supply of people willing to care for family dependents in a home was bound to affect hundreds of thousands of American families, not just a few rich matrons in Beverly Hills.

When I spoke with Eugene Pugliese in 1995, he denied that his legislative handiwork had contributed to a nanny shortage. "They say about child care that 'an American won't do it.' But there isn't anything you can't get an American to do, if you pay them enough. If you pay *me* enough, *I'd* do it."

One female staffer working for Democratic congressman Charles Schumer saw the issue differently. "I had a baby in 1989," she told me in a telephone interview, after being assured of anonymity. "I had just been through the experience of looking for a nanny in the Washington area, as well as having friends who were going through it. I *knew* that it was not true that you could find Americans for these jobs. I had placed an ad, not mentioning salary, in the *Washington Post* for a housekeeper, and out of about seventy calls, *two* were from Americans. About 90 percent of the responses were from illegals. You can't talk to anyone who doesn't know about this—my neighbor, my friends, all of them have illegal help. I even had one employment agency say to me, 'It's too bad you have to have somebody who's legal—we have some great Filipinas.'"

Like other mothers, I too had discovered that Americans don't want these jobs. And no wonder: the hours are long, the pay is low, the conditions are lonely, and the societal respect is nil. Many of the women who might be interested have children of their own, and no one to care for them. Black Americans in particular are understandably dead set against repeating their mothers' and grandmothers' unhappy history of working for white women in servile, dead-end jobs. In 1972, 40 percent of full-time domestic workers were black—more than 500,000 women. By 1995, fewer than 17 percent of household workers were black—137,000 women.

Many immigrants come from a different, more desperate place. They may have left their own children back home and are more than willing to put in a few years in other people's homes in return for a chance at a better life. Some actually prefer to live in, because they can save money faster and feel relatively secure from the Immigration and Naturalization Service. The work is frequently unpleasant and exploitative, but that has been the history of the immigrant in the United States from the beginning, and people who see a job as a stepping-stone are more willing to endure it for a while than those who see it as a trap.

In sum, reducing the number of nannies legally admitted from abroad effectively dried up the supply of legal, in-home care providers in the United States. But not a peep of protest was heard from the American women who would be affected.

Every previous restriction on immigration had brought the affected American employers to Washington, D.C., to object, more often than not successfully. When agricultural growers complained about a 1986 ban on hiring undocumented workers, for example, the government responded by allowing more than 1 million undocumented farmworkers to qualify for legal status. The 1990 law itself opened the doors wider to foreign professionals, including managers, computer programmers, and marketing specialists, in response to complaints from corporations that they needed employees from abroad for those well-paying jobs.

But the restrictions on at-home caregivers, a serious impediment to the livelihood of a large percentage of professional women in this country, were not challenged by a single women's organization. "There was no letter, no phone calls, nothing submitted to any congressman on this subcommittee, saying that because of what you guys are doing, it's going to be harder than ever for working women to find reasonable child care, to keep their jobs," Pugliese told me. "Nobody's called about this but you."

The only voices raised came from the immigration bar, which makes a living helping clients bring workers into the country. One attorney, Carolyn Killea, appeared on a Washington, D.C., radio show in the summer of 1990 and accurately predicted what was going to happen. "Working women, who are trying to get care for their children, for older family members, and handicapped family members, are going to feel these provisions the most," she declared prophetically, "because they are relying on largely immigrant women to enable them to work. . . . This law is an accident waiting to happen."

"I told anyone who would listen that we were going to do ourselves out of the next generation of women leaders," she later recalled. "I never expected to be proven right so soon, with the Zoe Baird case."[4]

Zoe Baird was general counsel at Aetna Life and Casualty when President Bill Clinton, before his inauguration, announced that she was his choice for attorney general. Shortly thereafter, Baird herself revealed that she had hired two illegal aliens as domestic staff and failed to pay the required Social Security taxes on their wages. This was a civil violation, and one of Baird's advisers had told her that it might be similar to a parking ticket. Years before, back in the early 1970s, it had come out that William Ruckelshaus, then deputy attorney general, had a foreign woman with an improper visa working in his home. His wife, Jill, was blamed for the oversight, and the matter was quickly passed over.

The offense was not something that had been red-flagged by the FBI's routine background checks, and it was not something that any male appointee had ever thought important enough to bring up. The hearings on Baird's confirmation in January 1993 revealed, however, that her maternal obligations were of great interest to the Senate Judiciary Committee, the same all-male body that had grilled Anita Hill. The senators were particularly curious about how many hours Baird spent away from her four-year-old son, Julian, inquiring when she left home in the morning and when she got home at night. "I must have been out of the room when those questions were asked of Ron Brown," commented Delissa A. Ridgway, president of the Women's Bar Association of the District of Columbia.

Zoe Baird's interrogators were unaware of the lengths to which Baird and her husband, Paul Gewirtz, a constitutional law professor at Yale, had gone to find legal child care. In 1990, the year after Julian was born, Baird had been named the top lawyer for Aetna, at a salary of $507,105. (The couple's combined income was $660,345.) The pair obviously could afford a full-time nanny, and they originally hired an American citizen who worked for them for five months before quitting with two weeks' notice.[5]

The couple then placed this ad in three local newspapers:

> Child Care Nanny. Live-in Nanny for 7 Mo. old Boy in warm family setting. Light housekeeping, cook dinners. Long term position with appreciative family in beautiful home. Non-smoker. Driver. Citizen or green card only. Require child care references.

They received not one response.

They contacted an agency and flew in an American candidate from Texas at their own expense. She refused the job, she explained, because she didn't feel comfortable working for a Jewish family. There followed a series of frustrating interviews with other applicants sent by agencies. One said that she had decided not to leave her current job; one took another job before the scheduled interview; one had a negative reference from her employer; one admitted that she smoked. The couple finally hired a woman who quit after a few days, explaining that she was homesick.

An acquaintance who had lunch with Baird around this time told me that she was not surprised to learn that Baird and Gewirtz had "nanny problems." It appeared to her that the couple was looking for someone to be on duty virtually every waking hour, a person who would be a de facto parent to the infant. This woman remembers thinking, "She's not going to find someone like that, even a live-in."

Finally, an agency sent a Peruvian woman named Lilian Cordero, who, Baird felt, would make a suitable caretaker for Julian. Cordero wanted to negotiate a job for her husband as well, so Baird and Gewirtz agreed to take him on as a driver, even though they didn't think they really needed one.

This was the summer of 1990. Professor Gewirtz was not teaching, so he assured his busy wife that he would handle the legal work involving the Corderos—whereupon he stepped into a Kafkaesque legal and bureaucratic maze that confounded even a Yale law professor.

Gewirtz was first told by an immigration lawyer that he couldn't pay Social Security taxes on the Corderos' wages until they had Social Security numbers, and they couldn't have numbers until they had permanent residency status, or green cards. Several months later Gewirtz filed for a labor certification for Lilian Cordero (certifying that no American citizen had been found for the job). This was approved, and he then filed an application with the INS for a green card. In October 1992 Cordero was approved for a green card, to be issued when her number in the visa application waiting list came up. But by this time, her husband had deserted her, and in November she too left the household. After Baird was nominated attorney general, the couple paid about $12,000 in back taxes and fines.

That was Zoe Baird's crime. But hiring illegal help, a civil violation, was not her real transgression. A few weeks after her nomination was rejected by the Judiciary Committee, her mentor, Lloyd Cutler, told me, "It was *women* who killed her appointment. The committee was deluged with angry calls and letters from women, denouncing her in the worst possible terms."

The grassroots attack on Baird was in stark contrast to the utter silence with which women had greeted the passage of the immigration law. Some female writers opined that Baird came across as a cold person. ("Compared to whom? Warren Christopher?" wondered one Washington female attorney.)

Other working women betrayed their resentment over the fact that Baird had not made the kinds of career sacrifices that they had—turning down promotions or choice assignments—in order to have more time with their children. Women who followed the drama closely told me they believed that this was what hounded Zoe Baird out of Washington more than anything else. There was a "we've paid; now *she* has to pay" quality to the attacks on her. (Baird's workaholism was never in question; she had called presidential aide Howard Paster at 8:00 P.M. on Christmas Eve to strategize about her confirmation, to the disgust of Paster's wife.)

Not one major women's organization stepped up to the plate for Baird, despite the blatant double standard that was being applied to her case. With their own memberships bitterly divided over the affair, no national group wanted to risk taking a controversial stand on behalf of a beleaguered corporate attorney who had never been particularly active in women's causes.

Then there was the liberal guilt factor, as thick as smoke at a barbeque. "There was some skittishness about the class thing," Warren Leiden told me. "I met with some women at the American Bar Association who were very interested in doing something about the housekeeper/nanny shortage. But there was this sense that it was somehow selfish and inappropriate for women to be seeking solutions just for themselves, for what many saw as a privilege."

I ran across this guilt phenomenon one day while skimming the Internet. I came across an ongoing conversation among female academic economists on the touchy subject of household help. Constance Newman of the University of California at Davis had suggested that to be entirely politically correct, a professional woman should consider not hiring any domestic help. Newman's proposal had unleashed an anguished uproar from computers from coast to coast. One correspondent logically noted that "short of doing all the household and childcare oneself, which is clearly not possible, the only alternative to offending Constance's sensibilities is to hire men to do those tasks."

Once Baird's case achieved notoriety, no one, male or female, who had ever hired an undocumented worker or failed to pay Social Security taxes for an employee could be safely considered for top public office. A new penalty was added to all the others attached to motherhood. A friend of mine, a forty-year-old public policy analyst, saw this immediately. "Just when we are on the verge of moving into real power," she lamented, "they invented a new reason to keep us out."

Kimba Wood, the next candidate for attorney general, had broken no laws at all, but because she had hired an undocumented child-care worker before 1986, when it was legal to do so, she was forced to withdraw.

The legacy of the Baird fiasco continues to punish working parents. Women—and some men—with young children are still being disqualified for judgeships and high government positions because they have a "Zoe Baird problem," shorthand for having run afoul of one of the myriad laws regulating household workers. In 1994 I had a conversation with Clarine Riddle, a former attorney general of Connecticut, who was then assisting Senator Joseph Lieberman in selecting candidates for the next available federal judgeship in that state. "I interviewed about twenty-five people, the overwhelming majority of them women," she told me, "and more than half had some kind of nanny problem in the past, mostly the failure to pay Social Security taxes." Riddle explained that the new disqualifier hurt women far more than men, because virtually every working mother needs a nanny, while many men can count on their wives to take care of the kids. She believes that the number of women appointed to judgeships in the 1990s was significantly lower than it might have been had this controversy never erupted.

Interestingly, the issue of immigration restrictions never became a focus of media attention at the time of the Zoe Baird affair. Attorney Killea says that she was contacted by several women television reporters who wanted to do a show on the immigration roadblock, but "then they'd say, 'By the way, I have a nanny. Should I do this show?' I would tell them the INS will look at you, and if something is not completely [on the] up-and-up, they could put your nanny into deportation proceedings and cite you for employer sanctions. And then what happens to your kid?" No one did the show.

It would be absurdly simple to alleviate the shortage of legal nannies. If home-care workers were simply reclassified—correctly—as skilled, they would fall into a category for which visas are readily available. One wonders why this solution did not occur to any of the American women's organizations. It did occur to one woman, however.

When the 1990 immigration law began to take effect, Priscilla Labovitz, an immigration lawyer in suburban Washington, D.C., decided to challenge the Department of Labor's definition of a nanny's job. One of her cases involved an English nanny who wanted to enter the United States to work for a couple in northern Virginia. The woman had two years of formal training in the care and development of children and seven years of child-care experience. Labovitz filed an application for Labor certification, asking that the applicant be considered a "nanny," which she described as a skilled occupation. She explained that the job's purpose was "to care for, and supervise the development (physical, intellectual, moral) of, children during most of their waking hours." The various tasks included teaching two young children social skills, conferring with their doctors, transporting them to appointments, preparing nutritious meals; in short, all of the services that parents provide.[6]

In her statement on the application, the mother explained that she was the owner and operator of a publishing company and had to take three- or four-day business trips about twice a month. Her husband, an investment banker, also had to travel frequently and unexpectedly. The mother stated that "because of our national failure to place sufficient value on the early development of children," she had encountered a shortage of professionally trained American nannies. She said that she had called every one of the fourteen nanny programs in the country and been told that there were lengthy waiting lists for their graduates. While waiting to find the right person, both she and her husband had cut their jobs back to thirty hours a week. Labovitz's effort to certify the English woman as a skilled worker was denied on the grounds that the parents, by asking for a person with two years of training plus experience, were asking for more than the job required.

In the meantime, Labovitz had applied to the Department of Labor requesting that the "new" occupation of "nanny" be established and coded as "skilled," requiring two years of formal training plus child-care experience. Normally, requests for new occupational categories take a couple of weeks to be OK'd. In this case, several months went by before the request finally came back in April of 1994. It had been approved.

"I was ecstatic," Labovitz recalled during an interview in her office. "The decision was published in the newsletter of the American Immigration Lawyers Association, and I got calls from all over the country. It meant that people meeting the standards would have to wait only about a year for a visa.

"The first thing I did was call the Department of Labor and ask them to reconsider [the English nanny's] application in light of the change. The woman I spoke with congratulated me, and said, 'I thought you were right all along.'

"Then about fifteen minutes later, the woman called back. 'We're going to deny the cert,' she said, 'and he [her superior in the regional labor certifying office in Philadelphia] says we'll fight you all the way.'"

A week later, the Department of Labor officially reversed its decision to create a new occupational category. In a letter to Labovitz, a bureaucrat in the department's occupational analysis center explained that the original decision was "based on insufficient fact-finding and research." According to immigration attorneys, there is little chance that Congress will remedy the situation given the current climate of hostility toward immigration.

Labovitz says that she now tells people who are working as nannies and who want to get a green card to go to college and study something *other than early childhood development* for two years and then apply as a skilled worker. As she puts it, "We've created an absolute disincentive for foreign-born workers to get training in child care."

With qualified caregivers shut out of the country, the only in-home workers who are currently allowed to enter are au pairs. Originally intended to be a form of cultural exchange, the au pair program offered girls a chance to live with an American family and study at a local institution in return for some service. But over the years, it has become more of a conveyor belt bringing in female teenagers to serve as cheap domestic help. These girls are allowed to care for infants after only twenty-four hours of instruction in child development and one day of safety training. Their contracts allow them to work ten hours a day, forty-five hours a week, at wages of little more than $3 an hour, plus room and board and a small educational stipend.

Three years before the Louise Woodward case in Boston, another nineteen-year-old au pair, a Dutch girl, was accused of shaking an eight-week-old baby to death in Virginia. The jury deadlocked in the girl's trial for manslaughter, and she was subsequently convicted of a misdemeanor and sent home. In the wake of that incident, the federal government proposed much tougher standards for au pairs. But 3,500 people, most of them mothers, wrote letters complaining that the new rules would raise the cost of au pairs and limit the hours they could work. Faced with this outcry, the government backed down and dropped a couple of the proposed new requirements. One of these would have prevented anyone under the age of twenty-one from caring for infants of less than two years old.[7] Had this regulation been adopted, Louise Woodward and Matthew Eappen would never have met.

The Canadian Solution

Just across the border in Canada, there is no shortage of trained caregivers. When the country went through its own at-home care crisis several years ago, a decision was made to open the doors to qualified foreign workers. Temporary work permits are now granted to persons with either six months of classroom training in early childhood development or four years of on-the-job experience. They must live in, and after a couple of years on the job, they can apply for permanent resident status in Canada.

Apparently, the Canadian government had been influenced by an alliance of several forces that are missing on the American scene: women's groups who focus on care; organized foreign-born child-care workers; and political pressure from affluent two-career couples. In the United States, by contrast, there is so little support for paid at-home care that when the Commission on Immigration Reform issued a sweeping report in 1994, it contained no recommendations at all on the subject.

Carolyn Killea believes that the only way to do anything about the issue is to frame it in a new light. "We have this debate," she said. "Should a mother stay at home with her kid or hire someone? Are rich women taking advantage of poor women; are they paying them enough? But these are the wrong questions—they divide women and set them against each other. The right questions are: What is this work [of care]? How important is it? And how is it going to get done?

"We have to look at our presumption in America that child care and home care are work that a woman cannot delegate; that somehow a home and a child are inseparable from a woman's person, and that doing this work is like washing her dirty underwear; a personal service to herself, and not to her husband. I didn't hear anyone criticize Zoe Baird's husband for not quitting his job at Yale to take care of their child. But once you take the position that this is a woman's personal obligation, then women are in a brown bag and they're never going to get out. We'll never have women leaders. We've reached our peak, and gone as far as we can go. . . . Women are now opting out of the labor force because they can't handle everything. If we want to have women in positions of power, if we don't want men to be the rulers forever, then those women can't be the cookie-baking, at-home mothers of the myth; someone else is going to have to take over that role."

Killea's point is backed up by research. A recent survey of senior executive women in the largest American corporations found that 93 percent of those with children had relied on in-home child care—and considered this the most important factor enabling them to combine a career with a family life.[8]

Legitimization of the profession of at-home child care is also in the interests of the women who do the work. The combination of lax standards and an illegal labor force makes it much easier for workers to be exploited. Few laws protect even legal household workers. (Domestic workers were not covered by Social Security until 1950, and the minimum wage did not even apply to them until 1974.) Vacations and medical insurance are rarities. And despite the Zoe Baird–inspired crackdown on Social Security, the IRS reported in 1995 that many employers are still not paying their nannies' Social Security taxes.

Eugene Pugliese claimed that he would do the job of raising children if it paid enough, but it doesn't. His own wife had to quit her job to stay at home, primarily because they couldn't find reliable and legal care for their two children. "The last thing I need," he said, "as chief counsel of the House immigration subcommittee, is an illegal immigrant working for me. . . . Anyway, what's so great about going out to work every day?"

Shortly before this conversation, in the wake of the 1994 Republican takeover of Congress, Pugliese lost his position as a congressional staffer on the Hill. For the moment, neither he nor his wife had a job. I had to wonder—did that give him pause, or at least a moment's regret, for having made legal child care so hard to find?

CHAPTER 13

"It Was Her Choice"

> What look like female values are regulations of society at large: to protect, conserve, love and rescue life. It is because these are demanded as actions and attitudes from individual women and not from a social structure that women are oppressed.
>
> —Poet Frigga Haug, "Daydreams"

I was listening to a radio show recently, and a woman who had just written a book was being interviewed. She was asked if her life had turned out as she had expected.

"Oh no," she replied. "I thought I was going to become a professor of literature, and then chairman of my department, and then maybe when I was fifty or so, dean. Instead, I . . . basically I'm a soccer mom."

"Do you have any regrets?" came the impossible question.

I could imagine the thought balloon: "As if I'm going to say on National Public Radio, with my husband and children and who knows who else listening, that I regret what I've done with my life."

"No, I don't regret the sacrifices I've made for my children," the woman said. "It's all been more than worth it."

There it was in a nutshell: the cover story. The sidelined ambitions, the compromises mothers live with that their husbands never had to make, all justified on the grounds of women's choice. What women choose is so important precisely because women bear a disproportionate share of the costs of child-rearing. If they do this willingly, there's no problem. It's their choice. No one "made them do it," so no one has to do anything about it.

A few years ago, a reporter from a big-city newspaper told me that his wife used to be his boss before she quit to raise their two children. She now makes one-fourth his salary, working as a part-time consultant. The loss of economic independence troubles her, he said, then added after a pause, "but it was her choice."

Anita Blair, an attorney active in an antifeminist women's organization, has compared a woman who wants to work and raise a family with a male marathon runner in her law firm. Because of the demands of his training, he didn't put in the same long hours as others in the firm, and as a result, he didn't make partner. But that was his choice, she brightly explained at a press conference called to poo-poo the gender wage gap. Obviously no one, she thought, be they a marathon runner or a conscientious parent, deserves to be promoted if they choose to put a priority on something other than their job.

Even a liberal critic like *Washington Post* columnist Richard Cohen has invoked the "choice" argument. In 1995, he observed that the well-meaning Clinton administration had few females in its inner circles. Cohen's conclusion: "Something besides discrimination seems to be at work at the White House and maybe in corporate America as well. Could it be that women choose to go into other fields? Could it be that some of them—who knows how many?—interrupt, abandon, or curtail their careers so that they can raise children? Could it be that some choose to give their husband's career primacy? To say no to any of these questions is to defy both common sense and the evidence all around us."[1]

So reasonable on its face, this view assumes that raising a child is just another lifestyle option, like choosing to run long distance or play serious tennis. The consequences of those decisions are private, of no concern to the rest of us. If the people who opt to nurture and educate the next generation are systematically handicapped in the labor market, if they find it hard to make a decent living or get ahead without neglecting their children, why should we care? It's their choice. But if raising children well is more important than running fast, and if female equality is important, the "it's their choice" argument is completely inadequate.

The big problem with the rhetoric of choice is that it leaves out power. Those who benefit from the status quo always attribute inequities to the choices of the underdog. The current rhetoric about choosing motherhood sounds suspiciously like the 1950s rhetoric about "happy" women. "Most women are happy at home; they don't want to have to compete with men; they don't want too many responsibilities; they like caring for kids. . . ." The modern version of the old "true woman" argument—the true woman appreciates that her proper place is in the home—is the "choice" argument.

But mothers' choices are not made in a vacuum. They are made in a world that women never made, according to rules they didn't write. To take just one example, what many mothers really want is a good part-time job, yet there is no rich and vibrant part-time labor market in the United States; as one observer has commented, we have many more choices in breakfast cereals than we do in work arrangements.[2] To take another example, married working mothers, as we have seen, pay the highest taxes in the country on their earned income, in addition to the mommy tax. Mothers obviously played no role in writing a tax code that takes most of their earnings away from them. But this heavy taxation powerfully affects their choice of whether to work or not.

A relative lack of power also leaves mothers, especially those who resign from full-time jobs, with most of the menial household chores. Unmarried couples living together tend to share the housework fairly equally. But after the first child arrives, traditional gender roles have a tendency to harden like concrete. The dynamic suggests that the most important choice a mother can make is in her choice of a mate. When the female graduates of three of Harvard's professional schools in the 1970s were surveyed in the 1990s, those who had managed to pursue their goals said that the critical factor enabling them to have a career and a family was a husband who supported them at home. Many of those whose careers had run aground after they had children made it clear that they had not had such a helpmate; for some, the kind of man they married had fatally sabotaged their plans.

Experienced women know this rings true. Dr. Rita Colwell, a microbiologist who became the first woman to head the National Science Foundation, is married to a fellow physicist. She has the following advice for younger women: "What I think you have to do is find someone who is interested in you as a partner, not as a domestic." (But what should one do about a man who wants a partner *and* a domestic?)

Talk of choice not only overlooks power but also ignores the pain embedded in mothers' tough trade-offs. Numerous psychotherapists, social scientists, and others who have had in-depth professional contact with American mothers can testify to the marital tensions and sense of loss that often lie just beneath the surface of their lives. My own conversations with dozens of women who decided to stop working or cut back after they had children uncovered a tangle of complex, mixed feelings. Most felt firmly that they had done the right thing for their children by putting their own pursuits aside. The women cherished the time they spent with their children and the deeply gratifying knowledge that their efforts were producing happy, thriving individuals. We are defined by our responsibilities, and those who are defined by their commitment to a child often earn a deep sense of accomplishment.

But at the same time, the women were clearly suffering from the renunciations they had been required to make.

One mother told me that she felt "confident that the children are better off for my not working full-time," but that she was "not so proud of myself with the public at large. Leaving the business world took a toll on my self-esteem. . . . When people ask 'what do you do?' I say 'consultant,' although I haven't consulted on anything for years.

"When I went off to college my mom gave me the book *Sisterhood Is Powerful*. She wanted me to do something with my life. When we think about what 'doing something with your life' means, it's all about external things: a job, money, prestige. With a child, it's the internal rewards: it's holding their little bodies in your arms. . . . I'm confused. What really bothers me is not being able to provide my daughter with a role model for all that a woman can do."

Clearly, women who have had a taste of the worlds that are now open to them are keenly aware of the huge discrepancy between the status and perquisites attached to many "male" jobs and those accorded a caregiver. Elizabeth Best, we'll call her, is a thirty-eight-year-old former copy editor at the *Washington Post* who decided to stay at home with two children, a five-year-old and an eighteen-month toddler. "We are the very women who were successful in what the women's revolution was all about, which was to be able to get out there and be the equal of the guys," she said during an interview in her backyard in Bethesda, Maryland. "And suddenly, you're back in the female world. It's a shock . . . raising children is still part of a relatively low status world. *Everything* was gone once I started to stay home. In my new job as a mother I had no salary and no professional contacts. There were no more movies, no more dinners out, no work clothes. . . . It was as if everything were being taken away from me.

"I hope this doesn't sound self-pitying, because self-pity is not what I felt. Anger is what I felt. You can sit behind a desk in an office and *proofread* and be paid $50,000 a year. . . . You can enjoy freedom and respect. Or you can stay at home and do work that is a thousand times as important and not only not get paid, but almost have your privileges as an adult stripped from you."

"I would have worked part-time," she adds, "but there were no part-time opportunities at the *Post*."

To most women choice is all about bad options and difficult decisions: your child or your profession; taking on the domestic chores or marital strife; a good night's sleep or time with your child; food on the table or your baby's safety; your right arm or your left. No wonder many mothers talk about "surrendering" to motherhood, as if it were a gigantic defeat that it is better to accept than to fight.

And the women whose sacrifices are mainly their self-esteem and equality in marriage are the "lucky" ones. What about the mothers who have no choice but to entrust their children to untrustworthy caretakers? Is this really their choice, or society's choice?

It is suggestive how few people talk about choice in this broader sense; how few liberals or conservatives question the choices that male legislators make, when they write tax codes that confiscate mothers' earnings; the choices that employers make, when they resist a shorter working day; the choices that husbands make when they act as if child care were wholly their wives' responsibility. These are the choices that frame and drastically shrink the choices a woman is able to make.

What Women Want

What would a real choice for women look like? An interesting series of polls at Williams College sheds some light on this question. For several years the students in Economics 203 at Williams have asked their classmates about their expectations for family and work. Not surprisingly, the women desire pretty much the same things their mothers wanted back in the late 1960s and 1970s: marriage, children, a husband who shares the child-rearing, and a fulfilling career on a part-time basis while the children are home. One is tempted to say: good luck.

The undergraduates are asked to predict how many children they will have, how many hours a week they and their future spouse plan to spend with their children, and how many hours a week they plan to be in the labor force at various times in their lives.

In 1994 the Williams women anticipated careers in traditionally masculine fields, from business to science and engineering, and on average they rated building a career as more important than having children. Yet they did not have a traditionally masculine view of what would happen when they did have children. They did not want themselves or their spouse to miss the parenting experience.

The women overwhelmingly expected to work part-time while their children were under five years of age, and most didn't want to work a forty-hour week until their children were eighteen. But they wanted a similar commitment to the family from their spouse. Of all the possible work situations for married couples with preschool children, the women rated highest the marriage in which both partners worked part-time. This marriage model, of course, is extremely rare in the United States today.

The men interviewed had a different idea. They too expected their wives to work part-time while the children were young, but envisioned themselves working more than forty hours a week. Their highest rating for a marriage with preschool children was one in which the husband works full-time and the wife does not work at all outside the home. This ideal describes more than one-third of all marriages with young children.

Both the men and the women thought the least desirable arrangement while children were under five was one in which both husband and wife worked full-time—which is the most common pattern among American married couples with preschoolers.

The Williams polls point to two conclusions. First, most families in this country are raising children under conditions that neither spouse considers ideal or would have chosen had they had better choices. And second, young men are more likely to get what they want out of life than young women. The male ideal of a traditional family approximates reality, while what the women want is still an unattainable dream. "Women's aspirations for demanding careers are not consistent with their anticipated home situations," noted the student pollsters.[3]

A few years down the road, when many of these girls marry, become mothers, take on most of the costs of child-rearing, and watch their independence slip away, someone is sure to say, "Well, it was her choice."

Choice, Swedish Style

For years I had heard stories about "Sweden," an almost mythical paradise where men believed in equality and did more housework and child care than anywhere else in the world. Could this really be true? And if so, why? Former Vikings could hardly have a unique gene for domesticity. Had the Swedes found a formula that could be adapted to American culture? I went to Sweden to find out.

Two days after my arrival, I had dinner with Staffan Movin and Karin Grute, a young couple with one child, a thirteen-month-old boy named Andreas. The family lived in a comfortable two-bedroom apartment overlooking the rooftops of Sodermalm, a neighborhood in Stockholm that reportedly has the highest density of children in Europe.

Karin told me that she had just finished a full year at home with Andreas, on a paid leave from her job as a marketing executive for the Stockholm airport. For that year of mothering, she received a check from the government each month amounting to 75 percent of her salary. Cradling Andreas, she explained that she was gradually introducing him to day care, staying at the center with him for a couple of hours every day until he was happy in the group.

When Andreas was settled, Karin planned to return to her job on an 80 percent schedule, a statutory right of every parent of a child under the age of eight. "My boss says that I can only work a shorter schedule until Christmas, but that's not how it's going to be. It's going to be longer," she said, with the confidence of someone who knows the law is on her side.

Staffan took Andreas into his lap as we sat down to eat and described his part in caring for his son during the baby's first year. "I got ten days off in the beginning—that is the leave reserved just for fathers. I also took another [paid] month at home. And from now on I'll be working an 80 percent schedule like Karin. She'll stay home Mondays, and I'll be home on Fridays, so Andreas will only have to be in day care three days a week."

Staffan is an independent marketing analyst, giving him some flexibility in arranging his schedule. Arrangements in other families vary. "Two or three couples are doing what we are doing; in another family the mother stayed home for several months, then the father was home for three or four months," Staffan said. "One woman stayed home a year, and now the man is taking over." One older businessman I met in Sweden told me that his young male executives typically took two months' paternity leave.

But many new fathers don't take more than the first ten days of paid paternity leave. As Staffan explained, "It's very tough if you work for a small company or for an American or French or German company. The multinational companies have very little respect for the Swedish custom. You're expected to have your wife at home."

The phrase "the Swedish custom" stuck with me. Swedish men are obviously presumed to be far more than a paycheck to their families. In almost every street scene, on almost every subway platform, I saw at least one man pushing a baby carriage. One executive I met was taking a six-month paternity leave. I was told about the director of a major food chain who had his secretary tell everyone who called on Fridays that he took the day off with his family. One of the judges on the Supreme Court even took a leave from the bench when his wife had a baby.

According to surveys, virtually all Swedish men between the ages of twenty-one and sixty feel an obligation to participate in the unpaid work of the household.[4] And time-use studies confirm that they do so to a degree unmatched anywhere outside Scandinavia.[5] Agneta Stark, an economist at the University of Stockholm and one of the country's leading feminists, happily assured me that "younger fathers are not only caring for children; they are also doing the housework associated with children: cooking, shopping, cleaning up."[6]

For decades feminists have argued that women will never be able to achieve full economic equality until men share the time-consuming unpaid work at home. But most men have dragged their heels. Part of the reason, undoubtedly, is that child care is accorded so little respect or accommodation. But it may also be that caring work is so little valued because so few men do it. Few men in positions of authority have any firsthand experience caring for children and therefore no basis for understanding just how difficult and important a job it is. Their ignorance helps perpetuate a system that takes the work for granted.

In recent years, the issue of male involvement in children's lives has taken on greater urgency as fatherlessness has become a serious concern. All over the world, men have been withdrawing from the institution of the family and reducing their financial support of children. Almost half of all children in Sweden and Denmark, and roughly one-third of American, British, Canadian, and French children, are born out of wedlock. This, combined with a rapidly rising divorce rate, means that an increasing percentage of children are being supported by mothers alone. The trend is so worrisome that the question of how to reengage fathers with their offspring has become a major topic of debate on both sides of the Atlantic.

In both Sweden and the United States, most people agree that while children can do perfectly well with one competent parent, those who have the love and support of both their biological parents have the best possible start in life. But the Swedish and the American approaches to this issue are diametrically opposed.

In their efforts to encourage male participation in family life, the Swedes use carrots, rather than sticks. Instead of declaring war on "deadbeat dads" or calling for a moral crusade, the pragmatic Swedes have looked to social science for hints on how to prevent fathers from drifting away from their children.

Swedish studies indicate that the risk of fatherlessness begins—and is greatest—at birth. The arrival of a child often puts severe stresses on a relationship. As a former Swedish government official told me, "When a baby comes, a man doesn't necessarily gain a child, he loses a wife. There are many divorces and splits at this time." And roughly one-third of the Swedish men who separate from their families soon after a birth have no contact with the child one year later.[7] In the United States as well, most fathers who play little or no part in their child's life disappear during his or her early years. What might make these men bond with their children?

We know that the more time a parent spends with an infant, the more attached the two will tend to become. In the United States, this research has looked almost exclusively at the mother-infant dyad, but in Sweden, researchers have learned that when fathers spend time with their children in those critical first months, they too will be more likely to become involved parents. Fathers with early attachments and responsibilities are more apt to pick their children up at day care, devote time to them on weekends and evenings, and remain active parents even if they are subsequently divorced or separated.

Goran Swedin, an obstetrician and family therapist, is the head of maternal and child health care at Ostersund County Hospital, where he runs a training program for new fathers. His goal is to encourage men to develop a primary-care relationship with their children at an early stage. According to Swedin, many fathers say that "when they are able to take a greater part in the situation at home, they won't leave their children. They might divorce their wife, they say, but never their children." Swedin believes that this is the key to children's well-being in societies with a high degree of personal freedom and high divorce rates. "Divorced kids do rather well if they don't lose one parent," he told me. "If we can maintain close contacts between father and child in the early years, we will probably have a better chance of keeping two parents in the picture for years to come."[8]

Since the 1970s, ten days of paid leave have been set aside for new fathers after childbirth, in addition to twelve months of paid leave that can be shared by both parents. (In the United States, by contrast, paid paternity leaves are extremely rare, despite all the handwringing about absent fathers. In a 1997 survey, *Working Mother* magazine could uncover only thirty-two American companies that offered any leave specifically for fathers.)[9] Interestingly, Swedish men did not initially jump at the chance to go home and bond with their newborns. Despite a media campaign featuring a well-known Swedish weight lifter as a stay-at-home dad, only 25 percent of fathers in the 1980s took more than the ten days that were reserved for them. After an intensive media and public information campaign, that percentage increased to more than 40 percent. Still, as late as 1994, twenty years after the introduction of paid parental leaves, only 11 percent of the total number of days taken off work to care for newborns were taken by men.[10]

In 1992 the Swedish government appointed a special government commission to investigate why men were not opting for more dad duty. One of the members of what became known as the Fathers' Commission was Greger Hatt, a writer who later became a speechwriter and adviser to Social Democratic prime minister Ingvar Carlsson. I spent an afternoon with Hatt, a tall, lean, affably intense man of thirty-four, in an office in Stockholm's Old Town.

Hatt had taken a twelve-month leave with each of his three children, then ages ten, seven, and three, and he shared parenting with both his current and his former wives. While he was a speechwriter, from 1994 to 1996, he told me the prime minister "would inquire, before setting up an afternoon meeting, whether I had to fetch the kids from day care and if so, he would set up the meeting for the next day."

Hatt, who seemed to be on a personal mission to win equality in the home for fathers, had spent little time with his own father as a boy. "I saw him at seven at night and sometimes not at all," he told me. "He was uninvolved in the family, and that was partly my mother's doing. She discouraged it—admittedly it didn't take much—but she made it difficult. He tried doing some cooking, maybe four times, and every time she ridiculed him unmercifully for months afterwards. I understand all this psychologically; [it was] the only place where she had any influence.

"In my childhood there were no men at all. In Sweden all most children see is women: their mother, then the women at the day-care center, their teachers in the lower grades, nurses. . . . A lot of boys don't meet a daytime man until they are ten years old. . . . It is a real apartheid system."

The Fathers' Commission wanted to break this gender segregation down by altering the factors responsible for it. These included employers' demands on men's time and older family members' expectations that fathers would be purely breadwinners. But the commission was surprised to discover that the single most important factor in determining how much time a father spent with his children was the mother's attitude. The key variable was the mother's education—a proxy for her position in the labor market. The more money she earned and the more fulfillment she found outside the home, the more space she was willing to create for the father within it.

As Swedin explained, "Whether a man shares in parenting is not dependent on the man's income or position. It's the woman's income and position that counts. . . . We've seen that underprivileged, unskilled women want to have their time with their children and are not so eager to share the parental leave with their husbands. In families with higher education and qualifications, there is a definite tendency to share the leave. In the final analysis, it's the woman who decides."

Indeed, whenever I asked people why Swedish men do more caring for children than men elsewhere, I was told that the reason was Sweden's "strong women." That is, relatively well-educated, high-earning women.

Even among Sweden's sizable minority population, including many immigrants from traditional Middle Eastern societies, the income of the woman determined the domestic participation of the man. At first the members of the Fathers' Commission had assumed that men from more patriarchal cultures would take lower rates of paternity leave. But it turned out that the immigrants had the same rates as native Swedes. "Culture was less important than economics," Hatt told me. "The woman often had her own business and couldn't take off as easily as the man, or he was unemployed, or he had the more flexible job. I myself know two couples, one from Iraq and the other from Lebanon, where the man does everything at home." He added that "the families for which it was economically rational to share parenting did so. That was our most interesting finding."

Nevertheless, Hatt admitted, women still have a lingering proprietary feeling toward their children. He attributed this not to biology but to their still tenuous foothold in the labor market. "It is not unnatural for women to feel that children are their property if the workplace is the property of men." To undermine these attitudes, the Fathers' Commission decided to engage in a little social engineering. It recommended that three months of the twelve months' parental leave be reserved for men only. (Three months were also to be for mothers only, but in practice mothers were taking almost all of the twelve months anyway.) If a father didn't take his three paid months off, the family would lose them.

"We thought that if the state is paying for twelve months of leave, at least three ought to be reserved for fathers," Hatt explained. "In the first month you only have time to find out how things work. In the second month you develop your own routines, and by the third month you begin to really communicate with the baby."

The proposal unleashed a national outcry. The chairman of the conservative youth league said it was "grotesque." The commission was accused of trying to legislate social revolution. Some women's rights activists complained that now men were trying to have everything, the best-paying work and the mother's job as well.

To the surprise of the members of the commission, the most vociferous protest came from women.

"We had piles of letters and many, many phone calls from women," Hatt related. "Some said this is infringing on breast feeding, even though the average for that is six months in Sweden. Women said 'my husband can't take paternity leave, he has such an important job'; or 'he can't handle our baby'; or 'I am home and he is a farmer, why should he be at home?'" Hatt claimed that not one single man phoned him to complain.

The government decided to ask the legislature for only one "father's month" instead of three, to be reserved exclusively for men. This measure passed quickly, in the spring of 1994. Since then, the great majority of new fathers have taken a month off, at 80 percent of pay, during their child's first year (on top of their ten days after childbirth). Many take the time in the summer, simply extending their vacation. Others use the month's worth of free days to work four-day weeks.

"It was a breakthrough," says Bengt Westerberg, the Liberal Party leader who was the principal driving force behind the father's month. "Before, very few fathers did anything like this. But there has been very little opposition since 1994. Sometimes people say we should get rid of the leave, but just as many say we should extend it."

The father's month may be largely symbolic, but it is important nonetheless. I asked Anna Wahl of the Stockholm School of Economics, an authority on gender patterns in business, whether she thought the father's month made any real difference.

"It moves the norm a little," she answered. "It creates pressure on young men; now they have to explain why they're not going to be at home." And it confirms "fatherhood as important in itself. It's not just anyone taking care of the child; it's the father. It says that he's irreplaceable."

Goran Swedin says his work with fathers has convinced him that involving men in child-rearing "creates a process in which everyone is happy. More equal parenting is obviously in the best interests of women. They can deepen their professional life if they know they have a coparent they can trust with their children. It draws men closer to their children. And studies show that children who have frequent contact with fathers as well as mothers learn different patterns on how to solve challenges in life. They are less afraid of strangers. I believe they are going to be more flexible in difficult situations and have a wider emotional and social repertoire."

The interesting question here is why the worldwide problem of absentee fathers has been interpreted in Sweden as a call for equal parenting while in the United States the same phenomenon has prompted cries for a return to traditional marriage, complete with breadwinner husband and stay-at-home wife. How did a land with more than its share of harsh patriarchs—as depicted in director Ingmar Bergman's unforgettable film portrayal of his own cold, distant father—morph into the country of the Fathers' Commission, an official body charged with breaking down age-old gender roles?

The reforms that set Sweden down this road started to take shape in the 1960s. The original driving force was not feminism, or men demanding an equal right to diaper babies, but a labor shortage. During the Great Depression of the 1930s, the Swedish birthrate had plummeted, giving rise to fears of depopulation; by the 1960s there were not enough native Swedish men to fill the demand for workers.[11] The country was faced with the choice of importing literally millions of people from Finland, southern Europe, and the Middle East or making it easier for

Swedish women to work outside the home. The issue was resolved in favor of native Swedish workers.

Women were offered generous maternity benefits and the right to work an 80 percent schedule as long as they had a preschool child at home. Later, in the name of gender equality, these rights were extended to men. And as women poured into the workplace during the 1970s, Social Democratic governments decided that every child should be able to find a place in a quality day-care situation. That goal has not yet been reached, but all Swedish families below a certain income do receive a check from the government to help cover the cost of child care.

These incentives to combine work and family succeeded. By 1986, more women were combining paid work and motherhood in Sweden than anywhere else in the world. Some 90 percent of mothers of children under age sixteen were working outside the home. The proportion of women quitting their jobs after childbirth fell to less than 10 percent.[12] Among university-educated Swedish men and women, the rates of participation in the labor force are now virtually the same.[13]

By creating so many incentives for mothers to work, Sweden has inadvertently addressed a problem that plagues the United States: poor unemployed women having babies they cannot support. "With all of our maternity benefits," Agneta Stark told me, "there is a very strong incentive for young women to have a job before they have a baby," she explained. "Without an earnings history, a mother receives only a small, flat payment, but if she has a job, she is entitled to a paid leave. Many young women are saying that they would like to stay at home with their children, but they want to have something to stay at home *from,*" says Stark. This suggests an approach to teen pregnancy that American policymakers have never considered.

The Swedish tax system also encourages women to work by taxing married men and women *individually* rather than jointly. A wife earning less than her husband is taxed at her own, lower rate, enabling the family to keep more of her earnings. In the United States, as we have seen, joint taxation makes it much less worthwhile for the lower-earning spouse to work.

Hands-on fatherhood is also made feasible by a relatively short workweek, compared to the United States. Not only do many Swedish parents enjoy enormous flexibility in scheduling their work, they have less of it to schedule. I spent an afternoon at a day-care center, and by 4:00 P.M. almost all of the forty-five children had gone home, a few with their fathers.

But the single biggest reason that Swedish men do more housework and child care is probably, as the Fathers' Commission discovered, economic. Or to be more precise, the high degree of economic equality between the sexes. Swedish women on average have higher incomes, vis-à-vis men, than women anywhere else in the world. Wives earn 39 percent of after-tax family income, the highest percentage in the world. In the United States, wives contribute on average only 26.5 percent of family income. Even in two-earner families with children, American wives still contribute only 32.5 percent of pretax income.[14] When people told me that Sweden has "strong women," this is what they meant.

When two spouses bring home close to the same income, the family stands to lose almost as much financially when the mother cuts back on her paid work as when the father does. This changes the conversation about who stays home and who remains employed, who picks the children up after school, who takes the child to the doctor, and so on.

There is also some tantalizing evidence that Swedish laws protecting women and children from the worst ravages of divorce have also strengthened the woman's hand in these conversations. In Sweden divorce is not a financial disaster for dependent family members. Child support is indexed to inflation and is backed up by what Mary Ann Glendon of the Harvard Law School has called "the most efficient collection system and the most generous package of benefits for one-parent families in the world," including free health care, a housing allowance, and a small cash grant per child each year. Since most mothers also work, the standard of living of women and their children declines by only about 10 percent after the parents divorce.[15]

With the weight of the law behind her, a woman who decides that her marriage is unsatisfactory is in a better position to do something about it. She can ask her husband to change—to do more housework and child care, for example. Or she can end the marriage without paying too high a financial price. This gives Swedish wives a certain confidence. The night I visited the Movins, Karin commented, "If I took all of the responsibility for this child, I would really be dependent on one person. A wife staying at home can't make choices of her own. She can't even get a divorce."

Unlike many Americans, the Swedes have accepted the revolution in women's roles and have eliminated much of the anguish American mothers feel when forced to choose between their work and their children. As one female journalist put it, "We haven't fully solved the problem of reconciling women's equality with raising children. But at least we think about the question, even if we don't have all the answers."

DESPITE FREQUENT AMERICAN predictions that the European welfare states cannot survive in the tough new global economy, everyone I spoke with in Sweden believed that the one area of government spending that isn't threatened is family support. The very suggestion of seriously cutting mothers' and children's benefits, I was told, "would be political suicide." Politicians of three different parties assured me, "No politician in their right mind would suggest it."

A major reason is, once again, strong women. Almost half the members of the Swedish parliament are women, as is half the cabinet, making Sweden the leading country in the world in female participation in government. One-third of the members of Sweden's parliament are parents of preschool toddlers, and schedules are organized so that members can combine governing and parenting.[16]

A number of studies confirm that large numbers of women in government do make a difference. To take just one example, there is a clear connection between the high percentage of women in Swedish local government and support given to shelters for battered women. And as lavish welfare states like Sweden seek ways to reduce public spending, a critical mass of women in government can ensure that family-friendly programs do not take the hit.

However their experiment fares, Swedish reformers have reason for optimism. "We are slowly moving into the third stage," Hatt told me earnestly. "In the first stage women were set apart in an apartheid system. In the second stage, in the 1960s and 1970s, women emerged by adopting male role models. In the third stage, we will have integration, and individuals will be free to assume any role they want. . . . Maybe in ten years we will be able to speak not only of the different strengths mothers can bring to leadership but the different strengths men can bring to parenting." Maybe so.

Mothers Divided Are Conquered

For now, in the United States at least, mothers' potential strength still lies dormant. In the course of reporting this book, I was struck, and admittedly surprised, by the deep reluctance of mothers to speak out or act up on their own behalf. For their children, they have no such qualms, but making demands for themselves still seems taboo. Many mothers don't even seem to believe that they deserve a fairer deal than they are getting. I reluctantly concluded that American mothers are their own worst enemies; and that this explains, more than anything else, why caring labor is so undervalued in this country.

I knew that women (like men) are divided, over the issue of abortion, and matters of class and race. And we know that many mothers of young children are too hard-pressed to have time to support women's causes—in many cases, even to vote. But it is nonetheless disturbing to find mothers actively engaged in sabotaging one another, blind to their common ground. Think about it: women against poor mothers on welfare; women against rich Zoe Baird. Women against their husbands' first wives; mothers embroiled in endless mommy wars. Working mothers aren't "doing their job" at home, while mothers at home don't have a "real" job. The net effect of all this belittling is to obscure the larger reality that mothers as a group are performing an enormous amount of essential unpaid labor.

Mothers have no shortage of critics, but precious few friends. "We have to cast child support as a children's issue," Leora Gershenzon of the National Center for Youth Law in San Francisco told me, echoing similar comments I had heard from half a dozen other activists. "If it becomes a woman's issue, it's a loser. Domestic violence is the only woman's issue that's a winner."

Working mothers are still singled out for attack, despite the fact that society increasingly expects mothers to be employed. Focus groups have revealed, for example, that most women do not believe that working mothers deserve any help in obtaining adequate child care. "To a person, women believe that child care is an individual problem," says Pat Reuss, a Washington, D.C., lobbyist for the NOW Legal Defense Fund. "They do not see it as something they could ask their state or the federal government for help with, or as something they can negotiate with their bosses for, or as a reason to join a union. Women really don't think they deserve help with this." Reuss likens this to the way women used to blame themselves for rape. "Women know finding decent child care is a problem, but they see it as a personal, private problem, and somehow their fault. With rape it was, 'I shouldn't have been there, maybe I was dressed too provocatively.' With child care it's 'maybe I shouldn't be working' or 'we made the decision to have this kid, now it's our responsibility.'"[17]

Given these attitudes, it is hardly surprising that no major women's organization has launched a serious campaign for subsidized child care and universal public preschool in the United States. Conservative women's organizations like Concerned Women for America, which claim to be pro-family, see public expenditures on early childhood care and education as a subsidy for working mothers at the expense of those at home. They oppose paid maternity leaves on the same grounds, although paid leaves would enable countless new mothers to stay home with their infants—a pro-family policy if there ever was one.[18]

Working mothers also told me, with predictable regularity, that their female bosses were often unsupportive. One young woman in her midtwenties volunteered this story: "Where I work, in a bookstore, it's the women who say, sarcastically, 'She's got kids, so she has to leave at five o'clock.' When one woman had a baby, the manager, also a woman, felt she wasn't planning to come back, so she hired someone else. The woman did try to come back, but she didn't have her job anymore. She had been pushed out."

Another young woman, who works for a foundation in Boston, told me she was toying with the idea of going on a 75 percent schedule so she could spend more time with her three-and-a-half-year-old daughter. But she was worried how her boss, a woman in her late thirties who had no children, would react. "She wants me to be more like her—all business," the young woman said. "My previous boss, a man, was more sympathetic. He even let me bring the baby in while I was nursing, as long as I got the job done."

Virginia Daley, the new mother who lost her job at Aetna, was done in by this lack of maternal solidarity. When Daley returned from maternity leave, she asked for but was refused a short workweek. According to Daley, she then started working by the book, going home after an eight-hour day. Daley's female supervisor had just had a baby herself, but her child was being cared for by a full-time nanny, freeing the supervisor, a hard-driving M.B.A. in her early thirties, to work nights and weekends. By refusing to do the same, Daley had in effect declared war on the corporate culture, and on her female boss, its loyal enforcer. In response, Daley's supervisor told her that "any woman who can't afford a nanny shouldn't have children."[19]

Mothers were also among the most vocal advocates of ending the federal entitlement to welfare. During the debates on welfare reform in 1995–96, mail poured into congressional offices from thousands of angry women, demanding cuts in the only federal program offering a guaranteed safety net for poor mothers and children. Focus groups revealed that many mothers deeply resented the benefits that welfare mothers received, even though welfare assistance would be their own last line of defense if disaster struck.

These feelings, similar to the expressions of resentment toward Zoe Baird, were at least understandable. Over the years the safety net for poor mothers and children had been expanded to include medical insurance, food stamps, and subsidies for housing, home heating, and child care. These kinds of benefits are not available to ordinary working mothers who struggle morning, noon, and night to stay afloat. No one was paying them to stay at home with their kids or helping them out with their bills. In fact, before welfare reform, government subsidies enabled more poor women than low-income women to be full-time homemakers. A welfare program that subsidized some women but not others to care for their own children inevitably bred bitterness.

But instead of demanding that all low-income mothers—or all mothers, period—should be entitled to a child allowance, medical coverage, and help with housing and child care, thousands of American mothers let their elected representatives know that they could safely reduce the protections for the very poorest. Instead of demanding a bigger pie so that everyone could have a slice, mothers demanded that the few crumbs that were on the table be swept away. And they were.

When the welfare issue came up for a vote in Congress in 1996, all but one female senator voted to end the federal welfare guarantee. Many mothers at home continue to insist that they have nothing in common with the kind of women who go on welfare. At one congressional symposium, when Senator Paul Wellstone wondered where the supporters of mothers at home had been when welfare reform forced millions of toddlers' mothers to leave the home for full-time work, conservative columnist Maggie Gallagher snapped, "I don't think mothers at home would appreciate being compared to welfare mothers."[20] They might not appreciate it, but the line dividing the two is mighty thin. In 1992 almost 30 percent of divorced or separated women were in need of government assistance. Most of them had been mothers at home.

As for the big feminist organizations, they have not exactly stepped up to the plate for mothers. Marjorie Sims, former staff director of the Congressional Caucus for Women, said that women's advocacy groups rarely contacted the caucus on behalf of caregivers.[21]

An attorney and legal affairs writer in New York City, the mother of a toddler, told me this story:

"I didn't want to go back to work after fourteen weeks with my child—the last thing I wanted to do after waiting so long was to turn my baby over to a nanny. But I quickly realized that there was no support in our society for this work. When the baby was about six months old I was bouncing against the walls, wanting to do *something*."

This woman wrote a letter to Patricia Ireland, president of the National Organization for Women, suggesting a march on Washington for paid maternity leave. She remembers writing, "You've marched for abortion rights, but more women become mothers than have abortions." What happened? She didn't even get a reply."

Two years later, in 1998, I checked NOW's Web site; paid maternity leave and subsidized child care weren't even listed as key issues.[22]

The strange indifference of many feminists to the inequities surrounding the most female of professions extends to the value of mothers' work.

Barbara Bergmann, an authority on women in the U.S. economy, has said that she cannot understand why including unpaid labor in the GDP deserves attention. "For me," Bergmann opined on Femecon, an electronic mail network of feminist economists, "feminism is about changing the division of labor rather than paying a little something to keep the present division of labor more tolerable and therefore in place."

Women's organizations of all stripes have also been indifferent to the issue of equality in marriage. When I first began to research the plight of divorced mothers, I assumed that various advocacy groups were out there fighting for family caregivers. I could not have been more mistaken. There were virtually none.

Diane Dodson, an attorney who has fought for divorce reform for years, filled me in on the reasons. "There is a pervasive fear of alienating men, and a 'rich white women' syndrome," she explained. "The big women's organizations don't want to be involved in anything that could be interpreted as women against men, and the smaller women's advocacy groups don't have the resources to do anything that doesn't focus on poor women or children," Dodson said. "Foundations that support the small advocacy groups don't want to fund anything that is too controversial and 'anti-male,' or that might be perceived as benefiting 'rich white women.'"[23] As she made clear, "rich white women" was a broad category that includes all females who aren't poor, downtrodden, or obviously oppressed. Dodson's comments were the first signal I had that somewhere along the line mothers in the United States who are not in absolute need have come to be seen as privileged. Their problems of inequality and dependency in marriage, and a lack of respect for their work at home, simply do not qualify them for much sympathy, even from their own.

Conservative women's organizations have no interest in wifely equality. And most feminist organizations are too strapped for money and too engaged in defensive battles, trying to hold the ground that has already been won, to take on any new campaigns. In sum, the major organizations purporting to represent the interests of women do not really speak for mainstream mothers. In effect, they are saying to mothers: "What's your problem? You've got a husband, a roof over your head, a job, and more money than the truly unfortunate. Your problem must be psychological."

This is, of course, exactly what was said to frustrated housewives of the 1950s and 1960s: "What are you unhappy about? You've got a husband, a nice home, children. What more do you want? If you're not happy, there must be something wrong with *you*."

In short, the disproportionate vulnerability of mothers is not seen as a major feminist issue, or as a pressing issue affecting children and our ability to invest in human capital; that is, in our economic future. Mothers are the true silent majority; too silent and too polite to become a cause. Mothers "have few advocates," explained one Washington-based advocate for the poor, "because they are not seen as a public problem."

It is hard to make a revolution if the beneficiaries themselves don't believe that their cause is worth fighting for. This bothers at least one old revolutionary: "Dignified motherhood is a feminist priority," writes Germaine Greer in *The Whole Woman*. Women must see a "future beyond joining the masculinist elite on its own terms. . . . There has to be a better way."[24]

Conclusion: How to Bring Children Up Without Putting Women Down

> The feminist task is neither to glorify nor discount the differences between men and women, but to challenge the adverse consequences of whatever differences there may be.
>
> —Christine Littleton

In the early spring of 1995, I attended an international conference in the fashionably faded Villa Schifanoia, a Renaissance estate in the elegant Florentine suburb of Fiesole. The topic was "The Cost of Being a Mother; the Cost of Being a Father."

The meetings were conducted in an ornate, high-ceilinged former theater hung with tapestries. Some fifty assembled scholars from Europe, the United States, and the United Kingdom listened through headsets to simultaneous translations as they sat beneath murals of cherubs playing lyres. Between sessions, the participants strolled through the grounds along avenues of stately cypress trees.

I had gone to this unlikely setting to get beyond the often sterile American debate over family values and the work-family conflict, by learning more about other advanced countries' policies toward caregivers. Were the Europeans really as successful as they are said to be in protecting mothers and children from poverty? Had they been able to promote caring for others without hindering women's progress in all the other arenas of work and life?

What I learned at this gathering, sponsored by the European University Institute, was heartening. First, despite severe budget cuts in virtually every European country, not one government was cutting its generous maternal and child benefits, with the important exception of reduced subsidies for child care in the former East Germany. In recent elections in both France and Norway, politicians had even competed over how to increase governmental support for families.

The American assumption that Europe can no longer afford its investment in good care for those who need it is clearly not shared by most Europeans. The public strongly supports policies that have kept poverty among children and their mothers substantially lower than in the United States. It is instructive to note that poverty among American white children alone is higher than the levels in western Europe.[1]

Moreover, the European debate seems to be more candid about the fact that family support issues are very much women's issues. The conference itself was organized around the idea that the costs of caring have to be better understood and more fairly shared between men and women and by society as a whole. Several commentators noted that unless this cost sharing occurs, women will never escape a precarious, semidependent economic status.

The implicit assumption in all of the papers presented was that caring needs to be conceptualized as work if it is ever to be properly valued socially, legally, or economically. By the same token, those who provide care, unpaid as well as paid, must be seen as productive citizens who deserve the same social rights as all other workers and citizens.

Despite its traditional trappings, western Europe is clearly out front in thinking about these issues. A 1992 Organization for Economic Cooperation and Development (OECD) report called for a revision of the current "social contract," which assumes that women can participate in the labor market as full-time competitors and still maintain a second unpaid job as the person responsible for home and children. If the experience of the past thirty years has taught us anything, it is that this is not possible. The report therefore recommended structural changes in the organization of paid and unpaid work in order to create more space for care. Examples of such changes include creating many more good part-time jobs, as the Dutch have done; and reducing the paid workweek, as France and several other countries have done.

The United States is not Europe, and Americans may never accept the kind of compassionate capitalism or caring state that western Europeans demand. But it doesn't strike me as beyond our reach to revise a new social contract as well. I can easily imagine adding care to our pantheon of national values, along with liberty, justice, and the pursuit of happiness through the pursuit of money.

But this will never happen unless women demand it. Women have to insist that caretaking and early education can no longer depend on their cheap or unpaid labor. And before that can happen, women have to understand that the true costs of care include their exclusion from full participation in the economy and in society.[2]

The only way women can achieve equal citizenship is for the entire society to contribute to the provision of a public good that everyone desires: well-raised children who will mature into productive, law-abiding citizens. And that means that all free riders—from employers to governments to husbands to communities—have to pitch in and help make the most important job in the world a top national priority—and a very good job.

Employers: Redesign Work Around Parental Norms

In a recent panel discussion on corporate leadership held by the *New York Times,* Lawrence A. Bossidy, the chief executive of Allied Signal, had this to say: "I do think the hardest deal in the world is for a woman to have two or three young kids and to work when her spouse works. . . . That takes a toll after a while. And I don't know what we in business have done yet to be able to resolve that."

The answer, of course, is very little. Here are some overdue steps business needs to take:

Give Every Parent the Right to a Year's Paid Leave

In 1997, American pediatricians officially recommended that new mothers breast-feed for a full year. This was a sick joke in a country that entitles new mothers to no paid leave at all. American mothers are guaranteed only three months' maternity leave without pay—forcing most working mothers to return to their jobs within a few weeks after giving birth, because they can't afford to take three months off without a paycheck.[3] As a consequence, poor mothers are far less likely to breast-feed than their better-off sisters, and infants as young as six weeks are going into day care, with some spending as many as ten hours a day in group settings. No other women or children in the industrialized world are forced to live under these conditions, which child development experts agree are deplorable, if not downright harmful.

Those concerned about family values or parental neglect of children could find no better place to attack the problem than by demanding a paid leave, which could be shared by both parents, of at least one year. This would do more to improve infant care, increase family income, enhance fathers' emotional ties to their offspring, and promote economic equality between husbands and wives than almost any other single measure.

More generous leaves allowing parents to stay home with a sick child are also essential. Fewer than half of working parents stay home when their children are sick, even though research shows that sick children recover more quickly when a parent is there.[4] According to a recent survey by the AFL-CIO, 54 percent of working women are not entitled to any paid leave for taking care of a sick child or other family member.

Corporate lobbyists have vehemently opposed the most minimal paid parental or family leaves, claiming that the cost would bankrupt American business. This is blatantly untrue. Generous paid parental leaves are a basic right in every other economically advanced nation, and in none of them does business have to foot the entire bill. In some countries the leaves are paid for by contributions of employers and employees to the national old-age insurance system; in others they come out of general tax revenues or some combination of taxes, Social Security, and employer or employee insurance funds.

The costs to the economy can be offset by reduced turnover and the creation of a wider labor pool of women who will remain in the paid workforce if they don't have to quit to take care of an infant or a sick child.

Shorten the Workweek

Experts estimate that roughly 5 to 7 million American children are left unattended at home every day. Why? Because parents of young children don't have the right to work a day that coincides with the school day.

In Sweden, parents can opt to work a six-hour day until their children are eight years old. In the Netherlands the official workweek is thirty-six hours, and workers have a right to a four-day week. The legal workweek in France was reduced from thirty-nine to thirty-five hours in 2000, and pressure is rising for the rest of Europe to follow suit.[5]

American parents have complained for years that they need a shorter workweek, but for many the workday is getting steadily longer instead. The average workweek has crept up to almost forty-eight hours for professionals and managers, and even so-called part-time work is now edging toward forty hours a week.

It always surprises people from other countries that the "rich" Americans allow themselves to be pushed so hard. Things were not always this way. In 1870, workers in the United States, Germany, France, Japan, and Britain all averaged roughly the same hours a year on the job. By the 1960s, the average American worker spent *less* time on the job than workers in any other major industrial nation. Today, the situation is completely reversed. Europeans work on average almost *nine* forty-hour weeks (350 hours) less a year than Americans.[6] This is another gift from unrestrained turbo-capitalism.

Despite their adamant opposition, American companies might discover gains in a shorter workweek. Overwork-related stress disorders, absenteeism, and turnover would surely be reduced, and productivity in some cases improved, as a number of French companies have already discovered.

Provide Equal Pay and Benefits for Equal Part-time Work

A shorter workweek would have to be accompanied by a federal law requiring companies to pay part-time workers at the same hourly rates as full-timers doing the same job, as well as prorated fringe benefits, including vacations, sick leave, and inclusion in company pension plans. Currently, only about 22 percent of part-time workers have any health insurance, compared with 78 percent of full-time workers, and only 26 percent have any private pensions, compared with 60 percent of full-timers. These inequities give employers a huge incentive to hire nonstandard workers—most of them mothers—on cheap, exploitative terms.

A model for ending the exploitation and marginalization of part-time work has been established in the Netherlands, where one-third of all jobs are now part-time. Dutch part-timers enjoy all of the benefits that accrue to full-time workers, on a prorated basis. The Canadian province of Saskatchewan has also set a precedent by becoming the first jurisdiction in North America to rewrite its labor laws to extend benefits to part-time workers.

Eliminate Discrimination Against Parents in the Workplace

Only eight states currently have laws prohibiting parental discrimination. Although such bias is hard to quantify, parents believe that it is widespread. One obvious example would be people who are penalized for declining to work overtime because of family responsibilities.

In the 1997 Massachusetts case of *Upton v. JWP Businessland* referred to earlier in this book, a single mother working as a store manager brought suit for wrongful dismissal after she was fired for refusing to work much longer hours than she had originally been hired to do, including all day Saturday. The woman argued that the compulsory overtime would prevent her from being an adequate mother to her son—indeed she would scarcely be able to see him. Yet the Massachusetts Supreme Judicial Court ruled against her. The court decided that state contract law permitted at-will employees to be fired "for any reason or for no reason at all" unless the firing violates a "clearly established" public policy. It found that Massachusetts had no public policy dealing with the responsibility of a parent to care for his or her child.[7] Perhaps it is time for governments to establish such policies.

Government: Replace the Welfare State with a Caring State

Equalize Social Security for Spouses

Under this reform, both spouses would automatically earn equal Social Security credits during their marriage. They would combine these credits with whatever credits they might have earned before or after marriage, for their own individual retirement benefits. This so-called earnings sharing would increase benefits for working and stay-at-home mothers alike, and for divorced women, who are among the poorest old people in the country.

Currently, the Social Security system penalizes anyone who spends time working as an unpaid caregiver, and anyone who earns significantly less than their spouse—that is, the great majority of married mothers. In 1992 Congress issued a report on the inequities surrounding women and retirement, with the intention of launching a national debate on the issue. But the expected debate never occurred. As soon as the new 1994 Republican Congress came into power, it abolished the Select Committee on Aging that had issued the report.

The avatars of free enterprise had a very different debate in mind. Soon we began to hear about privatization of Social Security: allowing individuals to keep and invest for themselves money that would have gone into the Social Security Trust Fund.

One of the versions of privatization favored by Republicans would allow a sizable portion of a person's Social Security contributions to be put into a so-called PSA: a personal savings account to be invested as he or she saw fit. At retirement everyone would receive a flat minimum stipend from Social Security plus whatever had accumulated in their PSA.

This scheme would mean that the spouse who makes the home, wipes the runny noses, kisses away the bruises, cuts the corners off her own career, and earns less money would not necessarily have a stake in the accumulated savings of her family. There would be no "family" savings, only "personal" savings. The millions of women who are primary caregivers would have smaller PSAs than their husbands, to match their lower lifetime earnings. If they wanted anything more than a below-subsistence retirement income, they would either have to go out and earn their own money to invest for themselves or have to "depend on what he felt like giving her," according to attorney Edith Fierst. It would be hard to dream up a more anticaregiver retirement plan.

If any version of privatization ever does occur, it should mandate an FSA—a family savings account—for all married couples with children, jointly owned by both spouses, rather than individual PSAs that would allow the big breadwinner to salt away most of the family savings and future retirement income as his own. An alternative would be simply to give Social Security credits to family caregivers. Both France and Germany give women pension credits for time spent out of the labor market caring for family members, young or old. During the 2000 election campaign such a "caregiver's credit" was proposed by Vice President Albert Gore. He would credit any stay-at-home parent with $16,500 annual income for up to five years. This would lift the benefits of as many as 8 million people, almost all of them mothers, by an average of $600 a year.

Offer Work-Related Social Insurance Programs to All Workers

The artificial distinction between "members of the labor force," who work for wages, and those who provide unpaid care should be abolished. A "worker" would be defined as anyone who either is employed in the provision of goods and services or is engaged in the unpaid provision of care and services to dependent adults and children. Primary caregivers would be considered to be "in the labor force," and eligible for temporary unemployment compensation and job training in the event of divorce, and workmen's compensation for job-related injuries.

Provide Universal Preschool for All Three- and Four-Year-Olds

A caring state would also guarantee that all children have access to developmental education in their critical early years. In the nineteenth century the United States led the world in establishing free public education for all children starting at age six. The early twentieth century saw the expansion of public education through high school. Yet the country has become a laggard in providing young children with the early education that can prepare them for success in school and in life. This failure to invest in human capital is surely one major reason why one out of every six adult Americans is functionally illiterate.

The remedy is universal preschool for all American three- and four-year-olds. We have seen that quality early education is beyond the means of most parents, just as most parents cannot afford the full costs of primary or secondary education. Even middle-class families are routinely priced out of licensed nursery schools and child-care centers. According to the Census Bureau, child care is the single biggest expense of young families, after housing and food.

Among low-income families, government-subsidized early education and child care is so scarce that only about one-twelfth of the poor families who are eligible for subsidies receive them, according to a 1999 study by the Department of Health and Human Services.[8]

No state offers universal early education to three-year-olds, and only one state, Georgia, offers subsidized preschool to every four-year-old (although in 2000 Oklahoma and New York were also starting to take steps in that direction).

The practical effect of this neglect is to deny an early education to poor children, who are the very ones who need it the most. Nationally, only 36 percent of three- to five-year-olds from families earning less than $15,000 a year attend any kind of prekindergarten, compared with 79 percent from families earning more than $75,000.

In France, by contrast, 99 percent of three- to five-year-olds attend preschools at no or minimum charge. The French government also finances a licensed network of subsidized crèches, where 20 percent of younger children are cared for in a family setting.

The French system cost $7 billion a year in the mid-1990s. A universal preschool program in the United States, similar to the one enjoyed by military families—free for children whose families are in the lowest income brackets and at sliding-scale rates for others—could easily cost $50 billion a year. But often overlooked is the fact that the costs would be partially recovered by the tax revenues generated by increased maternal earnings. Universal early education would generate hundreds of thousands of skilled teaching jobs, most likely filled by women. No other policy imaginable would do more to give children a more promising future, and boost the economy's long-term prospects.

Stop Taxing Mothers More Than Anyone Else

We know that children as well as women benefit when mothers have significant control over family income and some financial independence. With welfare reform, the country took a major step toward reducing mothers' dependence on government, but nothing has been done to reduce their dependence on men. One of the fairest, most effective ways of accomplishing this would be to lower taxes on mothers' incomes, as opposed to family tax cuts per se.

Edward J. McCaffery, a professor of tax law at the University of Southern California, has analyzed what he calls the "deep, complex, and pervasive gender bias of our tax system." The current tax regime, like the Social Security system, was set up between the 1930s and 1950s with a traditional male breadwinner, dependent female spouse in mind. To some degree intentionally, the tax laws discourage two-earner families at all income levels by taxing the lower-earning spouse at much higher rates than the primary earner.

The government could actually raise more revenue, without lowering families' income by a penny, by taxing married men more and married women less. Economists have discovered that in response to high tax rates, married women do shift from work outside the home to unpaid work in the home, while lower taxes, and more take-home pay, draw them back into the paid labor force. When taxes go up for married men, by contrast, either their work patterns are not affected by the change, or, if anything, the men work harder to make up for the loss of income.

As McCaffery puts it, by taxing a second income at the family's highest marginal rate, "we are doing *exactly* the wrong thing, if we care about utility, wealth, or women—that is, if we care about anything other than men alone."[9]

One simple way to remedy this tax bias against married working mothers is to restore separate filing of federal income tax returns, as was done in the United States before 1948. Separate filing, the most common method of taxing married persons in other advanced democracies, would currently put the first $10,000 earned by the secondary earner, usually the mother, in a zero tax bracket, rather than having every dollar of her income taxed at the family's highest marginal rate. Separate filing would also eliminate the anachronistic designation of one spouse as "head of household" and the other as "spouse." I may earn less money than my husband, but that doesn't make him the "head of the household" and me the "spouse." Let us file and be taxed (or not taxed) separately, as financial equals in the family.

A mother's taxes could also be reduced considerably by allowing her to deduct child-care expenditures. If business executives can deduct half the cost of meals and entertainment as a legitimate cost of doing business, then surely the family's primary caregiver should be allowed to deduct the cost of substitute child care as a business expense, which it certainly is.

A Child Allowance; or Social Security for Children

The big problem with tax deductions and tax credits for children and for child care is that tax breaks do nothing for the roughly 30 percent of parents whose income is so low they pay no federal taxes. Far better than tinkering with the tax code would be a *child allowance* paid to *all* primary caregivers of young children, whether they work outside the home or not. Such a "salary" for every mother is paid in a number of countries, including Britain and France, and is truly neutral regarding parents' decisions on how to raise their children, for the money can be used either to help pay for child care or to help pay the bills in households where one parent stays home.

A child allowance, with the check made out to the person who is the family's primary caregiver, would target children far more effectively than a "family tax cut." Tax cuts, including the child tax credit, increase the income of the major breadwinner—and not even that in families who earn too little to pay income taxes. Child-care deductions, for their part, don't help families where the mother provides the care. An allowance, or "family wage" paid directly to caregivers, would help all families with kids. It could be paid out of a Children's Trust Fund, similar to the Social Security Trust Fund, supported by a dedicated income stream, possibly including contributions from employers and employees, as in the case of Social Security. One version of the family wage idea calls it Social Security for Children.

Provide Free Health Coverage for All Children and Their Primary Caregivers

Another minimal element in a caring state is adequate health insurance for *all* dependents, including children as well as the elderly and disabled. An American journalist whose wife recently had a baby in Paris discovered how nice it is to live in a place that values maternal and child health more highly. "[I] have become French enough to feel, stubbornly," he wrote, "that in a prosperous society all pregnant women should have three sonograms and four nights in a hospital if they want to. . . . It doesn't seem aristocratically spoiled to think that a woman should keep her job and have some paid leave afterward. . . . All human desires short of simple survival are luxurious, and a mother's desire to have a slightly queenly experience of childbirth . . . seems as well worth paying for as a tobacco subsidy or another tank."[10]

Even in Britain, where the Darwinian struggle was invented, all new mothers receive several home visits from a nurse to ensure that everything is going well. Among other things, the nurses make sure that new mothers have a grasp of the techniques of successful breast-feeding. In the United States, by contrast, new mothers are routinely sent home from hospitals after one day, often knowing less about babies than they do about their cat. Recently, a young American mother was indicted for manslaughter because she didn't know enough about breast-feeding to realize that her baby was slowly starving to death."[11]

Add Unpaid Household Labor to the GDP

A final, and relatively cheap, step the government could take toward valuing unpaid child care would be to include it in the GDP. In the early 1990s, the United Nations Statistical Commission recommended that member countries prepare so-called satellite GDP accounts estimating the value of unremunerated work. Countries all over the globe are complying.

Why is the United States, where GDP accounting began, the hold-out in this movement?

Husbands: If You Want Her to Do the Work, You Have to Help Pay for It

Two-Tier Marriage

Most husbands deeply appreciate their wives' work in raising the children and running the household. But they like these services the way they are: free.

The law in most states supports this male preference. The income coming into the household legally belongs only to the person whose name is on the check. Marriage partners are more like two unrelated individuals who happen to be living under one roof than equals in an economic partnership. This puts almost all the financial risks of divorce on the spouse who has sacrificed her income potential for the sake of the family.

Current arrangements may not be a problem as long as no children are involved. The private financial agreements between two adults are their own affair; with the possible exception of a dependency created by a very long marriage. But society obviously has a huge stake in the well-being of children, an interest that calls for much greater financial integration in marriage than now exists.

I propose that in marriages that produce children, the economic union would kick into higher gear. In this second tier of marriage the two individuals would automatically become full economic partners in a common family enterprise. Both parents' income would legally belong to this new family unit, created by the birth or adoption of a child. The adults' income would become "family income," institutionalizing sharing and protecting the altruism necessary to family life.

This idea, which sounds radical, is in fact quite old-fashioned. The notion of the family as an economic unit—as a community sharing its joint resources—actually predates capitalism and the nuclear family and lasted well into the present century even in the United States. Barbara Beran, an acquaintance who grew up in a traditional Jewish household in the 1930s and 1940s in New England, remembers hers as such a family. During her childhood her entire extended family worked in her grandfather's tailor shop, and after World War II, in her father's army-navy store. She recalls that the money coming in was family money—a pool of income that "belonged to all of us; it didn't matter precisely who had earned it."[12]

"The law should recognize more clearly that the family is a unit, a fictitious person like a corporation is a fictitious person," says Beran. "A family should be able to open up credit cards, take out a mortgage, borrow, own things in common. . . . All salaries, pensions, and other income would go to the family; and if anything happened to break up the family, all of its members would have a claim on that income."

Beran, who married an engineer and raised three children as a homemaker, believes that making the family a legal economic unit would protect those who do the work of caring for dependent children and elders. "Today we've lost an important part of the marriage contract," she says. "Women may fulfill their part of the bargain, and raise the children, but then men are able to renege on their part of the bargain. After she has supported the children and the family, there is no quid pro quo from him to support her.

"If women are going to do this work, someone has to protect them financially. The whole name of the game in the traditional family structure was to tie the man down so he didn't run away from that obligation. Men should have to pay a price if they do that. . . . The key is to arrange it so that *no one,* husband or wife, can have kids without paying for it."

Equal Standard of Living After Divorces Involving Dependent Children

The family wage would continue after a divorce. The partners would share their joint income for a fixed period of time, depending on the length of the marriage and the ages of the children, so that all family members would have an equal standard of living as long as they are supporting dependent children.

The basic idea here is that a divorce should neither unduly reward nor penalize either parent or the children. Spouses pledge to share the risks and rewards of marriage, and by the same token, ld share equally in the risks and rewards of divorce. This basic of fairness, says law professor Joan Williams, would "raise the costs of traditional gender roles for *men,* so that men, like women, suffer long-term adverse consequences for family patterns that involve wifely dependence."[13]

Postdivorce income sharing has in fact become the centerpiece of a new divorce reform movement, led by predominantly female legal scholars.[14] Philosopher Susan Moller Okin argues that the arrangement should last "for at least as long as the traditional division of labor in the marriage . . . [or] . . . until the youngest child enters first grade."[15] Other proposals suggest one year of equal sharing of the couple's combined income for every two years of marriage.[16]

Congress could mandate the states to pass legislative guidelines on income sharing by parents after they divorce, just as it has mandated child support guidelines. Short of this, reformers believe that child support orders should at least be modified to include: (1) payments earmarked for college tuition; (2) cost-of-living and income adjustments; and (3) a presumption that custody reflect the time each parent spent with the children during the marriage (so that men could not threaten to take the children unless their primary caregiver agreed to less child support).

Transfer All Responsibility for Postdivorce Payments to a Single Federal Agency

This is the key to effective child support enforcement. One proposal put before Congress every year would have the federal government deduct court-ordered child support from paychecks, like taxes, and disburse them directly to parents. A similar system is used in many European countries, and it has been instrumental in minimizing poverty among single-parent households. In Sweden, for example, if a noncustodial parent's payments aren't made, an agency advances the amount of child support owed and then tries to collect this money from the delinquent parent. However much is collected, the family still gets to keep the advance. This puts the onus of collection where it belongs: on law enforcement.

In the United States, child support arrangements are still in the hands of more than fifty states and jurisdictions, whose collection systems are as efficient as the Russian economy. Custodial parents have to enforce the law themselves by taking on the costly and often futile job of tracking down child support evaders. This makes nonpayment of child support the only crime that the victim has to enforce at her or his own expense.

In the mid-1990s congressional Republicans actually considered charging custodial parents fees amounting to several billion dollars to have the government collect the court-ordered support they were legally owed. This is analogous to charging robbery victims for the cost of tracking down thieves. It is not surprising that the party that thought this up faces a serious gender gap.

The Republican leadership has never allowed a national collection system to come to a vote on the House floor. If it did, several legislators assured me, it would pass. In 1995 Marge Roukema, a New Jersey Republican, told me that "the tough part of child support is getting a bill out of committee. As long as it's only talked about in back rooms, it never goes anywhere. . . . the men find all kinds of reasons why you can't do this or that. But if we can get it to the floor, it's motherhood. They don't dare vote against it."[17] Her remarks echoed what I had heard elsewhere. In California, one children's advocate attributed the success of the state's effort to increase child support to publicity. "Shine a light on the people who wanted a rollback, and they all scattered," she said.

The Community

Provide Community Support for Parents

A striking feature of current attitudes toward parenting is the tendency to hold parents responsible for everything that goes wrong with their kids in the community, while maintaining that every parent should go it alone, without any help from the community or government.

Maybe it's time to reevaluate this frankly mean-spirited contradiction. Catherine Coon, a teacher, has some interesting thoughts on how the communities in which children are raised could be more supportive of parents. "Right now the caring function is entirely invested in this black box called the nuclear family. It's privatized, and it's invisible, psychically as well as economically. The question is how do we establish closer links between families and communities?" she wonders. "How do we break away from the private caring function in a new way that's not a day-care center in a company basement or a shopping mall, but a public green or common, a space where people can interact; a living, heart-beating, vital space with stability and coherence? Sports provide this to some extent, but we need more public spaces for parents and children.

"In Denmark, for example, they have a 'folk center' in every neighborhood. It is the focus for raising kids, with programs and support for parents from birth through nursery-school age. Leaving your kids at the center would be like leaving your kids at home; home would just be a bigger place. Our conceptualization of home needs to broaden."[18]

This vision might include:

- Public schools and supervised playgrounds open for before- and after-school programs coinciding with parents' working day.
- Local public libraries with free lending libraries of educational toys and games, safety equipment, and art supplies. Library-based counselors could help parents and family day-care providers plan their daily activities with young children.
- Community pediatric clinics that would offer free health care, including shots, and give parents information and classes on children's physical, intellectual, and emotional development.

Parent Education

Providing parents with the information and training they need for their crucial job is as important as equipping soldiers to carry out their mission. Parent education can change children's lives and enable more people to understand that child-rearing is a serious occupation. In a twelve-year study involving primary-school children from Seattle's most crime-ridden neighborhoods, the kids whose teachers and parents were coached on how to interest the children in school and teach them to interact socially showed a significant long-term improvement in behavior and academic achievement. The parents were encouraged to reinforce desirable behavior, rather than simply punish bad behavior; taught to discipline consistently; and shown how to help their children succeed in school.[19]

We all know that parents have a greater impact on their children's development than any other influence. According to scholars Christopher Jencks and Meredith Phillips, "Changing the way parents deal with their children may be the single most important thing we can do to improve children's cognitive skills."[20] But better-informed parents can also raise the level of surrogate care. When I asked Dave McNair, a manager of the largest nonprofit day-care provider in Washington, D.C., what the single most effective way to improve day care would be, his answer was immediate and simple: "Educate parents."

Only well-informed parents know enough to demand and maintain higher standards, he explained. "Lots of people, even parents, still think of what we do as baby-sitting. They don't understand what we provide: role models, basic development skills, socialization. . . . Parents and other relatives have to reinforce what we do in the centers. We talk to them, try to get them to visit, to get them to understand what the children need and what we are doing. But it's hard."[21]

(Just how hard was indicated by the head of another center in the District of Columbia, who told me that when she brought in a nurse to talk to a group of low-income parents, she discovered that many couldn't even read a thermometer.)

Taking a course on infant development could become a routine part of prenatal care and preparation, like taking Lamaze classes. For less educated, low-income parents, home visit programs have been shown to be effective, both in Britain and the United States. While governor of Arkansas, Bill Clinton initiated HIPPY, a Home Instruction Program for Preschool Youngsters. Paraprofessionals visited homes of welfare mothers weekly, providing lessons the mothers could teach their babies and reviewing the previous week's assignments.

Such programs increase mothers' sense of competence, enable them to understand the difference between developmental and merely custodial child care, and reduce the physical as well as cognitive risks to children. That kind of payoff should raise the question whether a mastery of the basics ought to be made mandatory of *all* caregivers, just as it is of all drivers.

Expand the Concept of Diversity to Include People with Caregiving Experience

In a truly diverse world, people with direct child-rearing experience should be well represented in positions of power. Every institution should ask itself not only "Do we have enough blacks, Hispanics, Asian-Americans, and women in our higher ranks?" but "Do we have enough people who have spent serious time with children?" Parenting, the most important job in the world, ought to be seen as a credential.

A female German parliamentarian once told NOW president Patricia Ireland that she had a dream in which she interviewed a young man. "Oh, you have such outstanding credentials," she told him, "but we are looking for well-rounded people. We see you have never spent any time with children. But there's still time. You're still young. Come back when you've had broader life experience."

EVEN IF ONLY a handful of these proposals were enacted, the most obvious result would be a massive shift of income to women—which is precisely why all of them have met with such resistance. But paying women for services rendered is precisely the point. Female caregivers have been the world's cheap labor for too long. They have been forced to be dependents for too long. This isn't fair, and it makes no sense in terms of the general welfare.

Whatever the cries of outrage, however loud the protests against each and every one of these ideas, remember one thing: a society that beggars its mothers beggars its own future.

Notes

Introduction

1. "Mother" is often used throughout this book to refer to anyone who is the primary caregiver of another person. Barbara Katz Rothman, in *Recreating Motherhood,* makes the fundamental point that motherhood is based on caregiving and nurturance, and that whoever provides these to a child are its real "mothers," be they men or women, blood relatives, adopted or foster parents, nannies or other paid caregivers, friends, or a combination of the above. Although women still overwhelmingly fill the maternal, nurturing role, men certainly can. The fact that relatively few do surely has something to do with the fact that caregivers are still seriously disadvantaged.

2. Shirley P. Burggraf, *The Feminine Economy and Economic Man* (Boston: Addison-Wesley, 1997), p. 64.

3. L. F. M. Groot, J. J. Schippers, and J. J. Siegers, "The Effect of Interruptions and Part-Time Work on Women's Wage Rate," *De Economist* 136, no. 2 (1988): 220.

4. This case is described in detail in Mona Harrington, *Care and Equality,* pp. 51–52, 153.

5. This 1999 Maryland case was brought to my attention by Laura Morgan, a national authority on child support at the National Legal Research Group in Charlottesville, Virginia. The case is *Dunlap v. Fiorenza,* 128 Md. App. 357, 738 A. 2d 312 (1999).

6. Economist Shirley P. Burggraf uses the term "feminine economy" to describe all the work of caring for dependents, from infants to the sick and the elderly. By far the greatest portion of the feminine economy involves caring for children, but elder care is rapidly increasing. A survey released in 1997 found that 22 million elderly people are being cared for by a relative, three times as many as only ten years earlier. Nearly one out of four households is engaged in caring for an aged relative. These caregivers, the great majority of whom are women, spend on average about eighteen hours a week at this often stressful task. One-quarter of them provide at least forty

hours a week of unpaid service to an elderly family member. (1997 Caregiving Survey, sponsored by the National Alliance for Caregiving, American Association of Retired Persons, and Glaxo Wellcome.)

7. For a discussion of these contradictions, see Nancy Folbre, "Holding Hands at Midnight: The Paradox of Caring Labor," *Feminist Economics* 1, no. 1 (spring 1995); and "Children as Public Goods," *American Economic Review Papers and Proceedings* 84, no. 2 (May 1994).

8. "Mothers Are Worth $508,700!" Press release put out by Edelman Financial Services of Fairfax, Virginia, May 1997.

9. *Human Development Report, 1995,* published by the United Nations Development Programme (UNDP) (New York and Oxford: Oxford University Press, 1995), pp. 96–97. Luisella Goldschmidt-Clermont and Elisabetta Pagnossin-Aligisakis, "Measures of Unrecorded Economic Activities in Fourteen Countries," UNDP Occasional Papers 20, New York, 1995, pp. 25–26. Also Robin A. Douthitt, "The Value of Unpaid Work in the System of National Income Accounts: A Satellite Account Approach," *Consumer Interest Annual* 42 (1996): 5. Douthitt calculated that in 1985 American women spent more time in home child care than was spent by all people working in retail, the third largest paid industry. In Australia, where the data on nonmarket activity are particularly good, unpaid child care at home in 1992 absorbed more hours of labor than any other industry, with the exception of wholesale and retail trade.

10. Women perform on average 51 percent of the total work done in industrialized countries and 53 percent in developing countries. These data are based on time-use studies collected for fourteen industrial countries, nine developing countries, and eight countries in eastern Europe. *Human Development Report 1995*, p. 88.

11. Mothers realize that they are a cultural anomaly. In focus groups conducted in the early 1990s among middle-income American women of all ages and races, 82 percent of the mothers and 66 percent of the nonmothers described themselves as "self-sacrificing." "Caring" was the most common adjective used by the women to describe themselves. "Caring" and "self-sacrificing" are not adjectives anyone uses to describe the broader culture. See Sherrye Henry, *The Deep Divide* (New York: Macmillan, 1994), pp. 57–58.

Chapter 1: Where We Are Now

1. John F. Sandberg and Sandra L. Hofferth, "Changes in Children's Time with Parents, U.S., 1981–1997," unpublished paper, Population Studies Center, University of Michigan, April 2000. See also Suzanne M. Bianchi, "Maternal Employment and Time with Children: Dramatic Change or Surprising Continuity?" 2000 presidential address, Population Association of America, revised June 2000.

2. In no known human culture have males ever had the primary task of rearing small children. According to two preeminent scholars of children's history, one of the few things that can be said with certainty, amid the "extraordinary variety" in

the historical treatment of children, is that "the vast majority of human infants have been and continue to be cared for primarily by females." N. Roy Hiner and Joseph M. Hawes, *Children in Historical and Comparative Perspective* (New York: Greenwood Press, 1991), p. 6. If this ever changed, writes Marion J. Levy, a sociologist at Princeton University, the implications would be more radical than the discovery of fire, the invention of agriculture, or the switch from animate to inanimate sources of power. Marion J. Levy, Jr., *Maternal Influence* (New Brunswick, N.J.: Transaction Publishers, 1992), pp. xix, 20–23.

3. Occupational data was supplied by Steve Hipple of the Division of Labor Force Statistics, Bureau of Labor Statistics, March 6, 2000.

4. Unpublished data from the March 1999 Current Population Survey, provided by Steve Hipple.

5. Female university graduates' labor force participation rates were provided by Agneta Stark, an economist at the University of Stockholm, during an interview in August 1997 in Stockholm.

6. The 80 percent figure is in Michael W. Trapp, Roger H. Hermanson, and Joseph V. Carcello, "Characteristics of Chief Financial Officers," *Corporate Growth Report* 9 (1991): 17–20. The 64 percent figure comes from Charles Rodgers of Rodgers & Associates, Cambridge, Massachusetts, the consulting firm that conducted the survey. Still another recent survey found that only 39 percent of male M.B.A. graduates had full-time working wives. In contrast, 89 percent of female M.B.A.s have spouses who work full-time. See "Women and the MBA: Gateway to Opportunity," a report released in May 2000 by Catalyst, a nonprofit research organization in New York City.

7. Charles Rodgers, personal communication, October 1994.

8. An even greater percentage of mothers of younger children are at home. In 1999, a little more than 40 percent of married women with children under age six were employed full-time, 20 percent worked part-time, and 38 percent were not employed at all. In only a little more than one-third (37.3 percent) of two-parent families with school-age children both parents are employed full-time, year-round. These statistics were provided by Steve Hipple of the Bureau of Labor Statistics.

9. More than 2 million American women work in a home-based business. They average twenty-three hours of work (in the business) a week.

10. Deborah Fallows made this comment during a panel discussion at the Harvard/Radcliffe twenty-fifth reunion in 1996, attended by the author.

Council of Economic Advisers, *Families and the Labor Market, 1969–1999: Analyzing the "Time Crunch,"* Washington, D.C., 1999, p. 4.

11. Louis Uchitelle, "As Labor Supply Shrinks, a New Supply Is Tapped," *New York Times,* December 20, 1999.

12. The sensational statistic first appeared in an article by William R. Mattox, Jr., who was then at the Family Research Council, a right-wing group whose stated mission includes "promot[ing] and defend[ing] traditional family values in print." In the winter 1991 issue of *Policy Review,* a publication of the Heritage Foundation, Mattox warned that "the biggest problem facing American children today is lack

of time with and attention from their parents." As his principal evidence he cited an alleged 40 percent decline between 1965 and 1985, based on a reading of data produced by John Robinson, a preeminent authority on how Americans use their time. Robinson later claimed that he had made a mistake, and that his 1985 numbers were in error, thus invalidating the 40 percent decline. For a discussion of this controversy see David Whitman, "The Myth of AWOL Parents," *U.S. News and World Report,* July 1, 1996, pp. 54–56, and William R. Mattox, Jr., "It's Not a Myth," *Policy Review* (September–October 1996): 3.

When I contacted Robinson in 1996, he was still furious over what he characterized as the "misuse of social science data by the family values groups. They take data out of context and use it to promote their narrow point of view." Robinson believes that exaggerated reports of a parental "time famine" are based on a willful misinterpretation of data by ideologues whose "agenda is to get women back into the home." When I contacted Mattox, he was still wondering whether Robinson's numbers had really been incorrect.

13. Council of Economic Advisers, *Families and the Labor Market*, executive summary.

14. Arleen Leibowitz, "Education and Home Production," *American Economic Association* 64, no. 2 (May 1974): 250.

15. W. K. Bryant and C. D. Zick, "Are We Investing Less in the Next Generation? Historical Trends in Time Spent Caring for Children," *Journal of Family and Economic Issues* 17, no. 3/4 (winter 1996): 365–91, especially p. 368. See also Council of Economic Advisers, *Families and the Labor Market*, p. 13.

16. Suzanne M. Bianchi, "Maternal Employment and Time with Children: Dramatic Change or Surprising Continuity?" p. 11.

17. Sharon Hays, *The Cultural Contradictions of Motherhood* (New Haven: Yale University Press, 1996), pp. 86–94. Hays's observations have been corroborated by data from the 1997 National Study of the Changing Workforce, revealing that women with relatively high wages actually spend *more* time in child care than women with relatively low wages. See Richard B. Freeman, "The Feminization of Work in the U.S.: A New Era for (Man) kind?" National Bureau of Economic Research, unpublished paper, 1999, p. 16.

18. Married working mothers spend only about *three* fewer hours a week directly engaged with each child; that is, reading, playing, cooking, bathing, dressing, and so on. Sandra Hofferth, personal communication, June 2000.

19. In one nationwide study of white married couples in the United States, the average workweek of the mother was eighty-seven hours; in a different study, it ranged from seventy-six to eighty-nine hours, depending on the age of the oldest child. Juliet B. Schor, *The Overworked American* (New York: Basic Books, 1992), pp. 20–21, 37.

A study at two high-tech companies in New England found that the average working mother had a total workweek of eighty-four hours, compared with seventy-two hours for working fathers and about fifty hours for married men and women with no children. Fran Sussner Rodgers, "Business and the Facts of Family Life," *Harvard Business Review* (November–December 1989): 125.

Studies in Canada have come up with an even greater leisure gap. The 1992 General Social Survey in Canada, which took into account both work in the home and paid work, found that married mothers worked on average *106.9 hours per week,* 21 hours more than fathers. Frances Woolley, *Research Notes: The Social Security Review and Its Implications for Women,* Canadian Advisory Council on the Status of Women, November 1994, p. 4.

20. John P. Robinson, "Who's Doing the Housework?" *American Demographics* (December 1988, reprint, 1993): 30–31.

21. Sharon Walsh, "Hosts Around Nation Thankful—for Takeout," *Washington Post,* November 26, 1998.

22. Candy Sagon, "Dinner TIME," *Washington Post,* March 3, 1999. It is possible that this survey, of more than 1,000 families by National Family Opinion Research, overstated the family dining experience. Many parents might be reluctant to tell a strange interviewer that "we don't have time to eat together more than once a week."

23. In 1998, employed mothers reported having six hours a week less sleep than nonemployed mothers (fifty-five hours compared with sixty-one hours) and significantly less free time (twenty-nine hours per week versus forty-one hours). Bianchi, "Maternal Employment and Time with Children," p. 16.

24. Anita Garey, telephone interview, December 11, 1998. Garey, an assistant professor of sociology at the University of New Hampshire, based her findings on interviews with women working in predominantly female positions, that is, nurses, nurses' aides, clerical workers, and administrative staff. The results are found in her book *Weaving Work and Motherhood* (Philadelphia: Temple University Press, 1999).

25. For all workers between the ages of twenty-five and fifty-four, the average number of hours worked rose to 1,980 a year in 1995, from a post–World War II low of 1,840 hours in 1982. The number of people working extremely long hours—forty-nine or more a week—has risen by as much as 37 percent since 1985.

26. In a nationwide survey of 2,011 American adults, conducted in 1999 by Peter Hart and Robert Teeter for the *Wall Street Journal,* fully 83 percent said that lack of involvement in their children's lives is a "very serious problem" facing society. In another survey, in 1997, by the Families and Work Institute, 70 percent of parents reported they didn't have enough time to spend with their children, period.

27. Hofferth, forthcoming; cited in Sandberg and Hofferth, "Changes in Children's Time with Parents," p. 6.

28. *Washington Post,* December 14, 1995.

29. Cheryl Russell, *The Master Trend* (New York: Plenum Press, 1993), p. 114.

30. Edward Walsh, "Drug Use Tied to Father's Role," *Washington Post*, August 31, 1999. In a *Newsweek* survey, 85 percent of teens said their mom cared "very much" about them; 58 percent said Dad cared "very much." Barbara Kantrovitz and Pat Winegert, "How Well Do You Know Your Kids?" *Newsweek,* May 10, 1999, p. 39.

31. W. Jean Yeung, John F. Sandberg, Pamela E. Davis-Kean, and Sandra Hofferth, "Children's Time with Fathers in Intact Families," unpublished paper, University of Michigan, March 1998 (revised September 1999), pp. 20–21. These findings are based on twenty-four-hour time diaries with a higher degree of accuracy than time-use data collected by other methods. The diaries were collected in two nationally

representative surveys of the American population—the 1997 *Child Development Supplement* to the *Panel Study of Income Dynamics*—and *The Time Use Longitudinal Panel Study, 1975–1981.* University of Michigan researchers analyzing these data found that in 1997 married fathers' direct engagement with preteenage children on weekdays (one hour and thirteen minutes) was 67 percent that of mothers' and on weekends (3.3 hours) was 87 percent of mothers'.

Researchers have learned that men are also doing more at home in Australia, Britain, the Netherlands, and all the Scandinavian countries. In Britain, the Netherlands, and Denmark, for example, men's share of housework, including child care, increased from around one-quarter in the 1960s or early 1970s to 35 to 40 percent by the late 1980s, according to British economist Heather Joshi. See Bianchi, "Maternal Employment and Time with Children," p. 24. Nevertheless, in Australia, a 1992 survey found that men provided only 22 percent of the direct care of children. Duncan Ironmonger, "Counting Outputs, Capital Inputs, and Caring Labor: Estimating Gross Household Product," *Feminist Economics* 2, no. 3 (fall 1996): 55–56.

32. Yeung et al., "Children's Time with Fathers in Intact Families," p. 20.

33. Richard Freeman, "The Feminization of Work in the U.S.: A New Era for (Man)kind?" Freeman's analysis is based on data derived from the 1997 National Study of the Changing Workforce.

34. George Akerlof, personal communication, December 9, 1997. These findings will appear in George Akerlof and Rachel E. Knorton, "Economics and Identity," *Quarterly Journal of Economics*, forthcoming.

Also see Jonathan Gershuny, Michael Gordon, and Sally Jones, "The Domestic Labor Revolution: A Process of Lagged Adaptation?" in *The Social and Political Economy of the Household* (New York: Oxford University Press, 1994), pp. 185–86.

35. Hays, *The Cultural Contradictions of Motherhood,* pp. 99–100. The mothers in this study spent on average four times the hours the fathers did on child care: 8.9 hours a day vs. 1.9 hours. Also see Masako Ishii-Kuntz and Scott Coltrane, "Predicting the Sharing of Household Labor: Are Parenting and Housework Distinct? *Sociological Perspectives* 35, no. 4 (1992): 629–47; and Cathleen D. Zick and W. Keith Bryant, "A New Look at Parents' Time Spent in Child Care: Primary and Secondary Time Use," *Social Science Research* 25 (1996): 260.

36. Joseph R. Meisenheimer II, "Employee Absences in 1989: A New Look at Data from the CPS," *Monthly Labor Review* (August 1990): 28–33.

37. The 1996 National Household Education Survey found that 41 percent of mothers, and only 15 percent of fathers, volunteered at school. Survey findings reported by Carin Rubenstein, "Superdad Needs a Reality Check," *New York Times,* April 16, 1998.

38. "Women's Commutes Often More Complicated," *Washington Post,* March 3, 1999. The survey in Washington, D.C., was conducted by the Metropolitan Washington Council of Governments.

39. Personal communication with Lynne Casper, Census Bureau, June 13, 1996. Also see David Nakamura, "Dads Who Rock the Cradle," *Washington Post/Health,* March 16, 1999.

40. This 1994 poll was conducted by Yankelovitch Monitor.

Chapter 2: A Conspiracy of Silence

1. Glass Ceiling Commission, *Good for Business,* Washington, D.C., 1995; Peter Kilborn, "White Males and the Manager Class," *New York Times,* March 17, 1995. See also the 1996 and 1997 surveys of the 500 largest American corporations by Catalyst, revealing that women hold only about 2 percent of top corporate positions however they are defined—by title, paycheck, or line responsibility.

2. Felice N. Schwartz, "Management Women and the New Facts of Life," *Harvard Business Review* no. 1 (January–February 1989): 65–76.

3. Felice N. Schwartz, *Breaking With Tradition* (New York: Warner Books, 1992), pp. 12–18.

4. *Ibid.,* pp. 32–33.

5. Claudia Goldin, *Career and Family: College Women Look to the Past,* Working Paper No. 5188 (Cambridge, Mass.: National Bureau of Economic Research, 1995). Goldin's survey was based on the National Longitudinal Survey, which has asked detailed questions of the same group of women since 1969. The Longitudinal Survey questioned more than 1,200 female college graduates in 1991, when they were between the ages of thirty-seven and forty-seven. Their demographic features closely match those of comparable women in the entire U.S. population.

6. Goldin defined "family" as having at least one child and "career" as hourly earnings higher than those of the *lowest* 25 percent of men of the same age and educational level. The figure of 13 percent represents women who met the required earnings test—the equivalent of $11 an hour, full-time—for three years in a row; 17 percent met the test for two consecutive years.

7. Renouncing motherhood still didn't guarantee a baby-boomer woman a corner office, a designer bank account, or academic tenure, however. Not even half of the *childless* women met Goldin's criteria of a career.

8. Betsy Morris, "Is Your Family Wrecking Your Career?" *Fortune,* March 17, 1997. Other surveys have found that neither male nor female managers believe that women with significant family responsibilities have much chance of succeeding in business.

9. Judith P. Walker and Deborah J. Swiss, *Women and the Work/Family Dilemma* (New York: John Wiley & Sons, 1993).

10. Nationwide, one-third of new mothers with annual income of $50,000 or more return to work after three months. They are *less* likely to stay home with a new baby than low-income new mothers, only one-fourth of whom return to work after giving birth. See Arlie Hochschild, *The Time Bind* (New York: Metropolitan Books, 1997), p. 28.

11. Walker and Swiss, *Women and the Work/Family Dilemma,* pp. 141, 197, 229, 231.

12. Catalyst, "Women and the MBA: Gateway to Opportunity," New York, May 2000.

13. Ellen Gabriel, personal communication, 1995. The Deloitte survey revealed that only about 10 percent of the women who left the firm dropped out of the labor force entirely. The great majority went to work full-time in less pressured

environments, primarily in the not-for-profit and public sectors. Some 20 percent left to work part-time, citing family responsibilities.

14. See *Working Mother,* October 1997.

15. *Wall Street Journal,* October 16, 1995. A partner in a major New York law firm with an eight-month-old baby reported in a separate survey that "the senior partners treat me as dead."

16. *Wall Street Journal,* April 9, 1996.

17. Natalie Angier, "Why Science Loses Women in the Ranks," *New York Times,* May 14, 1995.

18. Anne E. Preston, "Why Have All the Women Gone? A Study of Exit of Women from the Science and Engineering Professions," unpublished paper, SUNY at Stony Brook, New York, March 1992, p. 1.

19. Stephanie Dement, telephone interview, May 1995.

20. The estimate of the amount of venture capital going to female entrepreneurs is from Patricia Haig, American Association of University Women, July 30, 2000. The statistic on the wealthiest technology professionals is from a 2000 survey by the investment firm U.S. Trust Co. in New York City. The estimate that only 3 percent of Internet companies have a woman on their board is from a survey by Spencer Stuart in 2000.

21. *A Question of Equity: Women and the Glass Ceiling: A Report to the President and the Congress by the Merit Systems Protection Board,* October 1992, p. 21.

22. *Ibid.,* pp. x, 17, 22.

23. *Ibid.,* pp. 19–20.

24. National Institutes of Health, Office of Research on Women's Health, *Public Hearing on Recruitment, Retention, Reentry, and Advancement of Women in Biomedical Careers,* Bethesda, Maryland, March 2–3, 1992. Additional details on the status of women in the medical profession were provided by Vivian W. Pinn, Director, Office of Research on Women's Health, N.I.H.

25. Associated Press, "Young Female Doctors Reach Pay Parity," *Washington Post,* April 11, 1996.

26. As a result of these choices younger female doctors average $110,000 a year, compared with $155,000 for men the same age. *Washington Post,* April 11, 1996, p. A4.

27. Abigail Trafford, "Women's Gains in Medicine Not Reflected At the Top," *Washington Post Health,* March 28, 1995.

28. Michael J. Goldberg, "Top Officers of Local Unions," *Labor Studies Journal* 19, no. 4, (winter 1995): 13.

29. Innumerable factors play a part in a working mother's decision on whether to cut back on her career or not, including the flexibility of her employer, the supportiveness of her husband, the adequacy of her day-care situation, her income, and her stamina. I made an additional, although admittedly anecdotal, discovery after interviewing almost a hundred mothers who had decided to leave professional positions. As one, a former newspaper editor now staying at home with two small boys, summed it up: "I was a workaholic, and then I became a 'momaholic.' I think the

women who are most obsessive about their jobs may be the ones who become the most obsessive about their babies."

An exaggeration, perhaps. But it is suggestive that when the chemical company Du Pont looked into why a disproportionate number of female engineers were leaving the company, management found that it was the *best* performers, not the worst, who were leaving in search of more time for their families. See Arlie Hochschild, *The Time Bind* (New York: Metropolitan Books, 1997), pp. 30–33.

Chapter 3: How Mothers' Work Was "Disappeared"

1. A detailed history of women's unpaid domestic labor, and how it came to be redefined as industrialism spread, is described in Jeanne Boydston, *Home and Work: Housework, Wages, and the Ideology of Labor in the Early Republic* (New York: Oxford University Press, 1990).
2. Boydston, *op. cit.*, pp. 46–47.
3. Mary Wollstonecraft, *A Vindication of the Rights of Women* (Mineola, N.Y.: Dover Publications, 1996).
4. Nancy Folbre, "The Unproductive Housewife," *Signs: Journal of Women in Culture and Society* 16, no. 31 (1991): 465.
5. Charles Burroughs, *An Address on Female Education, Delivered in Portsmouth, N.H.,* October 29, 1827.
6. Ann Douglas, *The Feminization of American Culture* (New York: Alfred A. Knopf, 1977), pp. 74–75. The quote is from Lydia Sigourney's *Letters to Mothers,* written in 1838.
7. Quoted in Boydston, *op. cit.*, pp. 81–82.
8. Alexis de Tocqueville, *Democracy in America, Volume II* (New York: Vintage Books, 1945), pp. 223–25.
9. As Olivier Bernier wrote in *Pleasure and Privilege* (Garden City, N.Y.: Doubleday, 1981), a history of late-eighteenth-century Europe and America, "Middle class children would one day be expected to earn money and further the family fortunes; they had to be educated accordingly."
10. Mary P. Ryan, *The Empire of the Mother* (New York: Harrington Park Press, 1985), pp. 48–49.
11. Jane Rendell, *The Origins of Modern Feminism: Women in Britain, France, and the United States, 1780–1860* (New York: Macmillan, 1985), pp. 145–46.
12. *Ibid.*, pp. 209–10.
13. In the 1970s some feminist scholars viewed the cultural shift toward more intensive child-rearing as a step backward for women. Writing at a time when women were just emerging from "the feminine mystique," they concluded that the weighty importance suddenly attached to mothering sounded ominously familiar and repressive. The nineteenth-century "cult of motherhood" was characterized as the "bonds of womanhood," an enormous scam to keep women busy in the home while men monopolized the marketplace, the money, and the public power.

But even if the glorification of the role of the mother did play a part in channeling educated women away from public life, as it clearly did, that does not alter the fact that the feminization of child-rearing practices had profound economic consequences.

14. Wanda Minge-Klevana, "Does Labor Time Decrease with Industrialization? A Survey of Time-Allocation Studies," *Current Anthropology* 21, no. 3 (June 1980): 279.

15. Shirley Burggraf, *op. cit.*

16. Boydston, *op. cit.*, p. 102.

17. *Ibid.*, p. 104.

18. *Ibid.*, p. 114.

19. *Ibid.*, pp. 132–37.

20. Elizabeth Fox-Genovese, *op. cit.*, p. 57; Stephanie Coontz, *The Way We Never Were* (New York: Basic Books, 1992), pp. 52–53; and Robert Bellah, *Habits of the Heart: Individualism and Commitment in American Life* (New York: Harper & Row, 1986), p. 40.

21. Coontz, *op. cit.*, p. 55.

22. Boydston, *op. cit.*, pp. 162–63.

23. Elizabeth Griffith, *In Her Own Right: The Life of Elizabeth Cady Stanton* (New York: Oxford University Press, 1984), p. iii.

24. Theodore Stanton and Harriet S. Blatch, eds., *Elizabeth Cady Stanton as Revealed in Her Letters, Diary, and Reminiscences,* 1922, pp. 54–55, quoted in Reva Siegel, "Home as Work: the First Woman's Rights Claims Concerning Wives' Household Labor, 1850–1880," *Yale Law Journal* 103, no. 5 (March 1994): 1090–91.

25. Griffith, *op. cit.*, p. 91.

26. Boydston, *op. cit.*, p. 97.

27. Reva B. Siegel, *op. cit.*, p. 1113.

28. *Ibid.*, p. 1115.

29. Alice Kessler Harris, *Out to Work: A History of Wage-Earning Women in the United States* (New York, Oxford University Press, 1982), pp. 46–48.

30. Siegel, *op. cit.*, pp. 1083, 1183–85.

31. Folbre, "The Unproductive Housewife," pp. 474–75.

32. Siegel, *op. cit.*, p. 1092.

33. Folbre, *op. cit.*, pp. 483–84.

34. Cited in Barnet Wagman and Nancy Folbre, "Household Services and Economic Growth in the United States, 1870–1930," *Feminist Economics* 2, no. 1 (spring 1996): 43.

35. Folbre, "The Unproductive Housewife," pp. 478–79.

36. *Census of Great Britain, 1851,* quoted in Folbre, *ibid.*, p. 471.

37. *Census of England and Wales, 1961 and 1871,* quoted in Folbre, *ibid.*, p. 471.

38. Desley Deacon, "Political Arithmetic: The Nineteenth-Century Australian Census and the Construction of the Dependent Woman," *Signs* 2, no. 11 (autumn 1985): 34–35.

39. Siegel, *op. cit.*, pp. 1203–9.

40. The six states in which there is a legal presumption that marital property should be divided fifty-fifty are Idaho, Nevada, Arkansas, West Virginia, North Carolina, and New Hampshire. In these states a judge has to have a good reason for deviating from the principle of an equal division of property.

41. Reva B. Siegel, "The Modernization of Marital Status Law: Adjudicating Wives' Rights to Earnings, 1860–1930," *Georgetown Law Journal* 82, no. 7 (September 1994): 2197–99. Also see an analysis of this case by Joan Williams, *Unbending Gender,* pp. 18, 119–21.

Chapter 4: The Truly Invisible Hand

1. Clifford Cobb, Ted Halstead, and Jonathan Rowe, "If the GNP Is Up, Why Is America Down?" *Atlantic Monthly,* October 1995, p. 67.

2. These examples are cited by Gloria Steinem in her book *Moving Beyond Words* (New York: Simon & Schuster, 1994).

3. Herman Daly and John B. Cobb, Jr., *For the Common Good* (Boston: Beacon Press, 1989), p. 138.

4. I am indebted to Rita Brock, director of the Bunting Institute in Cambridge, Massachusetts, for calling my attention to the Aristotelian distinction between *oikonomia* and *chrematistics.*

5. Quoted in Daly and Cobb, *op. cit.,* p. 139.

6. World Bank, *Monitoring Environmental Progress,* Washington, D.C., 1995.

7. Roger Kubarych, personal communication, May 1996.

8. See, for example, Dale Jorgenson and Barbara Frameni, "The Accumulation of Human and Nonhuman Capital, 1948–84," in Robert Lipsey and Helen Stone, eds., *The Measurement of Saving, Investment, and Wealth* (Chicago: University of Chicago Press, 1989), pp. 227–85.

9. N. Gregory Mankiw, *Macroeconomics* (New York: Worth Publishers, 1997), p. 109.

10. Craig Ramey, quoted in Sandra Blakeslee, "Studies Show Talking with Infants Shapes Basis of Ability to Think," *New York Times,* April 17, 1997.

11. Marion R. Winterbottom, "The Relation of the Need for Achievement to Learning Experiences in Independence and Mastery," in J. W. Atkinson, ed., *Motives in Fantasy, Action, and Society* (Princeton, N.J.: D. Van Nostrand Co., Inc. 1958), pp. 453–78; cited in David C. McClelland, *The Achieving Society* (Princeton, N.J.: D. Van Nostrand Co., Inc., 1961), pp. 46–49, 342–45.

12. Gary S. Becker, *Human Capital* (3rd edition) (Chicago: University of Chicago Press, 1994), p. 209.

13. Gary S. Becker and Nigel Tomes, "Human Capital and the Rise and Fall of Families," *Journal of Labor Economics* 43, pt. 2 (July 1986): S5.

14. Burggraf, *The Feminine Economy,* p. 64.

15. Duncan Ironmonger, "Counting Outputs, Capital Inputs and Caring Labor: Estimating Gross Household Product," *Feminist Economics* 2, no. 3 (1996): 53. See

also Chris Beasley, *Sexual Economyths: Conceiving a Feminist Economics* (Sydney, Australia: Allen & Unwin, 1994).

16. IAFFE, *Newsletter* 3, no. 3, p. 10.

17. Nechama Mesliansky, personal communication, October 1993.

18. Cited by Ellen O'Brien, "Putting Housework in the GNP: Toward a Feminist Accounting?" unpublished paper prepared for "Out of the Margin—Feminist Perspectives on Economic Theory," conference in Amsterdam, June 1993.

19. Lloyd G. Reynolds, *Economics: A General Introduction* (Homewood, Ill.: Irwin, 1988); quoted in Marianne A. Ferber and Julie A. Nelson, *Beyond Economic Man* (Chicago: University of Chicago Press, 1993), p. 5.

20. Paul A. Samuelson and William D. Nordhaus, *Economics* (15th edition). (New York: McGraw-Hill, Inc., 1995), p. 417.

21. United Nations Development Programme, *Human Development Report 1995,* p. 88.

22. Nancy Folbre, personal communication, May 1995.

23. Elizabeth Enders, letter to the editor, *New York Times,* September 11, 1992.

24. UNDP, *op. cit.,* p. 98.

25. Quoted in the press release accompanying publication of the *Human Development Report 1995,* August 17, 1995.

26. Burggraf, *The Feminine Economy,* p. 1.

27. Nancy Folbre, *Who Pays for the Kids?* (London and New York: Routledge, 1994), especially pp. 108–16, 144–47.

28. Nancy Folbre, personal communication, July 1995.

29. Carol Lees, personal communication, September 1995.

30. Gloria Steinem, *op. cit.,* p. 240.

31. Marilyn Waring, *If Women Counted* (San Francisco: Harper & Row, 1988), p. 94.

32. Ironmonger, *op. cit.,* p. 149.

33. Nancy Folbre, "The Paradox of Caring Labor," p. 86.

34. Washington Feminist Faxnet, February 17, 1994.

Chapter 5: The Mommy Tax

1. This calculation was made by economist June O'Neill, using data from the National Longitudinal Survey of Youth. June O'Neill and Solomon Polachek, "Why the Gender Gap in Wages Narrowed in the 1980s," *Journal of Labor Economics* 11 (1993): 205–28. See also June O'Neill, "The Shrinking Pay Gap," *Wall Street Journal,* October 7, 1994.

2. The concept of the mommy tax was inspired by development economist Gita Sen, who has described the extra economic burden borne by women as a "reproduction tax."

3. I don't mean to suggest that old-fashioned sex discrimination, even against women who are able to perform as "ideal" workers, is not still alive and well, as numerous recent complaints, from the brokerage offices of Smith Barney to the

machine shops of Mitsubishi, can attest. Simply being female still sentences women in virtually every occupation and at every level to lower earnings than men in similar positions. But overt in-your-face discrimination has thankfully declined steadily in recent decades.

4. Jane Waldfogel, personal communication, October 1996.

5. Burggraf assumes that the more flexible parent's earnings average $25,750 a year, versus $55,750 for the primary breadwinner. She then multiplies $30,000 (the difference between what the two parents earn) by 45 (the years in a working lifetime) to get the $1.350 million. *The Feminine Economy and Economic Man,* p. 61.

6. Sue Headlee and Margery Elfin, *The Cost of Being Female* (Westport, Conn.: Praeger, 1999), p. 135.

7. Jane Lewis, ed., *Women and Social Policies in Europe* (Hants, England: Edward Elgar, 1993), p. 20.

8. The "typical" French mother is only out of the labor force for two years, one year after the birth of each child. Seventy-four percent of the mothers of children under three work for pay full-time, one of the highest percentages in Europe.

9. Hugh Davies and Heather Joshi, "The Forgone Earnings of Europe's Mothers," discussion papers in Economics, 1990, Birbeck College, London; also Heather Joshi and Hugh Davies, "Mothers' Human Capital and Children in Britain," *National Institute Economic Review* (November 1993): 52–53.

10. Martha Ritchie, personal communication, January 1995.

11. Sara Rimer, "Study Details Sacrifices in Caring for Elderly Kin," *New York Times,* November 27, 1999. The National Alliance for Caregivers estimates that the number of employed people who provide care for elderly family members will grow to 11 to 15.6 million in the first decade of the twenty-first century.

12. *Virginia V. Daley et al. v. Aetna Life & Casualty et al.,* August 12, 1994. Virginia Daley, personal communication, May 1996; Philip L. Steele, personal communication, October 2000.

13. Amity Shlaes, "What Does Woman Want?" *Women's Quarterly* (summer 1996): 10.

14. According to June O'Neill, an economist and former head of the Congressional Budget Office, "Full-time year-round workers are not likely to be representative of all workers. Women are less likely to be in this category than men." See June O'Neill and Solomon Polachek, "Why the Gender Gap in Wages Narrowed in the 1980s," *Journal of Labor Economics* 2, no. 1, pt. 1 (1993): 208–9.

15. U.S. Bureau of the Census, Current Population Reports, *Money Income in the U.S.: 1995,* Washington, D.C., March 2000, P60-209, pp. 46–49.

16. Robert G. Wood, Mary E. Corcoran, and Paul N. Courant, "Pay Differentials Among the Highly-Paid: The Male-Female Earnings Gap in Lawyers' Salaries," *Journal of Labor Economics* 11, no. 3 (1993): 417–41.

17. Christina Hoff Sommers, *Who Stole Feminism?* (New York: Simon & Schuster, 1994), p. 240.

18. The estimate of a 47 percent loss of lifetime earnings was presented by Hugh Davies at a session of the Allied Social Science Association in New York City on January 4, 1999. It is based on the British Household Poll Survey of 1994. Using earlier

data, Davies and Joshi calculated that the mommy tax on a typical British secretary was the equivalent of $324,000—not counting lost pension benefits. See Heather Joshi, "Sex and Motherhood as Handicaps in the Labour Market," in *Women's Issues in Social Policy,* ed. Mavis Maclean and Dulcie Grove (London: Routledge, 1991), p. 180. See also Heather Joshi, "The Cost of Caring," in *Women and Poverty in Britain: The 1990's,* ed. Carol Glendenning and Jane Millar (New York: Harvester Wheatsheaf, 1992), p. 121. Also see Heather Joshi and Pierella Paci, *Unequal Pay for Men and Women* (Cambridge, Mass.: M.I.T. Press, 1998).

19. Jane Waldfogel, "Women Working for Less: Family Status and Women's Pay in the US and UK," Malcolm Wiener Center for Social Policy Working Paper D-94-1, Harvard University, 1994.

20. Jane Waldfogel, "Understanding the 'Family Gap' in Pay for Women with Children," *Journal of Economic Perspectives* 12, no. 1 (winter 1998): 137–56. See also Waldfogel, "The Family Gap for Young Women in the United States and Britain," *Journal of Labor Economics* 11 (1998): 505–19. Looking at two different cohorts of young women, one averaging age thirty in 1981 and the other about thirty in 1990, Waldfogel found that the nonmothers' wages rose from 72 percent to 90 percent of men's between 1981 and 1990. But the wages of mothers rose less, from 60 percent to only 70 percent of men the same age during the same period. The more children a woman had, the lower her earnings, even with all other factors being equal.

Waldfogel also uncovered a wage gap of 20 percentage points for young women in the United Kingdom. Nonmothers at age thirty-three earn 84 percent of men's pay, while mothers earn only 64 percent. See Jane Waldfogel, "The Family Gap for Young Women in the US and UK: Can Maternity Leave Make a Difference?" Malcolm Wiener Center for Social Policy, Harvard University, October 1994, pp. 1, 20.

21. See Paula England and Michelle Budig, "The Effects of Motherhood on Wages in Recent Cohorts: Findings from the National Longitudinal Survey of Youth," unpublished paper, 1999.

22. Elizabeth Olson, "U.N. Surveys Paid Leave for Mothers," *New York Times,* February 16, 1998.

23. Christopher J. Ruhm, "The Economic Consequences of Parental Leave Mandates: Lessons from Europe," *Quarterly Journal of Economics* CXIII, no. 1 (1998): 285–317. Ruhm found that longer leaves (of nine months or more) were associated with a slight reduction in women's relative wages, but Waldfogel discovered that mothers in Britain who exercised their right to a ten-month paid maternity leave and returned to their original employer had wages no different from those of childless women.

See also "Working Mothers Then and Now: A Cross-Cohort Analysis of the Effects of Maternity Leave on Women's Pay," in *Gender and Family Issues in the Workplace,* ed. Francine Blau and Ronald Ehrenberg (New York: Russell Sage Foundation, 1997).

24. Heidi Hartmann, Institute for Women's Policy Research, personal communication, January 8, 1995. Hartmann's research has shown that fully 11 percent of women who have no paid leave have to go on public assistance during their time with a new baby.

25. Wood, Corcoran, and Courant, "Pay Differentials," pp. 417–28.

26. This 1993 study was coauthored by Joy Schneer of Rider University's College of Business Administration and Frieda Reitman, professor emeritus at Pace University's Lubin School of Business.

27. Joyce Jacobsen and Arthur Levin, "The Effects of Intermittent Labor Force Attachment on Female Earnings," *Monthly Labor Review* 118, no. 9 (September 1995): 18.

28. For a good discussion of the obstacles to mothers' employment in relatively well-paying blue-collar work, see Williams, *Unbending Gender,* pp. 76–81.

29. This survey of 1,000 workers was conducted by researchers at the University of Connecticut and Rutgers University, and was reported in the *Wall Street Journal,* May 18, 1999.

30. A survey of more than 2,000 people in four large corporations found that 75 percent of the professionals working part-time were women who were doing so because of child-care obligations. Only 11 percent of the male managers surveyed expected to work part-time at some point in their careers, compared with 36 percent of women managers. *A New Approach to Flexibility: Managing the Work/Time Equation* (New York: Catalyst, 1997), pp. 25–26.

31. There is other evidence that many so-called part-timers are increasingly working what used to be considered full-time—thirty-five to forty hours a week—for lower hourly pay than regular full-timers. See Reed Abelson, "Part-time Work for Some Adds Up to Full-Time Job," *New York Times,* November 2, 1998.

32. In the five years from 1988 through 1992, the number of women-owned sole proprietorships, partnerships, and similar businesses soared 43 percent, compared with overall growth of 26 percent in such businesses. *Wall Street Journal,* January 29, 1996.

33. Tracy Thompson, "A War Inside Your Head," *Washington Post Magazine,* February 15, 1998, p. 29.

34. Information on women-owned businesses provided by the National Foundation for Women Business Owners in Washington, D.C., September 2000.

35. Noelle Knox, "Women Entrepreneurs Attract New Financing," *New York Times,* July 26, 1998.

36. For the relatively low value placed on the caring professions, see Paula England, George Farkas, Barbara Kilbourne, Kurt Beron, and Dorothea Weir, "Returns to Skill, Compensating Differentials, and Gender Bias: Effects of Occupational Characteristics on Wages of White Women and Men," *American Journal of Sociology* 100, no. 3 (November 1994): 689–719.

37. On corporate attitudes toward part-time work for men, see the study cited in note 29. Another study found that 63 percent of large employers thought it was inappropriate for a man to take *any* parental leave, and another 17 percent thought it unreasonable unless the leave was limited to two weeks or less. Martin H. Malin, "Fathers and Parental Leave," *Texas Law Review* 72 (1994): 1047, 1089; cited in Williams, *Unbending Gender,* p. 100.

38. This study, by Linda Stroh of Loyola University, was reported by Tamar Lewin, "Fathers Whose Wives Stay Home Earn More and Get Ahead, Studies Find," *New York Times,* October 12, 1994.

39. Charles Rodgers, personal communication, October 1993.

40. Details of this story were provided by Cindi DiBiasi in November of 1995. When I contacted DiBiasi's former boss, Jack Hurley, he said that these conversations "didn't ring a bell." Neither did other tense encounters between the two. Hurley, who is now with the Freedom Forum in Arlington, Virginia, did remember calling DiBiasi to tell her that she was being taken off the medical beat and given general assignment. "The news director felt that Cindy was a stronger street reporter than medical reporter. The new assignment reflected that," he said.

41. Nancy Norman, a videotape editor who worked at Channel Nine while DiBiasi was there, confirmed her story, and told me that "most of the women at Nine stood behind Cindy." Norman herself sued the company for sexual discrimination and was awarded half a million dollars by a jury. She said it was easier for her to sue because she didn't have any kids.

42. Susan Pedersen, personal interview, June 1996.

43. Being a young mother obviously worked for Crittenden, who was affluent enough to have purchased a $1.3-million home in Washington, D.C., while still in her midthirties. But not many mothers enjoy such options.

44. Barbara Bergmann, personal conversation, January 4, 1999.

45. Joshua D. Angrist, "Lifetime Earnings and the Vietnam Era Draft Lottery: Evidence from Social Security Administrative Records," *American Economic Review* 80, no. 3 (June 1990): 313–31.

46. The United States is the only country in the world that offers *full* retirement to military reservists. In 1993 the cost to taxpayers was $1.9 billion. See Congressional Budget Office, *Reducing the Deficit: Spending and Revenue Options,* Washington, D.C., 1995, p. 64.

47. David O'Neill, "Voucher Funding of Training Programs: Evidence from the G.I. Bill," *Journal of Human Resources* 12, no. 4 (fall 1977): 425–45; and Joshua D. Angrist, "The Effects of Veterans' Benefits on Education and Earnings," *Industrial and Labor Relations Review* 46, no. 4 (July 1993): 637–57.

48. Williams, *Unbending Gender,* pp. 101–10.

49. The theory that much of the childlessness among educated American women is involuntary was supported by an informal class survey of the graduates of Harvard and Radcliffe class of 1971. Roughly one-fifth of both the men and the women were still childless in 1996, when the class was in its mid- to late forties. But many more women than men said they were childless because of "circumstances."

Chapter 6: The Dark Little Secret of Family Life

1. Unpublished data for 1995, Current Population Survey, U.S. Bureau of the Census; obtained from Bob Cleveland, Income Statistics Branch, Housing and Household Statistics Division, U.S. Bureau of the Census, personal communication, September 26, 1996.

2. Frances Woolley, "Intra-Family Inequality: Implications for the Design of Income Support," in *Research Notes: The Social Security Review and Its Implications for Women* (Canadian Advisory Council on the Status of Women, 1994), p. 3.

3. Rhona Mahony, *Kidding Ourselves* (New York: Basic Books, 1995), pp. 44–45.

4. Richard F. Curtis, "Household and Family in Theory on Inequality," *American Sociological Review* 51 (1986): 179. "Probably the single most widespread cause of male power," Curtis writes, "is the [fact] . . . that economic resources produced outside the family are brought into it by males, giving them internal power through control over resources. . . . Restriction of women to 'woman's sphere' denies them societal power by definition, and even reduces their power within the family" (p. 172). See also Jan Pahl, *Money and Marriage* (Basingstoke, Hampshire: Macmillan Education, 1989).

5. Robert Michelson, personal communication, March 1996.

6. Mahony, *Kidding Ourselves,* p. 18.

7. In 1999 more than 20 percent of the married mothers who were wage earners were the family's primary breadwinner. These data were provided to the author by Richard B. Freeman of the National Bureau of Economic Research in March of 2000.

8. In 1963, only 20 percent of married white women between the ages of eighteen and forty-four and 26 percent of young married black women contributed 30 to 70 percent of the family income. By 1993, three decades later, 47 percent of white wives and 56 percent of black wives were earning between 30 and 70 percent of the household income. These calculations, by Pamela Smock of Louisiana State University and Aimee Dechter of the University of Wisconsin, were reported in the *Wall Street Journal,* June 13, 1994.

9. Families and Work Institute, "Women: The New Providers," survey conducted by Louis Harris and Associates, Inc., May 1995, p. 31.

10. Edward J. McCaffery, *Taxing Women* (Chicago: University of Chicago Press, 1997), pp. 155–57. McCaffery estimates that "on average, two-earner families, at middle- and upper-income levels, sacrifice about 68 percent of the wife's lower salary to taxes and other expenses occasioned by her work" (p. 21).

11. Michael Boskin, "The Effects of Government Expenditures and Taxes on Female Labor," *American Economic Review* 64, no. 2 (1974): 251–56.

12. McCaffery, *Taxing Women,* pp. 146–49.

13. The 1999 income data is from the *Current Population Survey,* March 2000, Table PINC-04. It was provided by Ed Welniak of the Census Bureau. The information on the percentage of married women earning more than $50,000 was provided by Carmen DeNavas of the Census Bureau.

14. Barry W. Johnson, "Personal Wealth, 1995," *Statistics of Income Bulletin* (Internal Revenue Service, winter 1999/2000, p. 59).

15. Nancy Ann Jeffrey, "The New-Economy Family," *Wall Street Journal,* September 8, 2000, p. W1. In 58 percent of households earning between $500,000 and $999,999, there is only one breadwinner, according to data collected by the Federal Reserve Board, and 99 times out of 100, he is a man. Many of these men are married

to graduates of exclusive universities, which helps explain the apparent anomaly that while having a college degree *adds* $9,000 to woman's annual salary, a degree from a high-prestige school subtracts $2,400. See Natalie Angier in "Women, Men, Sex and Darwin," *New York Times Magazine,* February 21, 1999, p. 50. In short, while it is true that women with college degrees are more likely to be employed than less educated women, this is not the case in high-income families.

16. Women in households with incomes of less than $50,000 a year are twice as likely to make the decision to purchase a house on their own as women from households with higher incomes, for example. By a decided margin, working women are also more likely than homemakers to make independent financial decisions. Christy Harvey, "A Guide to Who Holds the Purse Strings," *Wall Street Journal,* June 22, 2000, p. A14.

Social scientists have also documented the relative subservience of the privileged wife. "Our own data suggest that women's economic dependency tends to increase with the husband's income," two sociologists concluded. See A. Sorensen and S. McLanahan in "Married Women's Economic Dependence, 1940–1980," *American Journal of Sociology* 93, no. 3 (November 1987): 662.

17. Carlotta Miles, personal communication, March 1996.

18. Hope Brock, personal communication, June 1996.

19. "It is clear that mothers invest more time and a higher percentage of their incomes in children than do fathers." Patrice L. Engle and Cynthia Breaux, "Is There a Father Instinct? Fathers' Responsibility for Children," the Population Council and International Center for Research on Women, February 1994, p. 1.

20. "When one takes into account all of its benefits, educating girls quite possibly yields a higher rate of return than any other investment available in the developing world." Lawrence H. Summers, "Investing in *All* the People," World Bank Policy Research Working Paper, Washington, D.C., May 1992, p. 5.

21. Steven Pinker, "Why They Kill Their Newborns," *New York Times Magazine,* November 2, 1997, p. 52.

22. Judith Bruce and Cynthia B. Lloyd, "Finding the Ties That Bind: Beyond Headship and Household," in *Intrahousehold Resource Allocation in Developing Countries: Methods, Models, and Policy,* ed. Lawrence Haddad, John Hoddinott, and Harold Alderman (Baltimore: International Food Policy Research Institute and Johns Hopkins University Press, 1997).

23. N. Cagatay, D. Elson, and C. Grown, "Gender, Adjustment, and Macroeconomics," *World Development* 23, no. 11 (November 1995): 1830.

24. World Bank, *Toward Gender Equality: The Role of Public Policy,* Washington, D.C., 1995, p. 59.

25. John Hoddinott and Lawrence Haddad, "Understanding How Resources Are Allocated Within Households," paper presented at the Canadian Economics Association Meetings, Ottawa, Canada, 1993.

26. Nicholas D. Kristof, "Asia Feels Strain Most at Society's Margins," *New York Times,* June 8, 1998.

27. Nicholas D. Kristof, "As Asian Economies Shrink, Women Are Squeezed Out," *New York Times,* June 11, 1998.

28. J. Bruce, C. B. Lloyd, and A. Leonard, *Families in Focus* (New York: Population Council, 1995), p. 33.

29. *Ibid.*, p. 7.

30. Duncan Thomas, "Intra-Household Resource Allocation," *Journal of Human Resources* 25, no. 4 (fall 1990): 635.

31. Bruce and Lloyd, "Finding the Ties That Bind," pp. 8–9.

32. Bruce, Lloyd, and Leonard, *Families in Focus,* p. 32.

33. Jonathan Friedland, "Mexico Tries to Take Politics out of Welfare and Focus on Neediest," *Wall Street Journal,* October 15, 1999, p. A6.

34. This story is related by Gilbert Steiner in his book *The Futility of Family Policy* (Washington, D.C.: Brookings Institution, 1981), pp. 102–11. Conservative solicitude for the two-parent family rests on statistics showing that children in two-parent households do better by many indicators than children in single-parent households. But as Mona Harrington points out in her book *Care and Equality,* all the statistics in the world showing that families are *always* better off with two parents cannot demonstrate that the particular fathers of the children borne by many low-income and/or unwed mothers are capable of contributing to the children's well-being. All too many of these men are unemployed, imprisoned, or too unstable to offer their families much in the way of support.

35. U.K. House of Commons Hansard, May 13, 1975; cited by S. J. Lundberg, R. A. Pollak, and T. J. Wales in "Do Husbands and Wives Pool Their Resources? Evidence from the U.K. Child Benefit," unpublished paper, August 1995, p. 9. This paper and a telephone interview with Robert Pollak are the primary sources for the story of the British child benefit.

36. *Ibid.,* p. 7. The Thatcher years reduced the value of the benefit after inflation, so that by 1999 child benefits were worth, in U.S. dollars, $23 a week for the first child and $15.35 for subsequent children—or a yearly "wage" of about $1,276 for a mother with two children.

37. *Ibid.,* pp. 15–20.

38. Robert A. Pollak, personal communication, May 7, 1996.

39. Pahl, *Money and Marriage,* p. 171.

40. Barbara Bennett Woodhouse, "Towards a Revitalization of Family Law," *Texas Law Review* 69 (1990): 245, 268–70.

41. David F. Charlow of Columbia College in New York City, quoted in Linda Matthews, "Divorced Father's Case Raises Difficult Issues of Who Pays Tuition," *New York Times,* November 15, 1995.

42. Sarah Blaffer Hrdy, *Mother Nature: A History of Mothers, Infants, and Natural Selection* (New York: Pantheon Books, 1999), pp. 8, 255, 379, 393.

43. Natalie Angier, "Primate Expert Explores Motherhood's Brutal Side," *New York Times,* February 8, 2000.

44. Hrdy, *Mother Nature,* p. 226.

45. Natalie Angier, *Woman: An Intimate Geography* (Boston: Houghton Mifflin, 1999), p. 351.

46. Hrdy, *Mother Nature,* pp. 379–80.

47. *Ibid.,* p. 255.

48. Mary Maxwell Katz and Melvin Konner, "The Role of the Father: An Anthropological Perspective," in *The Role of the Father in Child Development,* ed. Michael E. Lamb (New York: Wiley, 1981), pp. 155–86.

49. Scott Coltrane, "Father-Child Relationships and the Status of Women: A Cross-Cultural Study," *American Journal of Sociology* 93, no. 5 (March 1988): 1060–1095.

50. Scott Coltrane, *Family Man: Fatherhood, Work, and Gender Equity* (New York: Oxford University Press, 1996), pp. 190–91. Such cross-cultural comparisons do not, of course, explain which way the causal arrows run. In the societies where men have more to do with children, males may grow up with more balanced, relaxed masculine identities and have less need to lord it over females. Or the more status women have, the less stigma may be attached to tasks associated with females, and the more leverage women have to persuade men to help care for their offspring.

51. David Landes, *The Wealth and Poverty of Nations* (New York: W. W. Norton, 1998), p. 413.

52. Jesse Bernard, *The Future of Marriage* (New York: World Publishers, 1972), pp. 43–44.

Chapter 7: What Is a Wife Worth?

1. Deposition of Gary Wendt, October 1996, pp. 59–60.

2. Christine Lodewick, personal communication, 1998.

3. Tamar Lewin, "Fathers Whose Wives Stay Home Earn More and Get Ahead, Studies Find," *New York Times,* October 12, 1994.

4. Deposition of Gary Wendt, pp. 59–60.

5. Ann Laquer Estin, "Maintenance, Alimony, and the Rehabilitation of Family Care," *North Carolina Law Review* 71 (1993): 721.

6. Ann Laquer Estin, "The Case for Maintenance Reform," *The Colorado Lawyer* 23, no. 1 (January 1994): 54.

7. Joan Entmacher, personal communication, November 1996.

8. Betsy Morris, "It's Her Job Too," *Fortune,* February 2, 1998, p. 16.

9. See Greg J. Duncan and Saul D. Hoffman, *Economic Consequences of Marital Instability,* in *Horizontal Equity, Uncertainty, and Economic Well-Being,* ed. M. David and T. Smeeding (Chicago: University of Chicago Press, 1985), pp. 427, 437, 456.

10. Maggie Mahar, "Splitsville," *Barron's,* June 23, 1997, p. 32.

11. Cindy Williams, telephone interview, December 6, 1998.

Chapter 8: Who Really Owns the Family Wage?

1. The details of the "Jack and Jill" case were provided by Robin Bartlett. Bartlett's quotes are from a telephone conversation, April 30, 1995.

2. Annemette Sorensen, "Women's Economic Risk and the Economic Position of Single Mothers," *European Sociological Review* 10, no. 2 (September 1994): 178, 185.

3. Joan Williams, "Is Coverture Dead? Beyond a New Theory of Alimony," *Georgetown Law Journal* 82, no. 7 (September 1994): 2227–90.

4. *Ibid.,* p. 2283.

5. *Principles of the Law of Family Dissolution: Analysis and Recommendations,* tentative draft no. 1 (Philadelphia, Pa.: American Law Institute, 1995), pp. 144–45.

6. For a fuller description of the issue of compensation for caregivers, see Ann Laquer Estin, "Maintenance, Alimony, and the Rehabilitation of Family Care," p. 737.

7. This study is cited in Williams, *Unbending Gender,* p. 122.

8. Leslie Spillane, personal communication, September 1996.

9. Williams, *Unbending Gender,* p. 120.

10. Ralph T. King, "A Phone Fortune Is at Stake as McCaws Wrangle over Divorce," *Wall Street Journal,* August 7, 1996.

11. Ann Estin, personal communication, August 1995.

12. Ann Laquer Estin, "Maintenance, Alimony, and the Rehabilitation of Family Care," p. 737.

13. Joan M. Kraskopf, "Maintenance: A Decade of Development," *Missouri Law Review* 50 (1985); cited in Estin, *ibid.,* p. 735.

14. Eleanor E. Maccoby and Robert H. Mnookin, *Dividing the Child* (Cambridge, Mass.: Harvard University Press, 1992), p. 123; cited in *Principles of the Law of Family Dissolution,* p. 232.

15. Robert F. Kelly and Greer Litton Fox, "Determinants of Alimony Awards," *Syracuse Law Review* 44 (1993): 718–20.

16. Lynn Gold-Bikin, personal communication, 1997.

17. Diane Dodson, personal communication, October 1994.

18. Margaret A. Jacobs, "More Men Get Alimony, and More Women Get Mad," *Wall Street Journal,* July 30, 1997. During the decade of the 1990s, according to the Census Bureau, the number of people reporting income from alimony declined slightly, to 462,000. The average annual amount received rose from $6,566 to $10,266, not adjusted for inflation.

19. Ann Estin, telephone interview, August 1995.

Chapter 9: Who Pays for the Kids?

1. *Dunlap v. Fiorenza,* 128 Md. App. 357, 738A. 2d 312 (1999).

2. Maureen Pirog-Good, personal communication, 1996.

3. For a discussion and critique of the income-shares approach to child support, see Women's Legal Defense Fund, *Critical Issues, Critical Choices: Special Topics in Child Support Guidelines Development,* Washington, D.C., 1987; and *Essentials of Child Support Guidelines Development: Economic Issues and Policy Considerations,* Proceedings of the Women's Legal Defense Fund's National Conference on the Development of Child Support Guidelines, Queenstown, Md., September 1986.

4. Marilyn L. Ray, personal communication, 1996.

5. Mark Lino, personal communication, 1996.

6. Expenditures on the cost of children, by family income category and by region, are published annually by the U.S. Department of Agriculture, Center of Nutrition Policy and Promotion. See USDA, *Expenditures on Children by Families, Annual Report,* Washington, D.C.

7. Marilyn Ray Smith, personal communication, 1996.

8. Richard R. Petersen, personal communication, November 1996.

9. Eleanor E. Maccoby and Robert H. Mnookin, *Dividing the Child* (Cambridge, Mass.: Harvard University Press, 1992), pp. 116–31, 257–59, 264–65.

10. Drew Liebert, personal communication, January 1996.

11. Maureen A. Pirog-Good, "Child Support Guidelines and the Economic Well-Being of Children in the United States," *Family Relations* 42 (October 1993): 453–462.

12. Women's Legal Defense Fund, *Report Card on State Child Support Guidelines,* Washington, D.C., 1994, p. 19.

13. Diane Dodson, personal communication, October 1994.

14. Maureen A. Pirog-Good, "Child Support Guidelines and the Economic Well-Being of Our Nation's Children," Institute for Research on Poverty Discussion Papers, University of Wisconsin-Madison, February 1995. The formula was a percentage of the obligor's income, but still allowed some adjustment for time-shares. For example, a father with the standard 20 percent custody arrangement could have his support lowered by about 10 percent from the guideline.

15. Sonia Nazario, "Not with My Husband's Money You Don't," *Los Angeles Times Magazine,* December 3, 1995. In the midst of this massive struggle, one children's advocate said to me, "It seems like some of these fathers just don't want to pay for children unless they're sleeping with their mothers." Anthropologists and evolutionary psychologists have made the same observation. Geoffrey Miller of University College, London, has said that "if paternal instincts had evolved simply for the good of their children, fathers shouldn't care whether they're sleeping with the mother. These are their kids, they should be investing in them, acting like they recognize that the kids are vehicles carrying their genes. But the sad truth is that it's very hard to get a lot of men to pay child support" (Natalie Angier, "Author Offers Theory on Gray Matter of Love," *New York Times,* May 30, 2000).

16. Department of Revenue, Commonwealth of Massachusetts, *Report on the Child Support Guidelines,* Boston, 1993, p. 11.

17. Barbara Grob, personal communication, January 1996. The denial of the possibility of divorce is widespread. A randomly selected group of marriage license applicants in Virginia knew that almost 50 percent of all new marriages end in divorce. But when asked their estimate of the chance that their own marriage would break up, not one thought it could happen to them. See Baker and Emery, "When Every Relationship Is Above Average," *Law and Human Behavior* 17 (1993): 439; cited in American Law Institute, *Principles of the Law of Family Dissolution,* p. 176.

18. Sheila Jones Kuehl, personal communication, January 1996.

19. Sanford L. Braver, *Divorced Dads* (New York: Jeremy P. Tarcher/Putnam, 1998), pp. 28–33.

20. Shirley Craig, personal communication, January 1996.

21. Rebecca Leet, personal communication, 1995.

22. Linda Gail Stanton, personal communication, May 1995. For details of the Stanton case, also see Karl A. W. DeMarce, "Devaluing Caregiving in Child Support Calculations: Imputing Income to Custodial Parents Who Stay Home with Children," *Missouri Law Review* 61 (1996): 429–71.

23. Margo Green, personal communication, May 1995.

24. Estin, "Maintenance, Alimony, and the Rehabilitation of Family Care," p. 771.

25. Marilyn L. Ray, *New York State Child Support Standards Act, Evaluation Project Report 1993,* for the New York State Department of Social Services, Ithaca, New York, 1993, pp. xii–xix. See also William F. Ryan, Jr., and Mary Jane Moreau, "The Massachusetts Child Support Guidelines: Analysis of Their Impact upon the Courts and Families," *Massachusetts Family Law Journal* 7, no. 4 (November 1989): 78.

26. Jerilyn Borack, personal communication, April 1996.

Chapter 10: The Welfare State Versus a Caring State

1. Jane Lewis, *Women and Social Policies in Europe,* p. 14.

2. Nancy Folbre, "The Pauperization of Mothers: Patriarchy and Public Policy in the United States," *Review of Radical Political Economics* 16, no. 4 (1985): pp. 72–88.

3. All of this information supplied by Lynn Woolsey, personal interview, July 1996.

4. These details provided by Emma Mae Martin, telephone interview, June 1996. Also see Joel Handler, Letter to the Editor, *New York Times,* July 23, 1991.

5. Clarence Page, "Thomas Lied; Sister Isn't Welfare Queen," *St. Louis Post-Dispatch,* July 26, 1991.

6. Katherine Boo, "2 Women, 2 Responses to Change," *Washington Post,* December 15, 1996.

7. T. R. Reid, "Norway Pays a Price for Family Values," *Washington Post,* November 1, 1998.

8. A huge body of feminist scholarship has shed new light on the origins of the welfare state. The scholars of social welfare policy include Barbara Gordon, Nancy Folbre, Diana Pearce, Barbara J. Nelson, Mimi Abramowitz, and political theorist Carole Pateman in the United States, and Jane Lewis, Hilary Land, and Mary McIntosh in Britain.

9. Linda Gordon, *Pitied But Not Entitled* (New York: Free Press, Macmillan, 1994), p. 293.

10. Council of Economic Advisers, *Families and the Labor Market,* p. 8.

11. Michael J. Graetz and Jerry L. Mashaw, *True Security: Rethinking American Social Insurance* (New Haven: Yale University Press, 1999), pp. 116–17.

12. *How Well Do Women Fare Under the Nation's Retirement Policies?* a report of the Subcommittee on Retirement Income and Employment of the Select Committee on Aging, 102nd Congress, Washington, D.C., 1992, p. 12. A large majority of

women pay Social Security taxes for years, but when they opt to take benefits as a "dependent," they receive the same benefits they would have had had they never held a paying job at all.

13. See Burggraf, *The Feminine Economy,* pp. 124–25, for this last comparison.

14. Jacqueline B. and J. R. Stanfield, "Marc Tool's Social Value Theory and the Family," in *Institutional Economics and the Theory of Social Value: Essays in Honor of Marc R. Tool,* ed. C. M. A. Clark (Boston: Kluwer Academic Publishers, 1995), p. 217.

15. Graetz and Mashaw, *True Security,* p. 123.

16. Glenn Burkins, "U.S. Is Pressing States to Expand Jobless Benefits," *Wall Street Journal,* May 13, 1997.

17. Heidi Hartmann, Young-Hee Yoon, Roberta Spalter-Roth, and Lois Shaw, "Temporary Disability Insurance: A Model to Provide Income Security for Women Over the Life Cycle," paper presented at Allied Social Science Associations Annual Meetings, January 8, 1995, p. 7.

18. Jill Miller (executive director of Women Work!) citing 1989 data, personal interview, November 1993.

19. "American Women Workers: Organizing for a Changing Economy," Women Work! Public Policy Materials, November 15, 1993.

20. "Social Security Found to Save Third of Elderly from Poverty," *New York Times,* April 9, 1999.

21. Select Committee on Aging, *How Well Do Women Fare?* p. 23.

22. Graetz and Mashaw, *True Security,* pp. 117–18.

23. Shelley A. Phipps and Peter S. Burton, "Social/Institutional Variables and Behavior within Households: An Empirical Test Using the Luxembourg Income Study," *Feminist Economics* 1, no. 1 (spring 1995): 162–67.

Chapter 11: The Toughest Job You'll Ever Love

1. Data on preschoolers in paid programs in 1999 are from unpublished tabulations from the October 1999 Current Population Survey of the Census Bureau; cited by Suzanne Bianchi in "Maternal Employment and Time with Children: Dramatic Change or Surprising Continuity?" unpublished paper, June 2000.

2. Lynne M. Carter, *What Does It Cost to Mind Our Preschoolers?* U. S. Census Bureau, Current Population Reports, Washington, D.C., 1996, p. 1.

3. See Center for the Child Care Workforce, "Current Data on Child Care Salaries and Benefits in the U.S.," March 2000.

4. M. Whitebook, D. Phillips, and C. Howes, *The National Child Care Staffing Study Revisited* (Oakland, Calif: Child Care Employee Project, 1993), p. 11. This report is now available at the Center for the Child Care Workforce in Washington, D.C. Also see Rosemary Jordano and Marie Gates, "Invest in Workers for the Best Child Care," *New York Times,* June 21, 1998.

5. Paula England, *Comparable Worth: Theories and Evidence* (New York: Aldine de Gruyter, 1992), p. 164.

6. Paula England, personal communication, 1996.

7. Heidi Hartmann, "The Economics of Women's Work and the Affordability of Child Care," in *Breaking the Link: A National Forum on Child Care Compensation,* National Center for the Early Childhood Work Force, April 29–May 1, 1994, p. 14.

8. Judith Montminy, "Preschool Teacher Wins National Award," *Boston Sunday Globe,* April 28, 1991.

9. Testimony of Sheryl Adlin, executive director of South Shore Day Care Services, before Massachusetts House Ways and Means Committee, March 12, 1995.

10. Kathy Modigliani, personal communication, 1995.

11. Marcy Whitebook, personal communication, October 2000.

12. Cecelie Blakey, personal communication, February 1996.

13. Tony Marcano, "Accreditation Is No Guarantee on Day Care Centers, Study Says," *New York Times,* April 20, 1997.

14. M. Whitebook, D. Phillips, and C. Howes, *The National Child Care Staffing Study Revisited,* p. 11.

15. M. Whitebook, C. Howes, L. Sakai, NAEYC, "Accreditation as a Strategy for Improving Quality," CCW, 1997.

16. These figures are from material provided by Clark Anderson, a day-care organizer in Madison, Wisconsin (personal communication, October 1995).

17. The White House Conference on Child Care, briefing paper, October 23, 1997.

18. Ellen Galinsky, "Child Care: Reframing the Debate," testimony before the Senate Subcommittee on Children and Families, February 23, 1998.

19. Hartmann, "The Economics of Women's Work," p. 13.

20. Arleen Leibowitz, "Child Care: Private Cost or Public Responsibility?" unpublished paper, May 1995, p. 8.

21. Jonathan Rabinovitz, "New Scrutiny in Child Care Is Proposed," *New York Times,* March 1, 1996.

22. Jodi Wilgoren, "Quality Day Care, Early, Is Tied to Achievements as an Adult," *New York Times,* October 22, 1999, p. A16.

23. Christine Russell. "Early Help Improves Learning Ability, *Washington Post Health,* February 13, 1996.

24. Arleen Leibowitz, "Child Care," pp. 19–20.

25. Information on the Syracuse program was provided by Fight Crime: Invest in Kids, a national anticrime organization based in Washington, D.C.

26. Leibowitz, "Child Care," pp. 33–34.

27. Arleen Leibowitz, personal communication, 1996.

28. Ann Crittenden, "Fighting for Kids," *Government Executive,* December 1997, pp. 25–29.

Chapter 12: An Accident Waiting to Happen

1. Eugene Pugliese, personal communication, 1995.

2. Warren R. Leiden, personal communication, 1995.

3. "Women's Work—Up from .878." Report of the DOT Research Project, University of Wisconsin—Extension Women's Education Resources, 1975, p. 11.

4. Carolyn Killea, personal communication, 1995.

5. Sidney Blumenthal, "Adventures in Babysitting," *New Yorker,* February 15, 1993.

6. This and the following information was provided by Priscilla Labovitz, 1995.

7. Debbi Wilgoren, "New Regulations on Au Pairs Draw Criticism, Support," *Washington Post,* December 17, 1994. Additional details of this story were provided by Stanley Colwin of the State Department, the agency that administers the au pair program. Personal communication, 1997.

8. *Women in Corporate Leadership: Progress and Prospects* (New York: Catalyst, 1996).

Chapter 13: "It Was Her Choice"

1. Richard Cohen, "Beneath the Glass Ceiling," *Washington Post,* March 21, 1995.

2. Edward J. McCaffery, *Taxing Women* (Chicago: University of Chicago Press, 1997), p. 143.

3. Hilary Driscoll and Rachel Obenzinger, "Surveying Williams Students for Career and Family Expectations," unpublished paper for Economics 203, Williams College, May 1994. This paper was provided by Diane Macunovich, who taught Economics 203 class at Williams.

4. Jane Lewis, ed., *Women and Social Policies in Europe,* p. 7. The same surveys reveal that German men have very different attitudes about the gender division of labor. About 60 percent of German men said they preferred a homemaker wife (*ibid.,* p. 97). Until 1977 a German man could legally prevent his wife from taking paid employment if he felt this would be detrimental to family life. Alternatively, he could force her to earn money if his income was deficient. West German men had the last word on issues relating to children until 1980 (*ibid.,* pp. 99–100).

5. F. Thomas Juster and Frank P. Stafford, "The Allocation of Time: Empirical Findings, Behavioral Models, and Problems of Measurement," *Journal of Economic Literature* 29 (June 1991): 475.

6. Agneta Stark, personal communication, August 1997.

7. Goran Swedin, "Modern Swedish Fatherhood," in *Men on Men,* Equality Affairs Division, Swedish Ministry of Health and Social Affairs, Stockholm, 1995, p. 128.

8. Goran Swedin, personal communication, August 1997.

9. See *Working Mother,* October 1997 issue. One of the companies was Patagonia, which has an eight-week paid paternity leave.

10. Swedish Ministry of Health and Social Affairs, "Shared Power/Responsibility," in *The Government Bill on Policy for Equality Between Men and Women,* Stockholm, 1995, p. 14.

11. Bengt Westerberg, "Visions of an Equal Society—with a Focus on Men," in *Men on Men*, p. 136.

12. Suzanne A. Stoiber, *Parental Leave and Woman's Place* (Washington, D.C.: Women's Research and Education Institute, 1989), p. 52.

13. Unpublished data supplied by Agneta Stark, University of Stockholm.

14. Unpublished data provided by Bob Cleveland, Income Statistics Branch, U.S. Census Bureau.

15. Mary Ann Glendon, *Abortion and Divorce in Western Law* (Cambridge, Mass.: Harvard University Press, 1987), pp. 85–90. In the early 1980s, an unemployed single mother of two in Sweden had almost the same income as the average production worker. In England and the United States, in contrast, the typical unemployed single mother and her two kids had to live on *half* the income of the typical production worker.

16. Nora Boustany, "The Women Who Govern Sweden," *Washington Post,* June 27, 1997.

17. Pat Reuss, personal communication, 1995.

18. A spokeswoman for CWA said that there was one exception to the group's opposition to child-care subsidies. In 1996, during the debate over changes in the welfare law, the organization did support a state-level provision of child care to mothers moving from welfare to work.

19. When I asked Virginia Daley's superior if she had really said this, she replied, "I'm going to take a position of 'no comment.'" Ironically, not long after Daley's lawsuit was filed, she too left the company. The law doesn't even guarantee all new mothers an unpaid leave, because it only covers companies with fifty or more employees. A University of Michigan study shows that only 32 percent of the businesses not covered by the Family and Medical Leave Act offer leave on similar terms. The number of companies offering leaves of one year is actually declining, from a paltry 2 percent in 1997 to 1 percent in 1999, according to Hewitt Associates.

20. United States Senate Subcommittee on Children and Families, "Caring for America's Children," February 23, 1998.

21. Marjorie Sims, personal communication, 1996.

22. Before the November 2000 elections, NOW did send out a mail solicitation for funds, mentioning universal child care as one of the half-dozen top items on their legislative agenda.

23. Diane Dodson, personal communication, 1994.

24. Germaine Greer, *The Whole Woman* (New York: Alfred A. Knopf, 1999).

Conclusion: How to Bring Children Up Without Putting Women Down

1. International child poverty comparisons are from a study by the National Center for Children in Poverty at the Columbia School of Public Health and the

Luxembourg Income Study, a nonprofit group of scholars. See Robert Pear, "Thousands to Rally in Capital on Children's Behalf," *New York Times,* June 1, 1996.

2. For an elaboration of this point, see Mona Harrington, *Care and Equality* (New York: Knopf, 1999).

3. Jacob Alex Kierman and Arleen Leibowitz, "The Work-Employment Distinction Among New Mothers," *Journal of Human Resources* 29, no. 2 (spring 1994): 296. Unfortunately, another female boss who separated a new mother from her job was Washington senator Patty Murray, who had campaigned as "a Mom in tennis shoes" with the promise that as a woman she could understand other women's problems. But apparently not enough; her legislative aide Pam Norick was forced to resign after becoming pregnant with her second baby. The story is summarized by Clara Bingham in *Women on the Hill* (New York: Times Books, 1997), pp. 114–15, 253.

4. Alvin Powell, "Parents' Presence Helps Heal Children," *Harvard University Gazette,* November 4, 1999.

5. Suzanne Daley, "A French Paradox at Work," *New York Times,* November 11, 1999. In France not even managers are supposed to work more than thirty-nine hours a week.

6. Louis Uchitelle, "How to Succeed in Politics Without Really Working," *New York Times,* June 22, 1999.

7. See Mona Harrington, *Care and Equality,* pp. 51–52, 153.

8. Raymond Hernandez, "Millions in State Child Care Funds Going Unspent in New York," *New York Times,* October 25, 1999.

9. Edward McCaffery, *Taxing Women,* p. 197.

10. Adam Gopnik, "Like a King," *New Yorker,* January 31, 2000.

The mother was subsequently committed on a lesser charge and released on probation. Among the conditions of her release was a requirement that she attend parenting classes.

11. The mother, a poor, twenty-one-year-old living in the Bronx, was subsequently convicted of criminally negligent homicide, despite the fact that she had twice taken the baby to her HMO for checkups and been turned away because the baby's Medicaid card hadn't yet arrived in the mail. She was sentenced to five years' probation, including a condition that if she had another child during the probation period, she take parenting classes. See Katha Pollitt, "A Bronx Tale," *The Nation,* June 14, 1999; Nina Bernstein, "Mother Convicted in Infant's Starvation Death Gets 5 Years' Probation," *New York Times,* September 9, 1999.

12. Barbara Beran, personal communication, 1995.

13. Williams, *"Is Coverture Dead?"* p. 2286.

14. See, for example, Joan Kraskopf, "Theories of Property Division/Spousal Support: Searching for Solutions to the Mystery," *Family Law Quarterly* 23, no. 2 (summer 1989): 256.

15. Susan Moller Okin, *Justice, Gender, and the Family* (New York: Basic Books, 1989), p. 183.

16. See Jana Singer, "Divorce Reform and Gender Justice," *North Carolina Law Review* 67, no. 5 (June 1989): 1117–20; Jane W. Ellis, "New Rules of Divorce: Transition Payments," *Journal of Family Law* 32 (1994).

17. Marge Roukema, personal communication, May 1995.

18. Catherine Coon, personal communication, 1995.

19. Jane E. Brody, "Earlier Work with Children Steers Them from Crime," *New York Times,* March 15, 1999.

20. C. Jencks and M. Phillips, "America's Next Achievement Test: Closing the Black-White Test Score Gap," *American Prospect* (September-October 1998):44–53.

21. David McNair, personal communication, 1996.

Acknowledgments

My deepest debt of gratitude is owed to the dozens of mothers, fathers, and other caregivers who took the time to tell me their stories. Without their willingness to share their innermost thoughts and feelings, this book would literally not have been possible. A special thanks in this regard to Anna Dahlman and Ulf Karlsson, who offered me shelter when I discovered upon my arrival that Stockholm had no available hotel rooms whatsoever.

The book also owes its existence to an unsung army of feminist scholars. When I first conceived of this project, I knew from experience that all was not right in the world of the mother. But I wasn't sure that I could substantiate this personal impression, or base an entire book on my sense that caregivers are still not seen or appreciated as equal, fully productive citizens. As I soon discovered, all the evidence I needed to make this case was available, thanks to the work of countless academics and researchers devoted to women's issues.

In the past few years, a critical mass of mostly female scholars in economics, sociology, history, family law, political philosophy, child development, and anthropology have reinterpreted these disciplines to take into account the maternal experience, and to assert the value of early nurturing and care. This massive body of scholarship stands as a sweeping refutation of the charge that feminism has done little for ordinary women. On the contrary, the women who began their academic and professional careers in the 1960s and 1970s, thanks to the women's movement, have produced a striking reassessment of the traditionally female work of raising children. Their efforts to establish that this work creates enormous economic as well as social value will improve the lives of all mothers, whatever their life patterns.

I owe an intellectual debt to a few of these scholars in particular. Shirley P. Burggraf, of Florida A & M, was kind enough to share her insights before her own superb book, *The Feminine Economy and Economic Man,* was published. I am also grateful for the invaluable guidance of Nancy Folbre of the University of Massachusetts at Amherst, who introduced me to the world of feminist economics, and took the trouble to teach me the facts of life on the critical topic of "who pays for the kids." Heather Joshi of London University, and her coauthor Hugh Davies of Birbeck College, who pioneered the research into the economic costs of child-rearing, gave me a framework for understanding the price mothers pay, as did Jane Waldfogel of Columbia University, who vetted the chapter dealing with the mommy tax.

In the field of family law, no one influenced my thinking more than Ann Laquer Estin of the University of Colorado Law School and Joan Williams of American University, Washington College of Law. Their brilliant insights into the inequity of modern marriage and divorce were generously shared, in Williams's case, before she published her own book, *Unbending Gender.*

I am also deeply grateful for the help and/or inspiration of numerous other scholars, including George A. Akerlof; Iulie M. Aslaksen of Statistics Norway; Robin L. Bartlett of Denison University; Barbara R. Bergmann, Suzanne Bianchi and John P. Robinson of the University of Maryland; Nancy Birdsall of the Inter-American Development Bank and subsequently the Carnegie Endowment; Rita Brock of the Radcliffe Institute; Richard H. Chused of the Georgetown University Law Center; Kathleen Cloud of the University of Illinois; Karen Czapanskiy of the University of Maryland Law School; Robin Douthitt of the University of Wisconsin; Paula England of the University of Arizona; Marianne A. Ferber; Richard Freeman of the National Bureau of Economic Research; Anita Garey of the University of New Hampshire; Shoshana Grossbard-Shechtman of San Diego State University; Sandra L. Hofferth of the University of Michigan; Charlotte Koren of the Institute for Applied Social Research in Oslo, Norway; Arleen Leibowitz of the RAND Corp.; Kathy Modigliani of Wheelock College; Maureen Pirog-Good of the University of Indiana; Susan Pedersen and Theda Skocpol of Harvard University; Robert A. Pollack of Washington University; Reva B. Siegel of the Yale Law School; and Agnete Stark of the University of Stockholm.

I also particularly want to thank Robert Borosage of the Campaign for America's Future; Heidi Brennan of Mothers At Home; Nancy Duff Campbell and Marcia Greenberger of the National Women's Law Center; Constance Casey, Stephanie Diment, G. Diane Dodson, Joan Entmacher of the Women's Legal Defense Fund; Leora Gershenzon of the National Center for Youth Law; Heidi Hartmann and Catherine Hill of the Institute for Women's Policy Research; Debra Johnson, Carolyn Killea, Priscilla Labovitz, Alexandra Lowe, Nechama Masliansky, Nancy Polikoff of American University, Washington College of Law; Paula Roberts of the Center for Law and Social Policy; Lynn Schafran of NOW Legal Defense and Education Fund; Rosemarie Vardell of the National Center for the Early Childhood Work Force; and Marcy Whitebrook of the Institute of Industrial Relations, University of California at Berkeley.

Several knowledgable and incredibly helpful researchers within the Federal government made the task of finding the most up-to-date statistics a painless one. I especially relied on the good-natured assistance of Howard Hayghe and Steven Hipple of the Bureau of Labor Statistics; Lynne Casper, Robert Cleveland, and Carmen DeNavas of the Census Bureau; and Mark Lino of the Center of Nutrition Policy in the Department of Agriculture.

Many of my friends lent their support, their ideas, and their contacts; without them I can't imagine how I could have finished this lengthy project. A special thanks to Irene Addlestone, Rick Barton and Kit Lunney, Beth Bogart, Sara Day, Andy Dodds, Mary Edsall, Sandra Espinoza, Dorothy Fall, David Fenton, Geeta Rao Gupta, Eleanor

LeCain, Fran McLean, Shaun Murphy, Kathleen O'Banion, Pamela Peabody, Elaine Shannon, Christine Vinall, Deborah Weil, Tim Wirth, and not least, all the members of the workout group.

I also want to express deep appreciation to my agent Katinka Matson of Brockman Inc., my editor Sara Bershtel, and her colleague Riva Hocherman, three of the most capable people I've ever had the pleasure of working with.

Finally, a heartfelt thanks to my son, James Henry, who had to live with this book for what I realize to my horror was one-third of his life. The book most definitely would never have happened if it hadn't been for him. And a special salute to my husband, John Henry, who was a steadfast believer in the project from the beginning, even though we joked that the subtitle could have been "How to Take the Money From the Men and Give It to the Women."

This, I confess, is exactly what the book does advocate—for everyone's sake, of course.

Index

ABA Journal, 37
Abbey, Elliot, 181, 182
Abecedarian Project, 214
academia, 39–40, 102–3
accounting profession, 36
Achieving Society, The (McClelland), 74
adoption, 14–15
Aetna Life & Casualty, 91–93, 252
AFL-CIO, 259
African-American women, 56, 68–69, 108, 115, 222
after-school programs, 209, 272
agrarian society, 49
Aid to Families with Dependent Children (AFDC), 187–88, 193–94, 200
Akerlof, George, 24
Alberts, Dr. Bruce, 39
alimony, 112, 144–46
  "compensation" model of, 155–61
Allied Signal, 258
altruism, and economics, 71, 77
American Association of University Women (AAUW), 170
American Bar Association, 39, 161, 176
  Center on Children and the Law, 173
American Immigration Lawyers Association, 220, 229
American Law Institute (ALI), 155
American Revolution, 48
Anthony, Susan B., 53, 54
antidiscrimination laws, and parents, 107, 261
Aristotle, 67
Arizona, 198
Arkansas, 156
Aslaksen, Iulie, 76
Association for the Advancement of Women, 59
Astone, Angelo, 137
au pair program, 219, 229–30
Australia, 61, 76, 84–85, 95

baby boomers, 32–34, 104, 107–8
Baird, Zoe, 223–27, 231, 250, 252
Baker & Botts, 37
Ballmer, Steve, 2
Balzac, 8
Bangladesh, 122
Bartlett, Robin, 149–52
battered women, 114
"be a man" strategy, 29–35, 103, 104, 108
Becker, Gary S., 75–76
Beckley Cardy, 204
Beecher, Catherine, 52
Belgium, 200
Bellamy, Carole, 95
Beran, Barbara, 268–69
Bergman, Ingmar, 246
Bergmann, Barbara, 85, 254
Bernard, Jesse, 130
"Best, Elizabeth," 236–37
"better mother" effect, 123
Bianchi, Suzanne, 13
birthrates, 109, 246–47
Blackwell, Antoinette Brown, 54
Blair, Anita, 234
Blakey, Cecelie, 208
Borack, Jerilyn, 184, 185

Boskin, Michael, 116
Bossidy, Lawrence A., 258
Boston Edison, 15
Boston Globe, 206
Boydston, Jeanne, 52
Braver, Sanford, 177
Brazil, 122
breast-feeding, 258–59
Bright Horizons, 209
Britain, 50, 60–61, 95, 124–25, 201, 260, 266
Brock, Hope, 118
Brown, Ron, 224
Bryant, W. Keith, 20
"build the nest" vs. "scatter the seeds" conflict, 127–28
Bureau of Labor Statistics, 86, 221
Burggraf, Shirley, 2, 7, 51, 74, 75n, 78, 81, 89
Burkina Faso, 84–85
Bush, George, 116
business careers, 28–44
  childlessness of women in, 108
  and discrimination against parents, 261
  and full-time wife, 17
  and part-time work, 260–61
  started during marriage, 154
  see also corporations; managers; professional working mothers

California, 6, 64, 96, 157, 160
  child support in, 167–76, 179, 271
  Judicial Council, 176
  Judiciary Committee, 175–76
California Women's Law Center, 175
Canada, 76, 82–85, 200, 261, 230–32
Canadian Alliance of Home Managers, 84
Canadian Human Rights Commission, 80
capitalism, 49–50, 67–68, 74–75
Carbone, June, 155
career, 28–44
  and discrimination against parents, 99, 102–3
  -family trade-offs, 32–34, 238–39
  see also professional working mothers; and specific careers
caregiving. *See* child care; unpaid female caregiving
"caring tax," 91
Carlsson, Ingvar, 243
Catalyst, 30, 35, 97, 108
Catholic Charities Child Development Center, 202
census, 58–61, 82
Census Bureau, 59, 177, 221, 264
Center for the Child Care Workforce, 208, 209
Cherlin, Andrew, 26
Child, Lydia Maria, 54
child allowances or benefits, 50, 104, 124, 201, 252, 257, 266–67
childbirth, 242, 267
child care, 79
  at-home, paid, 218–32
  and disadvantaged children, 213–14
  expenses, not deductible, 115, 266
  and fathers, 24, 129
  in France, 90, 104, 264
  in Germany, 108–9
  industry, 202–17, 231
  lack of political support for, 251
  and medical schools, 42
  paid, forms of, 204
  and parental time, 8, 13, 9–21, 76
  professional vs. mother-provided, 213–14
  and Social Security, 194–96
  subsidized, 106, 108, 200–201, 214–15
  and unions, 44
  unpaid, measuring, 83, 84, 267–68
  and welfare reform, 84, 215
  in younger vs. older mothers, 103–4
  see also children and child rearing; day care; preschool and nursery school; unpaid female caregiving
Childcraft, 204
child custody, 48–49, 55, 56, 143–44, 270
child death, 128–29
child labor, 51n
childless women, 87–88, 94–95, 107–9
"child monitor," 221
child poverty
  in Europe vs. U.S., 50, 104, 257
  and social insurance, 200–201
  and welfare, 193–94
children and child raising
  and balance of power in marriage, 88, 112–13
  and child-care staff, 209, 210
  as "choice," 10, 233–55
  cost of, 81, 165–66
  devaluation of, 2, 4–7, 45–66, 74–78
  discrimination against, in workplace, 98–99
  and divorce settlements, 145–46, 150–53, 160, 268–70
  as economic assets, 49–51
  and fathers, in Sweden, 241–47
  fathers' control over, 48–49

children and child raising (*cont'd*)
financial penalty on anyone who spends time with, 6–7, 87–91
as focus of women's lives, 14
and human capital, 71–78
importance of, 2
and mangement and professional careers, 30–40
and marital dependency, 118–30
and mothers vs. fathers, 24–25
and mothers' lack of stature, 3
not considered work, 191–93
as obstacle to career, 3–4, 87–88
parental time with, 19–21, 23
postponing, 103
and reforms needed, 256–74
and Social Security, 194–96
spending on, by mother vs. father, 120–23
and strength of mothers, 129
and wage gap, 93–94
welfare of, and mother's earnings, 121–26
women's proprietary feeling toward, 244–45
and workweek, 260
see also child care; mothers; unpaid female caregiving
Children's Defense Fund, 195
Children's Trust Fund, 266
child suppport, 112, 126, 139, 144, 161–85
in California, 167–76
as children's vs. women's issue, 250
enforcement, 176–85, 270–71
guaranteed, 201
and "income shares" formula, 164–66
increase in, 177
and mothers who once worked full-time, 179–85
need for national, 188
need to reform, 270–71
and second family, 172n
and state guidelines, 163–65
in Sweden, 248
and welfare mothers, 189
child tax credit, 124
"choice," 16–17
argument, 233–38
real, 238–39
in Sweden, 239–50
chrematistics, 67
Churchill, Winston, 213
Clinton, Bill, 99, 223, 234, 273
COBOL (Common Business-Oriented Language), 41
Cohen, Richard, 234
Cole, Johnnetta, 14
college-educated women
and career vs. family, 29–35
labor force participation of, 17–18
and "mommy tax," 88, 89
see also education; professional women
college tuition, 126, 270
Colorado, 183n
Coltrane, Scott, 129
Colwell, Dr. Rita, 235
Commerce Department, 41
"commercialization" of marriage, 156–59
Commission on Immigration Reform, 230
community, 67–68, 271–74
compassion, and economics, 67–68
Compton, Ronald, 91–92
computer scientists, 41
Concerned Women for America, 83, 251
Congressional Caucus for Women, 253
Connecticut, 134, 157, 211
"conscientious mother," 68, 74
conservatives, 7, 14, 85, 87, 94, 130, 237, 245, 251, 253–55
Coon, Catherine, 272
cooperative housekeeping, 58
COPS (Coalition of Parent Support), 170, 171, 172, 174, 175
Cordero, Lilian, 225
corporate wives, and divorce, 136, 157
corporations
and fathers, 23, 243
ideal worker as childless, 87–88
problems of women in, 28–44, 252
reforms needed by, 258–61
Cosmopolitan, 60
"Cost of Being of Mother; the Cost of Being a Father, The" (conference), 256–57
coverture doctrine, 153–54, 193
Craig, Shirley, 177–79
credit, 63
Crittenden, Danielle, 103–4
Cutler, Lloyd, 225

"daddy tax," 105
Daley, Virginia, 91–93, 252
Dandrow, Ann, 211
Davies, Hugh, 94
Day, Carol Brunson, 212
day care, 273
regulation, 210–12
subsidized in military, 215–17
in Sweden, 240, 247
workers, 6, 205, 207–10
"deadbeat dad," 163, 176–85

Defense, Department of, 215
Democratic Party, 176
Denmark, 200, 241, 272
dependency, of mothers, 110–15, 192–93
  impact of, on children, 118–30
  problems with, 110–15, 270
  and taxes, 115–18
"dependents," married women defined as, 60–61
DiBiasi, Cindy, 100–103
Dictionary of Occupational Titles, 220
Diment, Stephanie, 40
disability insurance, 96
discrimination
  and displaced homemakers, 198
  and parents, 98–99, 102, 261
  and women's work, 220–21
disparate-action suits, 107
diversity, expanding concept of, 274
divorce, 133–85
  best states for mothers, 157–59
  and child support, 163–85
  and compensation for mother/caregiver, 153–61
  and equal income sharing, 269–70
  and marital property rights, 133–40
  and "opportunity costs," 80
  and parents' time with children, 23
  and professional working mothers, 140–47
  and right to family income, 268–69
  and Social Security, 196
  and spending by fathers, 126
  and standard of living of wife, 145–47
  and stay-at-home wives, 131–39
  in Sweden, 242–43, 248–49
  and welfare, 198
  women's right to, 55
  and working class, 149–53
  and young mothers, 103
  see also postdivorce income
"Divorce and Feminist Legal Theory" (symposium), 153–54
divorce courts, 138–39, 156–59
divorced men, standard of living, 147n
divorced mothers
  in California, 167n
  elderly, 199
  and "income shares" formula, 166
  lack of support for, 254
  and welfare, 185
divorce reform movement, 14, 152–55, 270
Dodson, Diane, 161, 168, 254
Dogon, 128
Dole, Elizabeth, 95

Eappen, Matthew, 230
early-childhood education, 251
  and poor children, 213–15
  and low pay and turnover, 207–9
  by mothers, 74
  universal, 263–65
earned income tax credit (EITC), 116, 123
earnings and income, 24
  and census, 59
  and divorce, 154–55
  and equality between sexes, 248
  gap, 5, 50, 88, 93–95
  and "income shares," 165
  loss, by mothers, 5, 7, 87–93
  of mothers, spent on children, 119
  pooling, in families, 112
  and postponement of childbearing, 103–4
  and productivity, 61
  sharing, in divorce, 269–70
  and taxes on mothers, 115–18, 265–66
  and women's rights, 55, 56, 63
  see also "family income"; "income shares"; postdivorce income; mommy tax; wages
East Germany, 108, 257
"economic man," 67, 68
"economic woman," 78–84
economists, 4, 24, 58–60, 67, 71, 74–84, 111, 214–15
  female academic, 78–84, 94–95
  and "New Home Economics," 75
  and value of unpaid mother's work, 61–63, 65–66, 76–78
economy, as "free rider," 7–9
Edelman, Ric, 8
education
  benefits for veterans, 105, 106
  parent, 272–74
Education, Department of, 126
education level of mothers
  and increased demands of child-rearing, 50–51
  and involvement of father with children, 244
  and loss of status and income, 27
  and mommy tax, 89
  and time spent with children, 19–20
education of children, 48
  divorced fathers and, 126

education of children (*cont'd*)
  by mothers, undervalued, 74
  and universal preschool, 263–65
elderly care, 83, 91, 223
elderly women, 199
Eli Lilly, 33
Emerson, Ralph Waldo, 11
employment gaps, 96–97
Enders, Elizabeth, 77
engineering, 40–41
England, Paula, 114, 205
English common law, 153–54
entitlements, 192–93
Entmacher, Joan, 139
Epstein, Robert, 132, 136
Equal Employment Opportunity Commission, 190
equality, in marriage, 58, 110–11, 133, 153, 248, 254–55
equal pay
  and part-time work, 260–61
  "for work of equal value" standard, 80
Equal Pay Act, 107
errands, 26
Espinoza, Rafael, 21
Espinoza, Rebecca, 21
Espinoza, Sandra, 21
Estin, Ann Laquer, 138–39, 159–61
Estrich, Susan, 28
Europe, 108, 200–201, 256–58, 270
Evans, Cheryl, 18

Fallows, Deborah, 18
Families and Work Institute, 210
family
  changes, in nineteenth century, 51, 53, 58
  and community, 272
  in economic theory, 62–63, 51, 111
  equality in, 55–56
  as "free rider," 9
  and human capital, 75–76
  and law, 36–39, 111, 139, 152–53, 268–69
  patriarchal, 48, 81
  two-parent, 81
family assets, in divorce, 6, 133–34, 139, 148, 152–53
family-care providers, 205, 210–12, 215–17
"family income," 6, 46, 120–21, 268–69
Family Research Council, 48n
family support, 126, 200, 249
family values, 7, 192, 200
family wage, 111, 149–61, 266–67
family wage gap, 95–99
Farr, William, 60
father(s)
  and capitalism, 50
  and child support, 5, 163, 167–76, 184–85
  earnings and power balance, 112–13
  and equal parents myth, 23–26
  and feminists, 14
  and monogamy, 128
  and parental leave, 245–46
  and "separate spheres," 48
  and spending on children, 121–22, 124–29
  stay-at-home, 113–14
  and strong mothers, 129–30
  in Sweden, 240–46, 248
  and time with children, 13, 19, 23–26
  unmarried, 185
  wages of, with working wives, 99
  work hours of, 18
Fathers' Commission, Swedish, 243–45, 248
fathers's rights groups, 126, 174, 177, 179
Fedders, Charlotte, 114
Fedders, John, 114
Felder, Raoul, 148
Feminine Economy and Economic Man, The (Burggraf), 78
feminists, 30–32, 46, 80, 83, 94, 124
  legal theory, on family and divorce, 153–54
  and mothers' issues, 7, 253–55
  and mothers' work, 58–59, 61–63, 85–86, 138–39
  and myths about fathers, 14, 23
  and property rights of women, 53–57
"feminization of poverty," 186
Fierst, Edith, 263
Fifi (chimpanzee), 127–28
Finland, 76
firewood, 84
first vs. second wives, 173–75, 250
First Wives Club (movie), 147
flexible hours, 36, 44, 91–92. *See also* part-time work
Flo (chimpanzee), 127–28
Floria, John, 46
Folbre, Nancy, 47, 77, 81, 85, 186
"folk center," 272
food, spending on, 121–22
food stamps, 187
foraging societies, 128
Fortune magazine, 139

401k plans, 93
France, 50, 84, 91, 104, 197, 200, 257, 260, 264–67
Freeman, Richard, 24
free market, 67–68
"free rider," 9, 64, 86, 258
French Revolution, 48
FSA (family savings account), 263
full-time employment, of mothers, 18–19, 239

Gallagher, Maggie, 253
Garbolino, James D., 175–76
Garey, Anita, 22
Gates, Bill, 2
GE Capital, 136, 137, 139
Gelernter, David, 48n
gender bias
  in GDP, 77
  in tax laws, 265
gender division of labor, 58, 62, 120
gender gap
  and "be a man" strategy, 103
  and rich, 117–18
  and Social Security, 199
Georgia, 157, 264
German census, 61
Germany, 50, 76, 84–85, 108–9, 197, 200, 257, 260
Gershenzon, Leora, 176, 250
Gewirtz, Julian, 224
Gewirtz, Paul, 224–25
G.I. Bill, 9, 106–7
Gilman, Charlotte, 61–63
Giving Tree, The (Silverstein), 1, 7
Glass Ceiling Commission, 29–30
Glendon, Mary Ann, 248
Gold-Bikin, Lynne, 161
Goldin, Claudia, 32–33, 34, 107–8
Goldman, Robert I., 148
Goldman, Vira, 148
Goodall, Jane, 127
"good-enough" parenting, 72–73
Gore, Albert, 263
Gormley, William, 210
government policy, 186–201
  vs. Americans' values, 5
  and child support, 176–85, 270–71
  and day-care quality, 210–13
  mothering not defined as work by, 186
  and nannies, 219
  new, needed, 262–68
  and rankings of women's work, 220
  and soldiers vs. mothers, 104–5
  in Sweden, 242–50
  and unpaid care as work, 6
  see also specific policies
government workers, 37–42
Grameen Bank, 122
Greeks, 67
Green, Margo L., 181–83
Greer, Germaine, 255
Grob, Barbara, 174
Grossbard-Shechtman, Shoshana, 213
Gross Domestic Product (GDP, *formerly* Gross National Product, GNP)
  need to include unpaid labor in, 83, 84, 254, 267–68
  unpaid labor excluded from, 65–66
  value of unpaid labor as percentage of, 76, 77
Gross Economic Product (GEP), 80
Gross Household Product (GHP), 80
Gross Market Product (GMP), 80
Grund, Francis, 49
Grute, Karin, 239–40, 248–49
Guatemala, 122

Haack, Peggy, 203
Hadza tribe, 128
Hamilton, Alexander, 47
Haq, Mahbub ul, 78
Hart, Gary (California state senator), 167–69
Hartmann, Heidi, 205
Harvard Business Review, 30
Harvard University, 2, 33
  female professional graduates, 34, 36–37, 235
Harvard Women's Law Association, 36
Hatt, Greger, 243–45
Haug, Frigga, 233
Haugland, Valgard, 192
Hays, Sharon, 20–21
"head of household," 60–61, 132, 266
Health and Human Services, Department of, 164
health insurance, 106, 187
  free, 50, 104, 252, 267
  and part-time work, 261
  and preschool teachers, 205
Herman, Alexis, 108
"he who earns it owns it" concept, 6, 111, 153–54
Hill, Anita, 108, 224
Hipmama.com (web site), 165
HIPPY (Home Instruction Program for Preschool Youngsters), 273

home-based businesses, 98
homemaker
"displaced," and job training, 198
as largest occupation, 17
long-term, and divorce, 158, 159
home visit programs, 273
household help, 226–27
household labor by wife, 26, 235
devalued by economists, 3, 52–54, 58–64, 75–80
see also unpaid female caregiving
household management, and "economics," 67
"housekeepers," defined, 59
"housekeeper wage," 79
housework, 22, 83
and men, 24, 248
and power in marriage, 112–13
sharing, and first child, 25
see also household labor by wife
housing loans, 106
housing subsidies, 50, 104
Houston Oilers, 99
Howe, Julia Ward, 59
Hrdy, Sarah Blaffer, 127–28
Huff, Dorothy, 217
human capital
created by child-rearing, 2, 51, 65, 71–78, 86, 119, 129
deterioration of wife's, during marriage, 4, 155n
and professional child care, 213–14
hunters and gatherers, 128
husband
changes needed from, 268–71
as owner of family property and income, 153–54
sharing child-rearing, 237–38
and working mothers, 235
Hyde, Henry, 188

Idaho, 156
Illinois, 210–11
Immigration and Naturalization Service (INS), 222, 225, 227
immigration law, 219–20, 222–25, 228
"imputation"
of income, 180–85
of value for nonmarket activities, 79
"income shares," 164–65, 166
"independence effect," 123
Independent Women's Forum, 87
India, 122
Indiana, 156, 171
infants, 19, 259
Information Technology (IT) workers, 72
Institute for Equality in Marriage, 148
Institute for Women's Policy Research, 197
International Women's Day, 82
Internet companies, 41
Iowa Supreme Court, 57
Ireland, 17, 201
Ireland, Patricia, 253, 274
Ironmonger, Duncan, 80
Israel, 84
Italy, 84, 200
Ivory Coast, 122

"Jack and Jill" divorce case, 149–53
Jackson, Bev, 202–3
Jacobson, Joe, 182
Jamaica, 121
Japan, 23, 260
Jencks, Christopher, 273
job(s)
market, child-rearing as handicap in, 3–4
ranking of women's, 220–21
-then-family pattern, 33
training, for "displaced homemakers," 198
see also careers; employment gap; occupations; work; working mothers
Johns Hopkins University study, 214
Johnson, Lyndon B., 67
joint marital property rights. *See* property, marital
Joshi, Heather, 94
judges
and child support, 163, 166, 172n, 179–85
and divorce and marital property, 133, 138–39, 142–43, 155, 158–61
"just a housewife," 60
Justice Department, 212

Kansas, 156
Kennedy, Ted, 219
Kennedy-Simpson immigration bill, 221
Kentucky, 158
Kenya, 121
Killea, Carolyn, 223, 227, 230–31
Kindercare Learning Centers, 204
kindergarten, 209
kitchen table states, 156
Koren, Charlotte, 76
Kubarych, Roger, 72–73
Kuder, Armin, 145–47

Kuehl, Sheila James, 175, 176
Kuznets, Simon, 65–66

Labor, Department of, 85, 220, 221, 228–29
labor laws, and part-time work, 261
"labor of love," 47
labor shortages, in Sweden, 246–47
Labovitz, Priscilla, 228–29
Landes, David, 129
La Petite Academy, 204
law
  and American values, 5
  and discrimination against mothers, 102, 107
  and divorce, 138–47, 151–61
  and equal rights, 55–56, 58
  and paid maternity leave, 96
  profession, 36–39, 160, 143–45
  and wage gap, 94
Laybourne, Geraldine, 30
Lees, Carol, 82–84
Leet, Rebecca, 179–80, 184
Leibowitz, Arleen, 19–20, 214–15
Leiden, Warren R., 220, 226
leisure
  gap, 22–23
  women's work as, 77, 79
Lesothoh, 95
Lewis, Jane, 186
Liberal Party, Swedish, 245
liberals, 31, 163, 226, 237
libraries, 272
Lieberman, Joseph, 227
Liebert, Drew, 167–70
Lino, Mark, 165
Littleton, Christine, 256
Livermore, Mary, 59
Lodewick, Christine, 135
Los Angeles Times, 172
Louisiana, 6, 64, 157
love, choosing, 16–17
Lucas, Rita, 154
Lucas, Robert E., 154
Luxembourg, 201

McCaffery, Edward J., 115–16, 265
McCann, Elaine, 215–16
McCaw, Craig, 159
McClelland, David C., 74
McNair, Dave, 273
Malawi, 121
managers
  long workday of, 22–23
  mothers as, 29–36
  with nonworking vs. working wives, 18, 136
manufactured capital, 71
market, "magic of," 67
marriage, 6, 24
  and compensation vs. alimony, 153–61
  and earnings, 110
  equality in, 55, 24, 140–47, 254–55, 268–69
  gift exchange in, 24
  as partnership, in divorce, 132–40
  power of money in, 112–14
  and Social Security, 262–63
  and taxes, 116, 265–66
  tensions, and "choices" of mothers, 236
  and two part-time workers, 238
  two-tier, 268–69
  and women's property rights, 55, 56 and women's work, 46, 58–62, 64–66
Married Women's Property Act (1848), 56
Marshall, Alfred, 61
Martin, Christine, 190
Martin, Clarence, 190
Martin, Emma Mae, 188–90, 191
Martin, Leola, 190
Martin, Mark, 190
Maryland, 5, 156
Massachusetts, 60, 157, 158, 172n, 183n, 261
  Supreme Judicial Court, 4, 261
maternity benefits, in Sweden, 247
maternity leave, 18, 34, 42, 44
  and employers, 95–97
  lack of support for, 251, 253–54
  need for paid, 259
  paid, in Europe, 50, 91, 95, 108
  and women scientists, 40
MBAs
  career-family dilemma of, 34, 35, 108
  male, 136
  wage gap, 94, 96
Mead, Margaret, 84
media, and immigration policy, 227
medicine, mothers in, 42–43
Mesliansky, Nechama, 76
Mexico, 122
Michelson, Robert, 113–14
Michigan, 157
microlending, 122
Microsoft, 41
middle-class
  and cost of raising child, 165
  and divorce, 140–47, 161
  and mommy tax, 89

Miles, Carlotta, 118
military, 104–6, 215–17, 264
Miller, Harris, 72
Minge-Klevana, Wanda, 51
Minnesota, 158
Mississippi, 157
Missouri, 160, 182
MIT, 40
Mitchell, Maria, 59
Modigliani, Kathy, 206–7, 208
Moll, Richard, 120
"mommy tax," 5, 87–108
  and Aetna, 91–93
  childlessness as ultimate, 107–9
  children harmed by, 125
  and choice, 235
  and divorce, 155, 160
  vs. France and Scandinavia, 50, 91
  in Germany, 108–9
  how to lower, 103–7
  and lack of paid maternity leave, 95–98
  for men, 98–99
  and second baby, 100–103
  in Sweden, 108
"mommy track," 31
monogamy, 128
Montana, 157, 158
Morgan, Laura, 183n
Morris, Betsy, 139
Morrow, Bill, 172–74, 176
mother-infant romance, 34
Mother Nature (Hrdy), 127
mothers and motherhood
  and capitalism, 49, 50–51
  and career-parenting dilemma, 16, 34–35
  cash stipends to, 123–25
  as choice, 233–55
  and conspiracy of silence, 28–44
  cost of being, 94–98
  current status of, 13–27
  devaluation of, 1–12
  and divorce law, 131–85
  divisions among, 250–55
  and economics, 65–86
  exodus of, from corporations and professions, 28–44
  and father's involvement with children, 24, 244
  and family life, 109–29
  and family wage, 148–61
  and feminism, 7, 46, 61–63, 253–54
  how to raise status of, 256–77
  inequality of, in divorce, 131–48
  and mommy tax, 87–108
  and paid leave, 258–59
  power of, in marriage, 112–13, 235
  and social safety net, 186–201
  and Social Security, 262–63
  status of, 2–3, 11–12, 128, 132
  strong, better for children, 119–30
  and supportive mate, 235
  and taxes, 115–18, 265–66
  time spent with children, 13–14, 19–21
  work of, devalued, 45–64
  see also child care; children; divorce; unpaid female caregiving; welfare; working mothers
Movin, Staffan, 239, 240, 248
MS magazine, 3
multinational companies, 240

nannies, 6, 50, 219–29
National American Woman Suffrage Association, 61
National Association for the Education of Young Children, 204, 210, 212
National Center on Addiction and Substance Abuse, 23
National Center on Women and Family Law, 76
National Institutes of Health (N.I.H.), female doctors study, 42–43
National Organization for Women (NOW), 253
National Woman's Rights Convention of 1850, 55
National Woman Suffrage Association, 54
National Women's Political Caucus, "Good Guy" awards, 91
negative income tax, 123
Netherlands, 17, 201, 260, 261
Nevada, 157
New Hampshire, 156
"New Home Economics," 75
New Jersey, 96, 126
Newman, Constance, 226
New Mexico, 6, 64, 157
New York Evening Call, 63
New York State, 56, 96, 159, 264
New York Times, 28, 88–89, 121
New York University, 40
New Zealand, 84, 95
Nickelodeon, 30
Nobel prize, 154
Nordhaus, William D., 77
North Carolina, 157
North Dakota, 157

Norton, Eleanor Holmes, 108
Norway, 76, 84–85, 191–92, 257

occupation(s)
  housewives without, 58–61
  nanny as unskilled, 228–29
  with nurturing skills, underpaid, 98
Ohio, 158
oikonomia, 67, 68
Okin, Susan Moller, 270
Oklahoma, 157, 264
Oldham, Sarah, 136, 139
Onorato, Patty, 206
"opportunity costs," 80, 95
Oregon, 156
Organization for Economic Cooperation and Development (OECD), 257
out-of-wedlock births, 241
overtime, 4, 97, 261

Pahl, Jan, 125
Papua New Guinea, 95
parental leaves, paid, 243–45, 258–59
parental payments, 192
parent education, 272–74
"parenting," 24
parents
  and community support, 271–72
  discrimination against, 98–99, 102, 107, 261
  and diversity, 274
  and economic theory, 75
  and work hours, 23
part-time employment, 18, 19, 96, 235, 237
  and equal pay and benefits, 97, 107, 197, 260–61
  in Europe, 257
  and fathers, 25
  and professional women, 28–29, 38, 42–43, 238
  in Sweden, 108, 247
  and unions, 44
Paster, Howard, 226
paternity, attempt to establish, 185
paternity leave, 240, 242–44
"pauperization of motherhood," 186
Pedersen, Susan, 87, 103
pediatric clinics, community, 272
Pekerti, Dr. Anugerah, 121
Pennsylvania, 126, 127
pension
  and caretakers for elders, 91
  and elderly women, 199
  as joint property, 154
  of mothers, 6, 89
  and part-time work, 261
Perry Preschool Project, 214
personal injury awards, 154
Petersen, Richard R., 166
Pewitt, Capt. Pamela, 217
Phillips, Meredith, 273
physical capital, 71
physicians
  and child support awards, 180–81
  mothers as, 35, 42–43
Pierce, Melusina Fay, 59
Pirog-Good, Maureen, 164
Pollak, Robert A., 125
polygamy, 128
poor and lower-income families
  and breast-feeding, 259
  and child support, 185
  and cost of raising child, 165
  and divorce, 150, 152, 161
  and early education, 264
  and independence effect, 123
  and maternity benefits, 247
  and mommy tax, 89–90
  and mother's control over money, 125
  and parent education, 273
  and taxes on working mothers, 116
POPS (Parents Opposed to Punitive Support), 170–71
postdivorce income
  and alimony, 158
  and child support enforcement, 163
  need for equal, 269–70
  payments, and single federal agency, 270–71
  sharing, 153–61, 270
postindustrial age, 72
poverty
  and elderly women, 199
  and microlending, 122
  and "mommy tax," 88
  and unpaid female labor, 8–9
  see also child poverty; poor and low-income families
power
  and "choice," 234–35
  in marriage, 111–15
pregnancy, 31
premodern societies, 129
preschool and nursery school
  in France, 50, 91, 104
  low pay of workers, 203–5, 208, 220

preschool and nursery school (*cont'd*)
subsidized, 200
universal, 214–15, 263–65
see also child care; day care
President's Council of Economic Advisers, report of 1999, 19
Presumed Equal, 36–37
primate studies, 127–28
Principles of the Law of Family Dissolution (ALI), 155
productivity, 110
definition of, 47
of homemakers, 58–59, 82–83
and New Home Economics theory, 75
of working mothers, 98
professional working mothers, 28–44
and divorce, 140–47
and time with children, 20–21
professions, and full-time wife, 17–18
Progresa program, 122
promotions, 42, 91
property, marital
in divorce, 156–57
and income, 154
and joint rights issue, 53, 55–58, 64
movement to consider earnings as, 153–61
and professional women, 141–42, 146–48
and Wendt divorce case, 133
women's right to, 46–47, 55–57, 62–64, 131–34
property management, 67
"protected speech" issue, 92
PSAs (personal savings accounts), 262–63
psychologists, and human capital, 74
"public goods," children as, 81
public interest law, 37
Pugliese, Eugene, 219, 221, 223, 231–32

"quality" vs. "quantity" of children, 127–28

rape, 251
Rathbone, Eleanor, 124
Ray, Marilyn L., 164
Reagan administration, 163, 190
REAL Women, 83
Reed, Charles, Jr., 195
Reich, Robert, 85
Reid, Margaret, 79
Reid, T. R., 192
Reno, Janet, 95
Report on Manufactures (Hamilton), 47
Republicans, 170, 211, 262, 271
retirement, 5, 78, 81–82, 262–63. *See also* pensions; Social Security
Reuss, Pat, 251
"Revolt of Mother, The" (short story), 54–55
Reynolds, Mel, 114
Richie, Martha F., 89–91
Riddle, Clarine, 227
Ridgway, Delissa A., 224
Ripken, Cal, 73
Robinson, John P., 22
Rodgers, Charles, 18, 99
Roosevelt, Theodore, 1
Ross, Maxine, 3
Roukema, Marge, 271
Ruckelshaus, Jill, 223
Ruckelshaus, William, 223
Rush, Benjamin, 50
Russell, Cheryl, 23
Rutkin, Arnold, 137, 138

safety net, 201
Samuelson, Paul A., 77
Sanders-Crabb, Lori, 169
Saskatchewan, 261
Scandinavia, 91, 126, 129
schools, 25–26, 122, 209, 272. *See also* preschool and nursery school
Schultz, Charles L., 67–68
Schultz, Theodore W. "Ted," 20, 86, 213
Schumer, Charles, 221
Schwartz, Felice N., 30–32
science, women in, 39–40
second baby, 99–103
"second shift," 52
second wives, 167, 169–74
Securities and Exchange Commission, 37–38
self-esteem, 236, 237
self-interest, in economic theory, 67–68, 77
self-made man myth, 52
seniority, 96–97
"separate spheres" doctrine, 47–48, 55
Shalala, Donna, 95
Shaw, Anna Howard, 61–63
sick child, 25, 100, 259
sick leave, 261
Sigourney, Lydia, 48–49
Simpson, Alan, 219
Sims, Marjorie, 253
single fathers, 26
single mothers
in France, 50

single mothers (*cont'd*)
and government policy, 201
and long work week, 23
in professions, 144–45
single-parents
benefits in Sweden, 248
and child support, 270–71
and tax policy, 116
Sisterhood Is Powerful, 236
small business, female-owned, 97–98
Smith, Marilyn Ray, 166
social capital, 71
Social Security, 91
changes needed in, 262–63
for children, 267
mothers penalized by, 5, 6, 77–78, 81–82, 192–96, 199
and paid household workers, 227, 231
taxes, and working mothers, 115, 116
Sommers, Christina Hoff, 94
South Dakota, 156
"specialist wage" approach, 79–80
Spillane, Leslie, 158
standard of living
and cost of having child, 166
after divorce, 149–53, 158, 160, 168, 248
Stanford Business School, 94
Stanton, Elizabeth Cady, 53–56
Stanton, Linda Gail, 180–82, 184
Stanton v. Abbey, 182–83
Stark, Agneta, 241, 247
states and child support, 184–85, 176–77, 271
and day care providers, 210–11
and discrimination against working parents, 4, 261
Statistics Canada, 83
status, loss of, for mothers, 236–37
Steele, Philip L., 92
Steinberg, Leah, 25
Steinem, Gloria, 26, 79, 82
Stivers, Jim, 174
stock options in divorce, 154, 156
Stone, Lucy, 54
Stone, Sir Richard, 66
Stowe, Harriet Beecher, 53
strong mothers good for children, 127–28
suffragists, 58
Summers, Lawrence H., 2
Swaziland, 95
Sweden, 108, 200, 201, 239–50, 260, 270–71
Swedin, Goran, 242, 244, 246
Swiss, Deborah, 34
Switzerland, 17
Tanzania, 128
Tavris, Carol, 131
tax(es), 132
cuts, vs. child allowances, 111, 266–67
on individuals vs. couples, 247, 265–66
on working mothers, 115–18, 235
teachers, 6, 25
TEACH program, 210
technology careers, 41
teenagers, 23, 247
Texas, 4–5, 158
Theobald, Robert, 65
third-person criterion, 79
Third World, 84
Thomas, Clarence, 190
Thompson, Dianna, 173
Thompson, Flora, 60
"threat point," 112, 113–14
Tierney, Judge Kevin, 134, 147
time for family, 22–23
"shares," and child support, 168–69
Tocqueville, Alexis de, 49
Town & Country magazine, 165–66
Treatise on Domestic Economy (Beecher), 52
"true woman" myth, 52
turbo-capitalism, 22–23
Turkey, 17
two-career families, 58, 265
two-tier marriage, 268–69

undocumented workers, 223, 227
unemployment insurance, 6, 192, 197, 263
Uniform Marriage and Divorce Act (UMDA), 135n
unions, 43–44
United Kingdom, 104, 125, 200
United Nations
report on women, 78
Statistical Commission, 84, 85, 267
System of National Accounts, 66
United States
child poverty in, 257
vs. France, 50
new social contract in, 258
policy changes needed by, 262–68
and women politicians, 126–27
and women's unpaid labor, 84–86
U.S. Congress, 59, 65, 84, 86, 123, 163, 177, 200, 219, 220, 229, 253, 262, 270
U.S. Senate
Judiciary Committee, 224
Subcommittee on Immigration and Refugee Affairs, 219

U.S. Supreme Court, 190
University of Michigan
  Law School, 37, 94, 96
  survey of single mothers, 23
University of Wisconsin Poverty Institute, 123
unmarried couples, and housework, 235
unpaid female caregiving, 6
  as basis of economy, 8–9
  and census, 82–84
  discounted and devalued, 44
  and divorce, 138–39, 155–61
  and GDP, 66, 267–68
  as "gift" in marriage, 160, 161
  information collected on, 84–86
  and invention of "unproductive housewife," 53–54, 58–64
  magnitude and value of, 73, 76–80
  no safety net for, 186–201
  and Social Security, 194–96, 199, 262–63
  and welfare, 193–94
  see also child rearing; household labor by wife
upper-income and rich families
  and child support, 184–85
  and cost of raising child, 165
  and dependency of mothers, 116–17
  and divorce, 131–40, 147, 148, 161
  and second-class status of wives, 118
  "white women" syndrome, 254
Upton, Joanna, 4
Upton v. JWP Businessland, 261

vacations, 261
venture capital, 41, 98
Vermont, 156, 157
veterans, 105
Villapardo, Aaron, 171
Villapardo, Dolores, 171–72
Villapardo, Eric, 171
Villapardo, Fred, 171–72
Villapardo, Irene, 171–72
Vindication of the Rights of Women, A (Wollstonecraft), 47, 48
voluntary unemployment, 180–81, 183n, 197
volunteer work, 84

Waerness, Kari, 72–73
wages
  of day-care workers, 203, 212–13
  "for housewives" idea, 10
  lost, for elder care, 91
  men's, and wives' unpaid labor, 52
  and money economy, 58
  for "women's" work, 80
  withholding, for deadbeat dads, 176–77, 179
  see also earnings and income
Wahl, Anna, 246
Waldfogel, Jane, 88, 95
Walker, Francis, 58–59
Walker, Judy, 34
Wall Street Journal, 117
Waring, Marilyn, 66, 82, 84
"warrior tax," 104–7
Washington Post, 23
Washington State, 127, 157, 158, 171
wealth creation, by mother, 67–68
welfare, 6, 187–90, 250
  and child support enforcement, 163, 169, 185
  child support seen as, 174
  demonization of, 191, 252–53
  and divorced women, 185
  vs. European systems, 191–98
  as threat to male control, 123
  reform, 200, 211–12
  as second-tier benefit, 193
  vs. unemployment insurance, 197
  and unpaid work of child care, 84
  and younger mothers, 104
welfare state, 186–201
  and discrimination against mothers, 192–98
Wells, Ida B., 54
Wellstone, Paul, 253
Wendt v. Wendt, 131–40, 147–48, 159
West Africa, 128
Westerbert, Bengt, 245
West Germany, 109
Westinghouse, 40
West Virginia, 156
Wharton School of Business, 31
white collar employees, 22–23
Whole Woman, The (Greer), 255
Who Pays for the Kids? (Folbre), 81
Who Stole Feminism (Sommers), 94
widows, 196, 199
Willer, Barbara, 210
Williams, Anthony "Tony," 68–71
Williams, David, 99
Williams, Joan, 6, 107, 149, 153, 154, 156, 162, 270
Williams, Lewis, Jr., 69
Williams, Lewis, Sr., 68, 70
Williams, Virginia, 68–71
Williams College, polls, 238–39

Wilson, Pete, 169
Winfrey, Oprah, 108
Winnicott, D. W., 72
Winterbottom, Marion, 74–75
Wisconsin, 156, 157
wives, at-home
  census erases from rolls of productive workers, 58–62
  and men's earnings, 17–18, 136
  see also divorce; household labor by wife; marriage; mothers; unpaid female caregiving
Wollstonecraft, Mary, 47, 48
Woman Engineer, 40
woman's congress of 1874, 59
women
  attitudes of, toward mothers, 250–55
  and Baird, 225–26
  begin working for wages, 56
  and custody rights, 48–49
  and judgeships, 227
  maximize well-being of children, 127–30
  and paid leave for fathers, 245
  poorer than men, 8–9
  productivity of, 47
  and Swedish labor shortage, 246–47
  proprietary feelings of, toward children, 244–45
  strong, good for children, 129–30, 248–50
  see also mothers; working mothers; and specific issues
Women and Economics (Gilman), 62
Women of Vision, 15–16
Women's Legal Defense Fund, 139, 161, 168
women's movement, 7, 13, 33, 63
  and equality in marriage, 254–55
  nineteenth-century, 53–58
  see also feminists
women's suffrage movement, 55
women's work
  census devalues, 58–61
  early feminists call for valuing with men's work, 55–56
  and GDP, 66, 78
  as "labor of love", 47
  see also child care; unpaid female caregiving
women's work, and *Dictionary of Occupation Titles,* 220
Wood, Kimba, 227
Woodward, Louise, 218–19, 230
Woolsey, Lynn, 188, 191
work (employers, employment)
  caring conceptualized as, 257
  choices, wanted by women, 238–39
  definition of, and cash income, 47, 58–60
  designed around masculine norms, 107
  discrimination against parents, 5, 98–99, 145
  enjoyable, vs. leisure, 79
  and family, in Sweden, 247
  vs. home split, in nineteenth century, 52–53
  need to redesign, 258–61
  nonmarket, how to value, 79–80
  policies, vs. Americans' values, 5
  "time-out" for mothers, in corporations, 30–31
  see also business careers; full-time work; part-time work; professional women; working mothers
work/family experts, 31
work hours, 22–23
  of mothers, 18, 34–35
  need to reduce, 257, 260
  in Sweden, 247–48
  of women vs. men, 8
working-class families
  and divorce, 149–53
  and handicaps on working mothers, 96–97
  and "mommy tax," 88, 96–97
Working Mother, 91–92, 243
working mothers
  absentee rates, 25
  and alimony, 160–61
  attacks on, 250–51
  and child support, 179–85
  and divisions among women, 250
  full-time vs. part-time, 18–19
  in Germany, 108–9
  hours, 18, 22, 34–35
  and leisure, 22–23
  and private child care, 219–31
  professional, 36
  sharing housework with fathers, 25–26
  in Sweden, 108, 247
  and wage gap with childless women, 94–98
  vs. welfare mothers, 252–53
  see also professional mothers; and specific issues, jobs, and types of work

workman's compensation, 6, 192, 197–98, 263
World Bank, 71, 140
Worthy Wage Day, 202
Wright, Martha Coffin, 54
WUSA-TV, 100–102
Wyoming, 157

yard work, 79, 83
Young, Marci, 209
Yunus, Muhammad, 122

Zero to Three, 202
Zick, Cathleen, 20

About the Author

Ann Crittenden is the author of *Killing the Sacred Cows: Bold Ideas for a New Economy.* A former reporter for *The New York Times* and a Pulitzer Prize nominee, she has also been a financial writer for *Newsweek,* a visiting lecturer at MIT and Yale, and an economics commentator for CBS News. Her articles have appeared in *Fortune, The Nation, Foreign Affairs, McCall's,* and *Working Woman,* among others. She lives with her husband and son in Washington, D.C.